Praise for *The Myth of the Great Ending*

"Too many books are called groundbreaking these days, but *The Myth of the Great Ending* truly is. Drawing from an impressive range of traditions and sources, Joseph Felser brings an intelligent voice of reason to the issue of doomsday prognostications. He illustrates persuasively that one person's doomsday can be another person's new beginning; the choice is ours."
—SUSAN RAY, author of *And Now for the Good News*

"Felser's well-researched and engaging writing takes us on a journey through humanity's perennial reinvention of the Myth of the Great Ending. He lifts the mask created by the Myth itself, bringing us face to face with a reality beyond the earthly veil."
—HAL Z. BENNETT, Ph.D., author of
The Lens of Perception: A User's Guide to Higher Consciousness

"What a relief to read a book by a Ph.D. who understands that the inner side of life is at least as real as the outer—and in many ways, is more critical to our future. And what a pleasure tò read a book that is profound and yet engaging. Are we in the last days? Those who are tempted to give in to despair, or even pessimism, should read *The Myth of the Great Ending.*"
—FRANK DEMARCO, author of, *Muddy Tracks: Exploring an Unsuspected Reality* and *The Sphere and the Hologram: Explanations from the Other Side*

"To find James Bond and Thomas Aquinas cited in consecutive paragraphs is both surprising and refreshing . . . Felser uses the myth of the 'end times' that has troubled mankind since the creation of the Mayan calendar (and perhaps even before then) to demonstrate that the idea of linear time being a progression from 'beginning' to 'end' is, as he says, 'not merely obsolete, but also clearly nonsensical.' . . . . *The Myth of the Great Ending* is very approachable, rich in revealing insights, and demonstrates firm control of a remarkable variety of materials drawn from across the centuries."
—RONALD RUSSELL, author of *The Journey of Robert Monroe* and
The Vast Enquiring Soul: Explorations into the Further Reaches of Consciousness

D1533494

"In *The Myth of the Great Ending*, Joseph Felser peels through layers of belief and mythology to reveal nothing less than the central underlying truth of reality creation, and he does it with a keen, affectionate intelligence that dissects the full spectrum of modern and ancient ideas. Not such a balanced and original voice has spoken in the world of consciousness studies since Jane Roberts herself lived among us."

— SUSAN M. WATKINS, author of *Conversations with Seth* and *What a Coincidence!: The WOW! Factor in Synchronicity and What It Means in Everyday Life*

THE MYTH OF THE GREAT ENDING

THE
MYTH
OF THE
GREAT
ENDING

WHY WE'VE BEEN LONGING FOR THE END
OF DAYS SINCE THE BEGINNING OF TIME

BY JOSEPH M. FELSER, PH.D.

HAMPTON ROADS

Copyright © 2011
by Joseph M. Felser, Ph.D.
All rights reserved, including the right to reproduce this
work in any form whatsoever, without permission
in writing from the publisher, except for brief passages
in connection with a review.

Cover design by Nita Ybarra
Interior design by Stewart A. Williams
Typeset in ITC New Baskerville

Hampton Roads Publishing Company, Inc.
Charlottesville, VA 22906
www.hamptonroadspub.com

Passages from *Journeys Out of the Body* by Robert Monroe,
copyright © 1971, 1977 by Robert Monroe. Used by permission of
Doubleday, a division of Random House, Inc.

Library of Congress Cataloging-in-Publication Data is available on request.
ISBN: 978-1-57174-645-0
WOR
10 9 8 7 6 5 4 3 2 1
Printed on acid-free paper in the United States of America

For Robert A. Monroe (1915-1995)
and
Jane Roberts Butts (1929-1984) and Robert F. Butts (1919-2008),

heroic pioneers in the exploration of human consciousness.

Myths are made for the imagination to breathe life into them.
ALBERT CAMUS, *"The Myth Of Sisyphus" (1955)*

Apocalypse does not point to a fiery Armageddon, but to our ignorance and complacency coming to an end.
JOSEPH CAMPBELL, *A Joseph Campbell Companion: Reflections On The Art Of Living (1991)*

The forlornness of consciousness in our world is due primarily to the loss of instinct, and the reason for this lies in the development of the human mind over the past aeon. The more power man had over nature, the more his knowledge and skill went to his head, and the deeper became his contempt for the merely natural and accidental, for that which is irrationally given—including the objective psyche, which is all that consciousness is not.
C.G. JUNG, *The Undiscovered Self (1958)*

CONTENTS

PROLOGUE

The Beginning of the End of the End of the World 1

CHAPTER ONE

Chicken Little and the Doomsday Machine 5

CHAPTER TWO

Apocalypse Now, and Then 23

CHAPTER THREE

Breaking the Circle, or Mending the Hoop? 37

CHAPTER FOUR

From Sacred Hoops to Time Loops 55

CHAPTER FIVE

Can You "In-See" the End? 75

CHAPTER SIX

To Thine Own Self 101

CHAPTER SEVEN

Into a Dark Forest 121

CHAPTER EIGHT

The Womb of Myth 133

CHAPTER NINE

Doing the Best You Can 159

CHAPTER TEN

Barrier-Breaker, World-Ender .177

CHAPTER ELEVEN

The Circle of Dreams and the Ends of Myth 195

EPILOGUE

Trust the Process 209

ACKNOWLEDGMENTS 211

NOTES 217

WORKS CITED 243

INDEX 259

THE BEGINNING OF THE END OF THE END OF THE WORLD

One day, after class, a student I'll call Cathy approached me in the hallway, as I was preparing to make my exit down the stairwell.

"Professor," she said tentatively, "do you mind if I ask you a question?"

"No, go right ahead," I replied. "Shoot."

Cathy was always the first to raise her hand in answer to a question, or to ask one of her own. She was bright, energetic—a quick study. I figured she wanted to know something about Plato, or perhaps she was worried about the upcoming midterm. But I figured wrong.

"What do you think of all this End of the World stuff? I mean, do you really think the world is going to end?" she asked.

I was stunned.

Cathy couldn't have known that I had just resumed work on this book after a long hiatus. Nor could she have known that, in a recent e-mail to a friend, I confessed how strange it was that suddenly all sorts of individuals I was encountering in my everyday life were bringing up the subject of apocalypse. I'd joked to her that I was becoming some sort of "doom magnet."

But I could tell from the look on Cathy's face that, to her, the subject was no joke. She was serious—deadly serious. I knew that I had to choose my next words very carefully. I didn't want her to think that I was belittling her or her concerns.

"No, I don't think that the world is going to end," I replied. "But why did you act as if you were afraid even to raise the question?"

"Well, it's just that someone in my astronomy class asked the professor about all these apocalyptic prophesies, and he got real angry. His face turned red. He said there was absolutely nothing scientific in them and quickly changed the subject. But I wanted to know what you thought."

"Since you've asked me a question, is it all right if I turn around and ask you something?" I replied. "If you really thought that the world were going to end, what would you do differently?"

Cathy paused, her face scrunched up in thought. "I think I'd just stay here in Brooklyn, with my family," she answered.

"And if you didn't believe that the world were about to end?"

"I'd transfer to another school—somewhere else, out of state, to finish my degree," she stated firmly, without missing a beat. "Then I'd go to law school," she added. "That's what I really want to do: I want to become an attorney. But I don't want to practice law. I want to go into politics. You know, make the world a better place, and all that. If it doesn't sound too corny."

"Not at all," I replied. Raising my arm with hand outstretched, I gave my professorial imitation of a sacred benediction. "Then go and become a lawyer," I intoned reassuringly. "Don't worry. Do what you really want to do. Don't act out of fear. The meaning of 'the end of the world'—it's not what you may think."

A look of relief washed over Cathy's face. She thanked me profusely as we said our hasty goodbyes and went our separate ways.

But as I trudged down the stairwell toward my office, I wondered: Was Cathy really convinced by my hearty reassurances? Or would her doubts—and fears—linger? How many of her generation were like her? How many more out there were living with an unchecked, and perhaps unexpressed, anxiety over a prospective cosmic cataclysm?

The mere thought of it boggled my mind.

Gadflies and Deep-sea Divers

Plato's great teacher, Socrates, famously stated that a philosopher must be annoying to be effective—like a buzzing gadfly that wakes up a sluggish horse catching a nap on a hot summer's afternoon. A society requires an irritant to wake itself up, to become aware of its destructive patterns, and—if it's not already too late—to initiate a change. It was too late for Athens. Is it for us?

The task at hand is not merely to "speak truth to power," but to question the core beliefs and values of our culture. Not only the attitudes of the elite, but also the prejudices and assumptions of the average person, are fair game. For most of us, as Socrates well knew, operate according to custom, habit, and tradition most of the time—that is, unthinkingly, with little or no critical reflection. Autopilot is our default position. We don't even know who set the controls or where we're going.

But what Socrates didn't quite reckon is that there is a much deeper source of culture than our rational intellect. Our consciously professed beliefs and values are but the tip of a vast and potentially dangerous iceberg. To be truly effective, it is not enough to be a gadfly; one must become a deep-sea diver. Not wings, but fins are what we need to grow if we are to get to the bottom of things: the myths.

Socrates more or less openly mocked the myths of his day: the philandering Zeus, the intra-Olympian warfare among the gods, etc. Centuries before television advertising, video games, and the World Wide Web, he fretted about the superior power of images to mold, influence—and, yes, corrupt—young minds unmoved by mere words, empirical evidence, and rational argument.

Despite his criticisms, however, Socrates failed to grasp either the source of the enduring power of those mythic images, or their larger, true significance. For that crime above all—his rank insensitivity—he met his martyr's fate by drinking the cup of hemlock prescribed by a jury of his Athenian peers.

No More Martyrs

We don't need any more superfluous martyrs. There have been far too many cups of poison already quaffed in the name of some higher truth. What we really need, right here and now, is a useful analysis of a contagion. Only then can I give a full and proper response to Cathy's question: What do you think of all this End of the World stuff? And that's what this book really is: the response I didn't have the time, or presence of mind, to give Cathy that day in the stairwell.

For my youthful, ambitious, but somewhat worried student is, unfortunately, in good company. I know because her story—or rather, her concerns—sounded so eerily familiar, so very close to home.

CHAPTER ONE

CHICKEN LITTLE AND THE DOOMSDAY MACHINE

There will be no more Time.
(Rev. 10:6–7)

There is no such thing in nature as an H-Bomb; that is all man's doing. We are the great danger. The psyche is the great danger.

C. G. JUNG, *Jung on Elementary Psychology* (1979)

On October 22, 1844, in a little town called Lincolnville in the state of Maine, a hundred or so local followers of the self-styled Christian prophet William Miller donned their white "ascension robes" and climbed majestic Mount Megunticook to await the Second Coming of Jesus.[1]

Alas, no Christ Triumphant swinging his terrible swift sword appeared on high in the clouds that day—or since, for that matter.

Much to his dismay, Miller had been proven wrong again. His first failed prophecy had been for March 21, 1844. As his followers grew increasingly restive and disenchanted with his faulty prognostications, his movement fizzled. Or did it?

Perhaps it only underwent a metamorphosis, for it could be argued that we have lived under Miller's spell ever since. We are, as it were, Millerites of the spirit—the letter be damned. For, despite the repeated abject failure of our most feverish apocalyptic prognostications, we remain steadfastly wedded to the titillating possibility of the End of Days. Nothing seems to disturb this robust belief.

Is there any good reason to suppose that, if the world doesn't end under some other apocalyptic vision, some new version of Millerism will not resurrect itself? Not if the evaporation of Y2K fears or the dashing of Millennial hopes in 2000 are any guide. The computers didn't break down. There was no Rapture. And yet . . .

No matter. Like a stealthy vampire on the prowl, the End of Time story rises again and again from the crypts of human consciousness to feed on the unwary, never to be vanquished—garlic, crosses, and wooden stakes notwithstanding.

The past sixty years have proven to be a particularly fertile period for Great Enders. First we had atomic Armageddon, Mutually Assured Destruction, and nuclear winter. However, long before the collapse of the Soviet Union, other players were warming up in the bullpen: Silent Spring, global warming, and climate change, followed by pole shifts, earth changes, extraterrestrial salvation from beneficent space brothers—or invasion from hostile aliens—and, lately, collision with Planet X. Not to mention peak oil, food-system collapse, global financial meltdown, global pandemics, and, of course, the War on Terror and the clash of civilizations.

The End is near. Or is it?

Waiting for Godot

Take, for instance, the Big Daddy of universal denouements—the end of the Mayan Long Count calendar—which began in 3114 BC and marks time in 394-year periods. This calendar is believed by some enthusiasts to herald the catastrophic destruction of the world as we know it, as, to put it as simply as possible, all kinds of rare celestial and terrestrial phenomena will create the conditions for a perfect cosmic storm that will bring the Great Ending, once and for all: game, set, and match.

This idea was originally championed in the 19th century by a French Catholic priest-turned-archaeologist named Charles Etienne Brasseur de

Bourbourg. But was this ex-priest merely guilty of an anachronism, reading backward the Christian belief in the Apocalypse into the Mayan astronomical cosmology?

Some Christian apologists argue that this projection is not necessarily an anachronistic error, as they are eager to find hints and anticipations of the "one true religion" sprinkled about, here and there, in earlier, so-called "primitive" religions. Presumably they were put there by a considerate God, who wished to prepare humanity for the real revelatory deal that would come later on.

Thus, as Saint Augustine of Hippo (354–430 CE), one of the early Church Fathers, opined: "What is now called the Christian religion, has existed among the ancients, and was not absent from the beginning of the human race, until Christ came in the flesh: from which time the true religion, which existed already, began to be called Christian."[2] Or, as the modern British philosopher R. G. Collingwood (1889–1943) put this same point: "Hence even the darkest heathenism is, as Christians have always said, an implicit, blind or caricatured Christianity."[3]

The notion that the Mayans were among the very first people to "get it right," apocalyptically speaking, was taken up in more recent times by the late Terence McKenna, the gadfly thinker who became an enthusiastic proponent of psilocybin mushrooms as the only viable path for the exploration of human consciousness. Based on his own mathematical and metaphysical calculations, McKenna forecast an end, not only to human history, but to time itself that would correspond to the Mayan prophecy.

In *The Archaic Revival* (1991), McKenna envisioned the Mayan calendar as heralding some sort of zygotic fusion of the computer and the psychedelic experience. He was admittedly pretty vague about what this would entail, but he proclaimed that humans would soon be able to project themselves into a mental, Alice-in-Wonderland world of pure imagination: a Wachowski-brothers-like Matrix—though one presumably innocent of all the dystopian, totalitarian hitches and glitches—with the mere click of a computer mouse. Our physical bodies would become mere secondary organs, and not very appealing appendages at that.

Like Karl Marx and other thinkers of his ilk who believe themselves to have discovered, not mere probabilities or sheer possibilities, but rather the ironclad, deterministic laws of necessity that dictate the course of future events, McKenna declared that this transfiguration is fated to be: "This isn't something human beings have to decide to do," he declared, "this is something that is happening!"[4]

Shadows of Things

What will be, will be. As the ancient Greeks said: "The Fates guide him who will; him who won't, they drag." In other words, like it or not, the End of Days is coming: It's a predetermined mass event, cosmically orchestrated, totally beyond our individual free choice or control. So, sit back, relax, and strap yourself in. You're either going to enjoy the roller-coaster ride, or else be terrified—it'll either be a joyride or a white-knuckle nail-biter—but, in any case, there's absolutely nothing you can do about it. So just hang on!

While some thrill-seekers seem eager to go along for the ride, many others are clearly terror-stricken at the prospect.

Ann Martin is an astronomer at Cornell University who runs a website that fields astronomical questions from the public. Of late, she's been inundated by anxious queries about impending global disaster. Martin says she gets e-mails from worried fourth graders who plead that they're too young to die. Even their parents are not immune to the fear. "We had a mother of two young children," Martin reports, "who was afraid she wouldn't live to see them grown up."[5]

To such frightened souls as these, the fatalistic mantra of "What will be, will be" offers cold comfort indeed at the imminent approach of the Great Ending.

You may recall that in Charles Dickens's classic tale of last-minute spiritual redemption, *A Christmas Carol*, that old reprobate Scrooge is forcibly led by the Ghost of Christmas-Yet-to-Come to view his own tombstone in the dark twilight of a life lived according to the misanthropic philosophy to which he'd theretofore been wedded. A terrified Scrooge implores the fearsome spirit: "Are these the shadows of the things that Will be or are they shadows of the things that May be, only?"[6]

Or perhaps they are just the insubstantial shadows cast on the wall by crude papier-mâché puppets manufactured—either by others, or perhaps by our very own subconscious minds—strictly for our entertainment. Not will be or may be, then, but rather, got to be—as in, "you've got to be kidding."

In other words, perhaps all this ballyhoo about the End of the World is just a lot of media hype, along with some good, old-fashioned American hucksterism, plus a dash of simpleminded hysteria thrown into the crock-pot for good measure.

Such snap diagnoses, while attractive to many critics, are perfumed with the condescending air of moral and intellectual superiority. It is easy, and perhaps tempting, to pretend to be above it all. Yet few of us enjoy an automatic immunity to the lure of the lurid.

I'm no exception to this rule. When I was younger—maybe eight or so—I'd hop into bed and switch on my magic carpet ride: a twelve-transistor radio with a tinny-sounding speaker. I'd plug in the earphone and—*whoosh!*—I was off. I loved listening to humorist Jean Shepherd tell tall tales about his youth and growing up in the Midwest. Some of my other favorite shows were interview programs that featured guests who spoke of exotic things like extrasensory perception, the search for the Loch Ness monster, UFOs, psychic surgeons, and haunted houses. Such topics were tinder to the fire of my youthful imagination. More than that, they spoke to my already awakened sense that there is far more to reality than meets the eye.

Sandwiched in-between, on Sunday night, was a show called *The World of Tomorrow*, which featured a preacher who evidently ran his own church, as there was always an advertisement at the end. Week after week, in stentorian tones, he delivered the same basic message: Repent, for the end is nigh. His sermons were peppered with anecdotes of everyday life—little moral parables—exhortations, and Bible quotations. But the idea was the same: The Lord is coming.

Now, I didn't believe in Jesus, and I wasn't worried about my eternal soul. Nevertheless, what always struck me was the note of absolute confidence in the minister's mellifluous baritone. This guy sounded as if he really *knew* something. He seemed so sure of himself, so dreadfully certain of his vision. Did he actually see the future—the world of tomorrow? Would we even want to know the truth if he did?

Imaginations can, and should, be stimulated. But they can also be warped—even poisoned—if we are not careful. The question is, of course:

How do we tell the difference? How can we open our imaginations without making them vulnerable to contamination by dangerous diseases and mass imbalances of the collective psyche?

Imagine That

Some may argue, however, that our imaginations are inherently perverse. From this it can be inferred that the root source of our seemingly endless fascination with the prospect of doomsday is hardwired into human psychology.

For example, Saint Augustine, the principal architect of the idea of Original Sin, believed that our enjoyment of tragic drama illustrates that we are all basically sadomasochistic voyeurs at heart. Our pleasure is to watch others suffer pain, the more exquisite the better. We get a cheap thrill out of feeling badly for them. "What miserable delirium this is!" he declared.[7] We enjoy their misfortune, even if they are fictional characters, because we feel superior to them even as they evoke our pity. Moral self-congratulation is the mask of the Peeping Tom.

It's true that we guffaw at the pratfalls of physical comedians like Buster Keaton, Charlie Chaplin, and Chevy Chase. We slow down on the highway to gawk at an accident on the opposite side of the road—"rubbernecking," as the traffic reporters refer to it. A video clip of one of those aging Las Vegas casinos being reduced to instant rubble by clever demolition experts is almost guaranteed to make the evening news for similar reasons. We are fascinated by disaster. We like to watch—and perhaps breathe a not-so-secret sigh of relief: At least it's them, not us.

Following this line of argument, the End of the World is the ultimate Vegas hotel collapse. Nothing draws spectators like a spectacle, after all. And what could possibly be more spectacular than doomsday? From classic films like *King Kong* (1933), *Godzilla* (1954), and *The War of the Worlds* (1953), to more recent offerings like *Armageddon* (1998), *Independence Day* (1996), *The Day After Tomorrow* (2004), *Apocalypto* (2006), *Cloverfield* (2008), *The Road* (2009), *The Book of Eli* (2010), and, of course, *2012* (2009), we are titillated by the prospect of having a safe ringside seat at the last cosmic picture show.

But is this sort of natural curiosity really so awful, degrading, and morbid—or, as Augustine would have it, "unholy"? Is it really fundamentally different from, say, wondering what it would be like to attend your own funeral?

Augustine's view seems unnecessarily dour. He regards the imagination as evil and perverse and out of control, because, for him, everything human is evil and perverse and out of control, and always has been—at least, ever since disobedient Eve wondered what it would be like to have wisdom and, in a daring act of imagination, took a bite of the apple and offered the rest to Adam.

For Augustine, you see, "natural" is a virtual synonym for "depraved." Even seemingly omnipresent, if often inconvenient, features of human existence like spontaneous sexual desire and death were not—at least according to him—part of the package deal of creation as God initially put it together. They were not part and parcel of his original intention. Rather, they were subsequent additions to the list of justly deserved divine punishments visited on the first couple and, by extension, on all of humanity, for eating that one piece of forbidden fruit.

But if we set aside such churlish notions, it is plain to see that the ability of images, either outwardly perceived by the physical eye or inwardly constructed and entertained by the mind's eye, to evoke certain kinds of more or less automatic responses in us has a prime survival value. That we may experience lust at the sight of a potential mate, or fear at the sight of a saber-toothed tiger, or tenderness at the sight of a helpless infant, is obviously good for the species in the actual world in which we live and have always lived— Eden notwithstanding. Not everyone who is sexually aroused by the image of an attractive prospect gets lost in pornography, however. Not everyone who can feel sympathy becomes addicted to television soap operas. We can, and do, choose how to cultivate and exercise our imaginations. We are responsible because we can decide to look the other way—or even not to look at all.

Just Do It!

If Saint Augustine's diagnosis of a corrupt imagination points to a possible link between a morally dangerous, pathological spectator psychology on the one hand, and the popularity of doomsday speculation on the other, there is yet another possible analysis—one that focuses on a somewhat different set of pathologies that inspire direct action rather than passive anticipation or strictly vicarious enjoyment.

Yes, there are indeed those overly enthusiastic End-Timers who, in their fierce urgency to respond to the final cosmic curtain call, decide to forgo waiting in favor of becoming more proactive in their cause. These actors attempt to force the curtain to go down: Ready or not, here it comes! Suicidal doomsday cults have thus proliferated like poisonous mushrooms sprouting on the underside of a rotting log.

In 1978, for example, more than 900 followers of pastor Jim Jones quaffed poisoned Kool-Aid when U. S. Congressman Leo Ryan led a delegation down to the jungles of Guyana to investigate the People's Temple cult—specifically, the accounts of Jones's sexual and psychological abuse of his flock. Ryan himself was assassinated at the hands of Jones's lieutenants on the tarmac of the Guyana airport.

In the 1990s, members of a Swiss Rosicrucian splinter group, led by a con man named Luc Jouret, took their own lives in a suicide pact. Adherents of the Heaven's Gate troupe in California, headed by the self-castrated former pastor, Marshall Herff Applewhite, believed that by shedding their lowly "vehicles"—to wit, their physical bodies—they would be transported aboard a hidden UFO that was concealed in the tail of a passing comet. Dressed in identical purple robes and Nike sneakers, they quaffed poison cocktails in order to speed their ascent to the skyborne Mothership—an updating of the Christian Rapture for a space-age sensibility.

For some, however, suicide was indeed too painless—so they turned to mass murder instead in hopes of hastening the arrival of the End Times. Followers of the Japanese Aum Shinrikyo cult, which professed an eclectic fusion of Buddhist, Shinto, and Christian beliefs, staged a poison-gas attack in a Tokyo subway, killing a number of innocent passengers as a prelude to Armageddon and a tribute to their guru, Shoko Asahara, who gleefully celebrated the "devotion" of his followers.

You could conclude, then, that End Time belief is no more than a useful tool wielded by power-seeking con artists in order to manipulate the pliable and fool the gullible. Case closed.

Yet this overly reductive view fails to explain why the foolish become fools in the first place and acquiesce to being manipulated. Nor does it account for how and why the cult leaders themselves—those who presumably know better, after all, because they're in on the trick—often succumb to the very spell that they successfully cast on others. Jim Jones, Marshall Applewhite, David Koresh, and many others have met the same fate as their most devoted followers: death.

If a fervent belief in an imminent End of the World often serves as a fruitful way to recruit, mobilize, and retain a loyal following, particularly in the face of real or imagined hostility from outside the movement, it's also true that many who long for or fear the End of Days, or who are deeply attracted to apocalyptic ideas, are not necessarily affiliated with any specific religious group, either as members or as leaders. The basis of this mysterious allure needs to be understood, and it can't be explained in narrowly reductive sociological or psychological terms, or solely in relation to cult dynamics. It must have a wider appeal. So the question remains: What is the source of our eerily magnetic attraction to the End of Days?

Times of Distress

Even when End Time belief doesn't inspire mass suicide, murder, bizarre eccentricity, or cultish fanaticism, there remains in all apocalyptic thinking a thick, slimy residue of dreadful gloom, seasoned with a pinch of barely suppressed, morbid glee at the prospect of the imminent arrival of the End. There is something decidedly unsavory, if not deeply unsettling, in our mad dash to the ultimate finish line, as if we just can't wait to get it all over with. Does this overriding need for "closure," in current parlance, perhaps furnish an important clue?

It may indicate that End Time hopes are a means of coping with, and an attempt to relieve, the pressures of some deep-seated anxiety. Furthermore, this unease may be a response to certain real, external conditions. "Historically," observed the great Swiss psychologist Carl Jung, "it is chiefly in times of physical, political, economic and spiritual distress that men's eyes turn with anxious hope to the future, and when anticipations, utopias and apocalyptic visions multiply."[8]

The last half century or so has certainly been a time of great upheavals and distress. The victorious end of World War II, punctuated by the exclamation points of the Holocaust horror and the atomic bombs dropped on Hiroshima and Nagasaki, left us with the nagging realization that anything is indeed possible where human behavior and its rationalizations are concerned.

Beneath the superficial "placidity" of the 1950s were percolating issues of race, religion, gender, and politics, which soon boiled over into the tumultuous '60s and '70s: Vietnam, the Civil Rights movement, the sexual revolution, feminism, gay and lesbian rights, political assassinations, the ecology movement, Watergate, and a cultural civil war over values and beliefs that continues to rage down to this day.

The increasingly fierce and fervent clashes over abortion, gay marriage, evolution versus creationism (and public education in general), the right to die, global climate change, etc., are skirmishes in an ongoing struggle for the very heart, mind, and soul of America—at least, as many on both sides see it. Champions of science and progress cannot quite believe that they are still fighting to teach evolution in public schools 150 years after Darwin published *The Origin of Species*, while advocates of the Old Time Religion do not even acknowledge the validity of the bedrock principle of the separation of church and state, which they regard as nothing but "a myth perpetrated by secular liberals."[9]

Secular democracy versus religious theocracy: For some, this is a war being waged, not between America and Islamist extremists, but within an America divided by rival, indeed mutually incompatible, worldviews. It is a clash between a modern, secular rationalism based on the humanistic values of individual free choice and scientific inquiry on the one hand, and a rigidly doctrinaire, authoritarian religious fundamentalism founded on biblical literalism on the other. Thus, for example, Joel McDurmon, the director of research for an organization called American Vision, advocates the execution of gay people because that's what the Bible says to do:

> The truth is, hate is an inescapable concept in every society.
> . . . The problem is that in modern society, we have let the liberals and heathen define the values for us. Instead of gathering our standards of what is to be loved and what is to be "hated" from God's word, we are supposed to accept the shouts of shame from liberals—shouts which derive directly from their rejection of God's word and replacing of God's standards with their own value system.[10]

These increasingly vitriolic and intransigent cultural disputes only serve to underscore what the late Dr. David Bohm, an eminent quantum physicist and thinker, described as a most dangerous "fragmentation [that] is now very widespread, not only throughout society, but also in each individual."[11]

Now, how can this be? Aren't we cultural warriors single-minded types?

Consider this: God's word, if it exists, must still be heard, recorded, filtered, and interpreted by our human minds. To disparage the point of view and values of the latter in order to glorify the former thus betrays a fatal inconsistency. Similarly, a view that aspires to be completely rational, but leaves out of its analysis—or utterly discounts and disparages—those widespread mystical experiences that suggest the whole may indeed be more than the mere sum of its parts, is itself incomplete, and therefore inconsistent. The conflict between us is thereby also within us.

According to Bohm, then, this fragmentation "is leading to a kind of general confusion of the mind, which creates an endless series of problems and interferes with our clarity of perception so seriously as to prevent us from being able to solve most of them."[12] We seem to have reached an impasse.

Is it any wonder that, in the midst of such confusion, frustration, denial, and lack of clarity, some of us—perhaps many—seek refuge, solace, or the resolution of apparently irresolvable difficulties in the yearning for an End to It All?

Could it be, then, that our steadfast belief in the End of the World is not so much an irrational obsession about the future as it is an eminently reasonable response to present world conditions? In this view, End-Timers are not falling back on a psychological coping mechanism, but are engaged in a scientifically sound extrapolation of certain current—and self-evidently ominous—trends. Is there, in short, more fact than fancy to be found in these prognosticative perturbations?

After all, there *was* a Cuban missile crisis. M.A.D. (Mutually Assured Destruction) *was* our avowed policy of nuclear deterrence. The supply of oil *will* run out. Global warming *is* taking place. The World Trade Center *was* destroyed, and the Pentagon *was* attacked, on September 11, 2001. A major economic crisis *did* occur in 2008. These are solid facts, not sheer fantasies, are they not?

To be sure, there will always be room for differing interpretations of and disputes concerning the facts. Debates still rage about the significance of events in human and natural history that took place decades, millennia, or even millions of years ago.

For example, scientists are still not sure what caused the extinction of the dinosaurs. Was it indeed the impact of a comet that led to climate change?

Here's another example: New forensic evidence raises questions about a familiar story from World War II—namely that Adolf Hitler, on April 30, 1945 as the Russians closed in on Berlin, committed suicide with his companion, Eva Braun, in their bunker by taking a cyanide pill and then shooting himself in the head. What recent DNA analysis reveals, however, is that the skull fragment with the bullet hole that was supposed to be Hitler's belonged to a woman under 40 years of age, not a man of 56.[13]

Even the most firmly established views thus remain open to revision.

Yet despite such controversies, no reasonable individual would question that Hitler is dead and that the Jurassic period is over. Similarly, if there's plenty of room for disagreement over the interpretation of certain recent events like 9-11, who would reject the general observation that the world is facing its share of major challenges? Ideas of disaster are not being conjured out of thin air, after all.

Or so the argument goes.

World Words

On the face of it, this is a reasonable position to take. Who can deny that we often find ourselves navigating treacherous waters through dire straits? The prophets of doom may be the ones who are courageously facing grim reality, while the rest of us self-deluded "Pollyannas" have our heads firmly planted in the sands of illusion.

And yet . . .

On closer inspection, "The End of the World" turns out to be a fairly slippery notion, a slyly mercurial phrase whose shape-shifting meaning is difficult to pin down. The term "world" itself is ambiguous, and so it is unclear what, exactly, is coming to an end. Is it the planet Earth, the solar system, the Milky Way galaxy, or the universe? If it is, say, the Earth, are we talking about its total destruction, or "just" a radical change in its landscape and environment? Will humans become extinct, or merely cease to be the dominant species in the planetary food chain?

Perhaps, however, "world" is a reference, not to physical nature, but to the human spheres of society and culture: our belief systems and institutional forms of group organization. In that case, is it the end of human civilization *per se*, or merely the end of American hegemony that haunts us? Do we dread the death of one particular religion—usually our own—or the end of religion itself? Or is it the cumulative transformational effect of technology that casts such a giant shadow?

The question is, do the various facts that fall under these different concepts compel us to envision the End, or does our image of the End compel us to find (or to create) data to validate our vision? In other words, do we see it because it is there, or is it there because we are determined to see it? If it is the former, the End is itself a fact to be—a future event. If the latter, it is something else altogether—a myth.

Myths of Myth

By "myth" I do not mean a lie or an exaggeration.

Joseph Campbell, the great expert on myth, used to say that this was the biggest misconception, as well as the greatest linguistic and mental hurdle, that people had to overcome. Our English word "myth" comes from the ancient Greek, *mythos*, which means story. Though I can inflect the spoken word "story" in such a way as to encourage or indicate disbelief—"Oh, she gave me quite a *story* about her whereabouts last night," for example—this is not the necessary implication. We all know that some stories are true, while others are false.

Moreover, we also know that stories are true in quite different senses. We expect one kind of truth from a newspaper report of the events of the day, and a very different type of truth from a novel populated by fictional characters enacting events that never actually took place except in the imagination of the author. In the former, we are reading at the literal level in search of factual truth; in the latter, images are being used symbolically to convey truths about the human condition. Myths, like novels and unlike newspaper reports, said Campbell, are metaphors.[14]

A myth, in the proper sense, then, is a story that has emotional resonance at the abyssal depths of the human psyche—for that is its very source, its point of origination in what Campbell called "the mythological zone." Myths—or what Carl Jung referred to as archetypes of the collective unconscious—are not mere facts in and of the outer world(s), but rather the inner perceptual lenses and mental windows through which all mundane facts are viewed and understood.

And perhaps, if some observers are right, even created.

The belief in the Great Ending is thus a myth in this specific sense. It is ultimately about a transformation of reality down to its metaphysical bones. To those enchanted by its magical spell, all of the other changes we have mentioned—social, cultural, geographical, and environmental—are mere signs and symptoms, either concomitants or harbingers, of the Big Change: the end of time and human history and the conclusion of the cosmic story that is the plotline of both.

That is why it makes no difference to those held tightly in the grip of their fascination with the End Time if a given predicted condition fails to materialize, or if the meanings of their key terms seem to slip and slide around a semantic ice-skating rink. The particulars are not really important, after all, for an overweening force that will sweep aside all particulars in any event is driving them to annihilation.

What, exactly, is that superior force?

The Doomsday Machine

In "The Doomsday Machine," an episode from the classic 1960s *Star Trek* television show, the starship *Enterprise* is threatened by a gigantic robot ship that smashes and consumes whole—including inhabited—planets and uses them for fuel, thereby enabling the killer machine to continue its murderous interstellar rampage.

After the *Enterprise* is attacked, Captain Kirk speculates that the killer ship is a doomsday machine—the 23rd-century equivalent of 20th-century nuclear bombs—manufactured by some alien civilization as a deterrent threat, ostensibly never intended to be used. But used, after all, in some long forgotten ancient war to end all wars. Now, with its makers long reduced to interstellar ash, it wanders the galaxy on automatic pilot, mindlessly fulfilling its preprogrammed mission of destruction.

Yet, as Jung states in the opening epigraph to this chapter, H-bombs don't grow on trees. The real doomsday device is the mind that is inspired to conceive, construct, and program the bombs for use. Our unfettered human imagination is thus the ultimate doomsday machine. "The psyche is the great danger," as Jung put it. We are possessed by an archetype, held fast in its clutches.

There is, unquestionably, great destructive force in nature—greater, in fact, than any single nuclear bomb. Our sun, for example, is a vast roaring thermonuclear furnace. And Jung, who spent his childhood in the mountainous Swiss countryside totally absorbed in his natural surroundings, knew this well from his own direct personal experience, as his memoir, *Memories, Dreams, Reflections* (1965) makes clear. People who live close to nature do not need instruction in its power.

But nature, being impersonal, is not intentionally malicious and does not operate from fear, ignorance, or willful self-deception—what the ancient Greek philosopher Plato dubbed "the lie in the soul." Nature is not dishonest. Nor does it act out of an emotional need for justice, "closure," or, less charitably, revenge. Only human beings—and their personal gods, modeled on their own foibles—do this:

> The voice of one crying in the wilderness:
> Prepare the way of the Lord, make his paths straight.
> Every valley shall be filled, and every mountain and hill
> shall be brought low,
> and the crooked shall be made straight,
> and the rough ways shall be made smooth;
> and all flesh shall see the salvation of God. *(Luke 3:4–6)*[15]

This, of course, is John the Baptist, citing the Old Testament prophet Isaiah, as he looks forward to the imminent establishment of Kingdom Come. But it is also the biblical passage quoted by Martin Luther King Jr. in his famous "I Have a Dream" speech, which he delivered in August 1963 at the Lincoln Memorial in Washington, D.C.—a key moment, if not a decisive turning point, in the Civil Rights movement and the fight for racial justice in the erstwhile social kingdom of America.

The Story of the Vanquished

The deep connection between the righteous anger of the prophetic biblical tradition and the Myth of the Great Ending raises some urgent questions.

If this myth is indeed an expression of certain deep-seated human desires, aren't those desires—and therefore the myth itself—necessarily universal, present in all times and places? In other words, hasn't it always and everywhere been thus? And, if so, would it not be naïve and unrealistic to expect this myth to change or disappear? How can we alter human nature?

Furthermore, would we want to, even if we could? For aren't those very same desires among our greatest and noblest aspirations? How can our thirst for justice—our relentless drive to rectify the apparent imbalance between good and evil in the world—be such a bad thing?

R. G. Collingwood once classified Christianity as an "anger religion."[16] He saw the development of this anger as a key step forward in the evolution of human consciousness. For no longer did we merely fear God and blindly obey Him. We became angry with the Old Man for creating a world that was, on reflection, manifestly unfair. After all, it was He who made Adam and Eve as flawed creatures capable of sin; and it was He who gave them—his hapless human children—over to the seductions of the wily serpent. And for this, Collingwood implies (undoubtedly with tongue planted partly, but firmly, in cheek, in true British fashion), Christ was rightly crucified when he had the temerity to show up in person to plead his case.

But is such righteous indignation indeed a step forward in the development of human consciousness? Or does it represent a wrong historical turn—a road better not taken, or at least, at this late hour, one closed for repairs?

In our usual way of thinking, religions with a single personal god as the creative source of all represent a "higher" form of spiritual understanding and insight than the older nature religions, with their dizzying array of spirits, deities, and demigods performing as agents of impersonal cosmic forces. But we may want to ask ourselves whether this evaluation is not merely the result of an unjustified bias. History, as they say, is the story of the vanquished as told by the victors.

Perhaps we need to go back to the beginning of the story. If we can make do without the anger, does it mean that the Myth of the Great Ending, as we now know it, is not somehow "hardwired" into the imagination of the human species after all?

CHAPTER TWO

APOCALYPSE NOW, AND THEN

> You have noticed that everything an Indian does is in a circle, and that is because the Power of the World always works in circles, and everything tries to be round.
>
> BLACK ELK, in John Neihardt's, *Black Elk Speaks* (1972)

Are all apocalypses created equal? Or, are some better than others? The question is whether there is a single, canonical Myth of the Great Ending, with only minor variations, or whether there are significantly different versions that embrace widely different, perhaps even mutually exclusive, meanings.

To answer this question, we must dig deep into our past. We must become archaeologists of the human mythic imagination. Who, indeed, were the creators, the original manufacturers, of the greatest stories ever told? And what served to fire up their imaginations to convert them into the very first doomsday machines?

If we want to know how to turn off the machine, we have to figure out how and why it got turned on in the first place.

We're All Goners

Alas, our greatest shaman-philosophers have been nameless. Truth to tell, they weren't even fully human.

According to scholars like Joseph Campbell and philosophers like Michael Grosso, the ritual burial sites of prehistoric Neanderthals—an innovation apparently without precedent—provide convincing evidence of a key transformation of prehuman consciousness.[1]

These corpses have been found carefully arranged in the fetal position, accompanied by tools and other personal possessions. The implication is a belief in the existence of a self-identity beyond that of the physical body, as well as the notion of a plane or realm of existence in which that "other" self continues to live and move and have its being.

Thus it is the fact of death, or rather the dawning human awareness thereof, that is the font of our most ancient metaphysical ideas—namely, the concepts of the soul and an afterlife in which each soul meets its justly deserved fate. Philosophy and religion alike were born in the recognition of endings within the context of an experience—provided by dreams, waking visions, and out-of-body ecstasies—of a continuing life beyond the earthly veil, or at least the great hope of one.

Could it be, then, that the Myth of the Great Ending arose simply as a logical extrapolation of this personal limitation to the wider reality? After all, if I meet an ultimate end, must not the world as a whole share a similar fate? And if my soul is rewarded or punished according to its record of deeds, must there not likewise be a general accounting of justice when the book of life is closed once and for all?

From this standpoint, it is no wonder that the Myth of the Great Ending is universal, found in virtually all cultures, in all times and places—and is thus, perhaps, both inevitable and necessary. For the death genie, once out of the bottle, can never be put back—as Pandora discovered the hard way. We're all goners, sooner or later.

The Denial of Death

There is, however, another possible, if somewhat less charitable, interpretation of the very same anthropological data. According to this point of view, our fixation on the Great Ending represents a flight from logic, not an expression of it. For those who regard themselves as hard-nosed skeptics, the myth is not a reasonable extrapolation of the truth of survival, but rather a psychological evasion of extinction.

This view is nicely dramatized in Woody Allen's 1977 film comedy, *Annie Hall*, in which Allen portrays Alvy Singer, a neurotic Manhattan comedian suffering from chronic romantic failure. In one scene, Alvy recalls a formative incident from his childhood, when his mother took him to see the family doctor because he'd read something in a science book that made him too depressed even to do his homework. The physician, Dr. Flicker, asks young Alvy if there's anything bothering him.

"The universe is expanding," Alvy replies morosely. "Well, the universe is everything, and if it's expanding, some day it will break apart and that will be the end of everything."[2]

The skeptical British philosopher Bertrand Russell once said that the only reasonable philosophy is one built upon the foundation of "unyielding despair,"[3] as we know that someday our sun will burn up and fry this world to a crisp before it sputters out. The end of the physical universe means the end of everything because, from the scientific standpoint—or rather, from the metaphysical assumption that many scientists embrace as if it were a proven empirical conclusion—only physical matter is real. Hence the ancients' notion of a soul that survives the death of the body and relocates to a nonphysical realm is sheer superstition.

However, we don't want to face our own inevitable demise or even the little ego-deaths of daily life—going to work or suffering romantic rejection—all of which presage and foreshadow our extinction. So we shift our attention to the cosmic scale of mega-extinction. We'd rather contemplate the impersonal destruction of the universe than face our personal limitations. From this perspective, philosophy and religion alike are resorts catering to cowards.

Perseverating on cosmic entropy is thus a dishonest and neurotic way of avoiding the unpleasant facts, especially that final insult added to the ultimate injury: we age, we croak, and we molder in the grave. "The worms crawl in, the worms crawl out," as the old song goes. "The universe is everything" is just a displacement stratagem. It is far easier to deal with than, "My body and the gratification of my ego are everything," because we are so vulnerable to injury. The Myth of the Great Ending is not, therefore, an expression of our longing for ultimate justice, but an evasion of the consciousness that each of us draws the short straw.

A Good Day to Die

But just who, exactly, are the neurotics? Certainly not those peoples who remained closest to their roots in "Neanderthal philosophy," namely the indigenous peoples we blithely used to derogate as "primitives." There is, in them, no avoidance of the fact of their own death, though there is a very different attitude toward it—one that would not put much lucre in the pocket of a Park Avenue psychoanalyst.

Here, for example, is a representative sampling of such "primitive" opinions:

> Chief Seattle, for whom the city was named, expressed this view most succinctly: "Dead?—I say. There is no death. Only a change of worlds."[4]

> When Black Elk, the Oglala Sioux holy man, sat down in 1931 with the poet John Neihardt to tell his life story, some of the holy man's older friends stopped by to contribute their recollections of the period of time when Black Elk was a young boy. As he recalled an encounter between the Sioux warriors and the U.S. cavalry during the successful campaign of Chief Red Cloud, one of those friends, Fire Thunder, recalled the battle-cry made famous by Crazy Horse: "Let us go! This is a good day to die . . . Hoka hey!"[5]

> "Do not grieve," advised the Omaha Chief Big Elk. "Misfortunes will happen to the wisest and best of men. Death will come, always out of season."[6]

Perhaps the best exemplar of the Native American attitude toward death is provided by the life and writings of Ohiyesa (or Charles Alexander Eastman, 1858–1939), whom Kent Nerburn, a leading authority on Native culture and history, describes as "one of the most fascinating and overlooked individuals in American history."[7]

A member of the Santee (eastern) tribe of the Dakota, or Sioux, Ohiyesa was raised in the traditional way in the woodlands and on the prairies. His father sent him off to white schools, however, where he learned English well enough to graduate from Beloit College and Boston University medical school. As Charles A. Eastman, he would become, as Nerburn notes, "an adviser to presidents and an honored member of New England society,"[8] though he later grew disenchanted with white civilization and returned to live in a more traditional tribal way in the forest woodlands of his native Minnesota.

In his book, *The Soul of an Indian* (1911), Ohiyesa dismisses the belief in a "happy hunting ground" as a postmortem destination of the soul as a modern corruption of, or Christian imposition on, true native ideas about death. While the Indians never doubted the existence of an immortal soul or spirit, he says, they preferred not to speculate too much about the exact nature of the afterlife.

"In our original belief," explains Ohiyesa, "we were content to believe that the spirit which the Great Mystery breathed into us returns to the Creator who gave it, and that after it is freed from the body it is everywhere and pervades nature." He concludes, matter-of-factly: "Thus, death holds no terrors for us."[9]

This frank acceptance of death—even, from our standpoint, what would count as its rank injustices—is characteristic of these peoples. And while they also have myths of Great Endings, the tone of these stories is in keeping with their matter-of-fact, unperturbed attitude toward individual death, and thus distinctly different from the feverish dread and ecstatic hope expressed in our own versions. Mythic variations thus turn out to be as significant as their similarities.

Folklore researchers Richard Erdoes and Alfonso Ortiz have collected many such stories of Native American versions of the Myth of the Great Ending. Fire and flood, they note, are popularly cited as the instruments of End Time destruction.

Yet, even in the blackest of times, there are rays of hope, evidence of worldly renewal, "for the end of this world does not mean the end of everything," they write, "but merely the passing of one state and the arrival of the next, just as other worlds were destroyed to make way for the one we live in now."[10] In other words, the end of *this* world is not the end of *the* world. The show must—and will—go on.

The Hopis, for example, believe that when the present world ends in worldwide conflict, only the place where the Hopi peoples live will be spared, and they will become the matrix of the new world.

Similarly, there is a story among the Brule Sioux that the Great Mystery created the Third World—the one in which we presently live—after he burned up the first one in flames and drowned the second in water. Neither effort proved to be satisfactory to the Creator. As he was making his third attempt, he was already musing to himself that someday there might have to be a Fourth World.

Even the Mayans, who, with their calendar, have provided the contemporary mythic imagination with the latest cultural peg on which to hang its apocalyptic yearnings, had a very different attitude toward this ending than might be supposed by present-day End-Timers. Anthropologist Sandra Noble, executive director of the Foundation for the Advancement of Mesoamerican Studies, notes: "For the ancient Maya, it was a huge celebration to make it to the end of a whole cycle,"[11] for they knew that the cycle would be starting up all over again.

Like Yin and Yang, life and death can never be separated in ancient ways of thinking. Where one is, the other is as well. The notion of an absolutely "final" victory over death—or change, or evil—is, therefore, foreign to their perspective.

"Cycle." This key term goes a long way toward explaining the ancients' matter-of-fact acceptance of death, which is light-years removed from the neurotic denial of an Alvy Singer, the obscene glorification of a Marshall Applewhite, or the manipulative fear-mongering of fundamentalist preachers like Pat Robertson and Jerry Falwell—hawkers of last-chance salvation at the ultimate Going Out of Business Sale: Burn now in Hell, or celebrate in Heaven as you await bodily resurrection!

All apocalypses are not created equal, after all. Not size, but rather shape matters. Implicit in the apocalyptic myths of indigenous peoples is an image—and, just as importantly, an experience—of time that is quite different from our own. Time, for them, is circular. "Everything the Power of the World does is done in a circle," Black Elk explained to his amanuensis, Neihardt:

> The sky is round, and I have heard that the earth is round
> like a ball, and so are all the stars. The wind, in its greatest
> power, whirls. Birds make their nests in circles, for theirs
> is the same religion as ours. The sun comes forth and goes

down again in a circle. The moon does the same, and both
are round. Even the seasons form a great circle in their
changing, and always come back again to where they were.
The life of a man is a circle from childhood to childhood,
and so it is in everything where power moves.[12]

Indeed, as Black Elk recalled, the wise human being imitated the circular
way of nature—which is also, incidentally, the way of spirit. "Our tepees
were round like the nests of birds," he said, "and these were always set in a
circle, the nation's hoop, a nest of many nests, where the Great Spirit meant
for us to hatch our children."[13]

Cosmic time, human history, nation, society, culture, and the life of the
individual—all embodied the same primordial shape: the circle. And since
all things on a circle's perimeter are equidistant from the central point, no
matter where you are in the cycle—and no matter who, or what, you are—all
are equivalent expressions of the World Power.

The Clockwork Universe

Not so for us, who regard time as a straight line. In the scientific version
of this idea, we move from the Big Bang to either the Great Whimper—in
which, as Alvy Singer whined, the universe keeps expanding until it just
disintegrates or fades away to nothing—or the Big Implosion, in which the
universe collapses back into itself, producing total annihilation. From the
religious (specifically Christian) standpoint, the parallel movement is from
Creation out of Nothingness to the Last Judgment and the End of Everything as We Have Known It.

Thus mainstream science and mainstream religion—as well as what some
like to think of as sheer "common sense"—all subscribe to some version of
linear chronology. While it's true that the theory of relativity and quantum
mechanics challenged both common sense and the Newtonian view of time
(we'll get to that part of the story a bit later), most mainstream scientists still
cling, often with dogmatic desperation, to the Newtonian picture and the
philosophy of the Enlightenment, which gave birth to modern science and
the modern world, and which is still the default position of our thinking.

In 1748, French physician and philosopher Julien Offray de la Mettrie published a slim volume entitled *Man: a Machine*. In it, he argued that his predecessor and fellow countryman, René Descartes (1596–1650), founder of modern philosophy (about whom I'll have much more to say in chapter 4), was wrong: There is no "soul," that is, mind or consciousness, apart from the workings of the physical body. "The soul and the body fall asleep together," he wrote. "As the motion of the blood is calmed, a sweet feeling of peace and quiet spreads through the whole mechanism."[14] Body and soul thus live— and die—as one.

It was de la Mettrie's view, not Descartes', that prevailed. His hard-nosed medical materialism expressed the general Enlightenment belief that the unfettered use of reason—the one true light—in and through individual experience (from the Latin, *experientia,* also the source of our word "experiment") would reveal the orderly operation of the universe to the human mind; and that order, at bottom, is mechanical. The universe as a whole is but a vast, complex machine, and the human body is a miniature version of this mechanism.

From Sir Isaac Newton and his cohorts, we learned that physical matter is composed of basic building blocks called "atoms," which were believed to be solid and indivisible—something like tiny indestructible billiard balls. These operated according to certain regular patterns called "the laws of nature," within the four dimensions of space and time. These laws govern the motion of atoms as they collide on the billiard table of the universe according to the principle of cause and effect, whereby a cause must always precede its effect, and every effect must have a prior cause. "Accordingly," writes renowned consciousness researcher Dr. Stanislav Grof, "matter evolved in an orderly way, moving from the past, through the present, into the future."[15] Linear time is thus a most logical conclusion of truly scientific thinking—at least if we operate from certain 17th-century premises.

Within this orderly cosmic trajectory, human history also came to be regarded as an orderly process unfolding in a linear fashion, and also, in moral terms, as an essentially progressive achievement. Though there are, to be sure, some definite bumps in the road.

For example, in the religious view of Christianity, between the glory of Creation and the triumphant awe of Last Judgment there lies the Fall in the

Garden of Eden. Adam and Eve disobeyed God's instruction not to eat the fruit of the tree of the knowledge of good and evil—an unfortunate turn of events that had to be rectified through an unquestioning faith and sheepish obedience to authority, both earthly and divine. But everything will turn out right in the end—at least for the chosen few eligible to receive forgiveness or what is called "salvation." As for the rest of us stubborn goats—well, there's hell to pay. But that's as it should be as well.

Monotheists of virtually all stripes—including Jews, Christians, and Muslims—naturally view their own worship of the one God as far superior to the earlier worship of many gods (polytheism) or nature (animism). The latter are collectively derided as "demon worship," "magic," or, in general, as "lower" forms of religion, while the honorific title of "higher" religion is kept strictly for their own faiths. In the proud monotheistic view, then, there has indeed been progress in religious development, but that has—quite conveniently—come to an end with the advent of monotheism itself.

Enlightenment philosophy, however, sees historical progress in starkly different terms. In this view, we have, slowly but surely, emerged from the dark swamps of all ancient religious superstition into the bright laboratory lights of rational scientific inquiry, and thus from slavery—both physical and mental, or political and intellectual—to freedom. Natural history, too, is conceived as a slow, gradual—if occasionally dead-end—development from lower, simpler forms of life, to higher, more complex forms, until, at long last, *Homo sapiens* triumphs in the competitive, cutthroat game of chance called evolution.

We Are the Champions!

This type of self-congratulatory triumphalism is called "Whig history," after the old British political party that supported parliamentary power, or democracy, over the older forms of absolute monarchy. The originator of the term, British historian Herbert Butterfield, defined "Whig history" as the tendency to "emphasize certain principles of progress in the past and to produce a story which is the ratification if not the glorification of the present."[16]

Science would not be happy with being lumped in with Whig interpretations of history. For science pretends to be a value-free inquiry, offering only a neutral description of how the world actually works, rather than any moral or evaluative judgments about that world. So it would vehemently deny that it sees evolution in nature as yielding what we call "progress."

Yet, science also makes no bones about insisting that the beliefs produced by its experimental methods are more reliable than those obtained through other means like intuition, guessing, or dreams. Scientific method yields genuine fact as opposed to pseudo-knowledge. It offers testable claims as opposed to unverifiable conjectures. It finds truth; it does not create fiction. Of course, the tacit assumption is that truth is *better* than lies or errors—for only the truth will set us free, and intellectual freedom is far preferable to the slavery of ignorance.

Now, these statements are qualitative; they are, in other words, judgments of value. Science as a form of inquiry, and as a cultural institution, is therefore implicitly wedded to a philosophy of historical progress, whether it wants to admit it or not. Value-neutrality is an illusion, an ideological mask worn to disguise our self-congratulatory and triumphalist view of human beings.

In sum: We are the champions!

We proudly congratulate ourselves on our moral, intellectual, and biological achievements: on being top dog in the food chain, on our enlightened, rational ways of thinking and acting that have proven so successful in creating wealth and power, or on having been given the gift of the best, most up-to-date version of divine revelation. Even the avowedly pious, from the Puritans to TV preachers, celebrate economic prosperity, interpreting it as a sign of divine favor.

Most of us, therefore, look down our cultural noses at the ancient circular models of time. We experience a collective shudder at what we think of as the "mindless repetition" endured or—heaven forbid—acquiesced to by our poor "primitive" ancestors—tortures from which we have been released by our notion of linear time and historical progress. This revulsion is expressed in both religious and scientific perspectives. "New and improved" is our mantra, from the New Testament to the latest technological gadget. As a consequence, we often wind up celebrating novelty for its own sake, and expect to find it around every corner.

And when we don't? Well . . .

An Unexpected Reverie

One morning, I was sitting at my desk, sipping my morning coffee, when I found myself slipping into a kind of spontaneous reverie. In this waking dream, I'm all excited about visiting a new exhibit at the museum. I walk into an enormous rectangular hall; before me sits an impressive sculpture, a huge intricate bronze piece. I amble on down the central aisle and, on the left, find another sculpture. Only something seems oddly familiar. Then I realize it's the same piece I just saw. Puzzled, I walk on. On my right is another bronze sculpture. But as I approach it, I see that it's the very same piece I've already seen twice before. I'm running down the aisle now, angry and indignant, half in a panic. Every piece is identical. "What kind of crazy fun-house museum is this?" I cry out. "Why would anyone build an exhibit like this?" But then the most frightening thought of all occurs to me: Maybe I'm the whacko, not them. Now I don't even trust my eyes. I just want out of this place.

The scene fades, and now I'm in a cavernous circular rotunda. At the center of the room sits a massive, intricate sculpture—the same one, I realize, that I glimpsed before. I'm standing on a turntable walkway that slowly revolves around the edge of the room, giving me a 360-degree vantage point on the sculpture. Each moment provides a slightly different view of the piece, and each complete revolution provides fresh opportunities to see details I previously had missed. I'm amazed: I'm not bored or frustrated at all. In fact, I feel certain that, no matter how many times I circumnavigate the sculpture, I will discover something of interest.

Round and Round

The museum, of course, is the Museum of Time. In this case, however, our usual expectations and values have been reversed. Or perhaps it may be more accurate to say that our perspective has been turned upside-down, as in the famous image of the Tarot card known as the Hanged Man, which depicts a man hanging by his right ankle from a wooden frame that some interpret as the mythical Tree of Life.

My initial visit to the exhibit—striding purposefully down the aisle in a rectangular hall—is our linear experience of time. But where we think we will find novelty and stimulation, we are instead inundated by a rapid-fire succession of superficial impressions—life in the digital age—that serve only to confirm us in our boredom and amplify our frustration, leading to burnout and a longing for escape. Death—or, more generally, the end of the world—is the only way out.

The rotunda, on the other hand, is a metaphor for the older cyclical experience of time: Round and round she goes, and where she stops, nobody knows—or cares. For surprisingly, this circularity presents heretofore-missed opportunities for penetrating beyond the surfaces to the hidden depths of things. Not the futile merry-go-round of existence of our fears after all.

This shockingly fruitful engagement with repeating patterns reminded me of the 1993 film *Groundhog Day*, in which actor Bill Murray portrays an obnoxious, egomaniacal Pittsburgh weatherman assigned—much to his unconcealed chagrin—to cover the annual Groundhog Day festivities in Punxsutawney, Pennsylvania.[17]

By a strange metaphysical twist of fate, Murray's character finds himself caught in a bizarre time loop. He is forced to relive the same day—Groundhog Day—with all its boredom, trivia, and encounters with cornpone locals, over and over. He finally comes to a series of breakthrough realizations about the limitations of his selfish, self-absorbed personality and his previous notions of happiness and success. He realizes, in short, that he's been an ass.

True to form, Hollywood presents this epiphany as a "happily-ever-after" moment—wherein lies the weakness of the movie's grasp of its own true message.

Contrast this with Carl Jung, who, in his important essay "The Stages of Life," argues that it is a mark of emotional maturity to realize that there are no such endings. "The serious problems of life," Jung writes, "are never fully solved."

But—and here is the kicker—according to Jung, this is a *very good thing*: "If it should for once appear that they are [solved], this is the sign that something has been lost." He concludes: "The meaning and design of a problem seem not to lie in its solution, but in our working at it incessantly. This alone preserves us from stultification and petrifaction."[18] This incessant labor is not a heavy burden, but a golden opportunity.

Such a realization would be equivalent, from the cyclical view of time, to arriving at the center of the circle—which is, of course, your own center, as well as the center of the world. And this can be done in any and every moment, wherever you happen to be on the circle's outer perimeter. Yet it also has to be done over and over—not like the futile gesture of Sisyphus, rolling his rock up the hill, but like the wind or the water wearing away the rock, penetrating ever deeper: year after year, decade after decade, epoch after epoch.

The linear versions of the Myth of the Great Ending have no truck or patience with such lack of finality, however. They demand that the problems of life be solved, once and for all, not simply for the individual, but for us all. It began in the Beginning and it will end in the End. Period. The crooked *will* be made straight. The rough ways *will* be made smooth. And that, at last, will be that!

The paradox, as Jung's comments suggest, is that the cyclical or circular form is not static; indeed, it is quite the reverse. The straight line—the proverbial arrow of time—is the icon of purposeful forward motion. But ultimately, it negates its own movement in an ironic annihilation of the very idea of process and change.

Following Jung, is this negation not a symptom of emotional immaturity? Could it be that the consciousness of human beings actually regressed rather than progressed in its development when we set aside the old cyclical view of time to embrace the linear model, with its distinctively hard-edged, apocalyptic versions of the Myth of the Great Ending? Was this, in other words, devolution as opposed to evolution? Such an interpretation runs directly counter to the received, self-consciously self-congratulatory view of our own illustrious history.

How, and why, then, did this momentous transformation occur? That is the question we must now address.

BREAKING THE CIRCLE, OR MENDING THE HOOP?

Thou art a soul in bliss; but I am bound
Upon a wheel of fire, that mine own tears
Do scald like molten lead.

W. SHAKESPEARE, *King Lear*, Act IV, Scene vii

Is the Myth of the Great Ending nothing more than the ultimate cosmic bailout plan for spendthrifts, thieves, and legions of the irresponsible? Do we—not unlike the Bard's poor, mad, tortured King Lear—make our own misery, and then have the audacity to cry out to the heavens for deliverance?

Such nerve recalls the classic case of the little boy who murdered his own parents in cold blood, only to plead for the court's tender mercy as he was being sentenced for his crime. "See, I am but a poor orphan!" he wailed. "Woe is me!"

That, as they say, is the textbook definition of chutzpah. Woe is us, indeed.

In our culture, the Myth of the Great Ending is often sold as the cure-all antidote to human woe. But is this eschatological balm nothing more than old-fashioned snake oil? Who profits from its sale? *Qui bono?* Who first patented the medicine, and who among the prophets keeps raking in the profits?

Inquiring minds, as they say, want to know.

As Told by the Victors

Because of our preoccupation—some might say obsession—with things that are tangible and measurable, it is easy and tempting to lose sight of the fact that we inhabit a world of abstractions that cannot be perceived directly by our physical senses. Typically, if we can't work on it in the gym, view it on an LCD screen, or park it in a garage, it's just not real. Certainly it's nothing to get hot and bothered about.

Yet our computers, cars, and even our very physical bodies—whose shapes and sizes reflect changing cultural standards of beauty and health—are expressions of ideas and images that possess three-dimensional qualities, albeit only in a strictly metaphorical sense. We speak of ideas being "weighty" or "solid." Back in the heyday of the 1960s, there was a familiar expression: "That's heavy, man!" The images of our dreams and myths have great "energy" and "power," but not the kind that the utility companies bill us for each month. These prime movers belong to an order of reality that is itself intangible and beyond measure: consciousness. So if we don't like what we see "out there," well, turn around and take a long, cold, hard look in the mirror.

Not many of us today are keen on accepting this kind of responsibility. If you have any shred of remaining doubt about this, just watch a few minutes—as few as humanly possible—of one of the many court TV shows. Or, if you have an especially strong stomach, try watching an entire episode of the evening news or *Dr. Phil*.

What you will learn from this brief experiment is that a sense of duty to others and self, a sense of honor, and indeed all such "old-fashioned" sentiments have evaporated like the morning mist. Too many today know no shame, as they have no concept of owning up to their actions. From Wall Street mega-predators who steal billions, to public officials who sell their offices to the highest corporate bidders, to unrepentant murderers and rapists who steal children from their parents, there is a startling absence of anything resembling genuine remorse, guilt, or even embarrassment at getting caught. Conscience has abdicated its role, leaving chaos in its wake. "Things fall apart; the centre cannot hold," laments the poet W. B. Yeats in "The Second Coming"—his own take on the Great Ending.[1]

But what if the center cannot hold precisely because we have lost the very concept of a center? Perhaps this disintegration has been a long time a-coming.

In Shakespeare's great play, *King Lear*, the king abandons his duty by literally abdicating his throne, on little more than a childish whim and an egocentric need to be flattered by his children (especially his favorite daughter, Cordelia), who are now ostensibly his supremely grateful heirs. As Lear's erstwhile kingdom and his own family disintegrate into ruinous conflict, treachery, and deceit, he descends into mordant self-pity, madness, and finally, death—his own great ending, which serves as a handy escape-hatch from the suffering of which he himself is the principal author.

Nothing, as it is said, exceeds like excess.

But here is the point: As the epigraph to this chapter reveals, the prime image of this excruciating misery is, of all things, the circle—the "wheel of fire" upon which Lear felt himself hideously bound. Evidently, by Shakespeare's time, Black Elk's circle had somehow acquired an altogether different—and diametrically opposite—meaning. The sacred "hoop" of the Oglala Sioux, which had been the icon of a world in harmonious balance for thousands, if not hundreds of thousands, of years, had become instead a symbol of a kind of self-inflicted and self-perpetuating suffering. Strange, is it not?[2]

According to Joseph Campbell, this unprecedented mutation had actually taken place long before. It occurred during the era identified by author Ken Wilber as the period of "the great axial sages," beginning with Pythagoras and the Buddha, and culminating with Jesus and Mohammed. In Wilber's view, this era represented the high-water mark in the development of human consciousness and its spiritual achievement. All that remained was the further refinement of these great insights.[3]

Yet, this is the very same era that Campbell terms the period of the "Great Reversal"—a time, he says, "when, for many in the Orient as well as in the West, the sense of holiness departed from their experience both of the universe and of their own nature," and instead "a yearning for release from what was felt to be an insufferable state of sin, exile, or delusion intervened."[4]

Thus, something pretty darned drastic, if not drastically depressing, occurred on the historical watch of those "great axial sages"—at least according to Campbell, who regards this reaction as a kind of childish foot-stamping, an extended cultural tantrum that continues unabated to this very day.

Who is right, then, Campbell or Wilber? Which was it: the Great Leap Forward, or the Great Reversal?

If Campbell is correct, this marked downshift into rank pessimism was the sour attitudinal cradle in which the so-called "higher" world religions of Christianity and Buddhism were conceived and born. Furthermore, this reversal was both embodied and reflected, says Campbell, in the altered significance of the old mythological imagery—and, in particular, of our old friend, the circle.

Whereas the circle or the spoked wheel had, once upon a time, been revered as a sacred symbol of power, glory, and delight, in the period of the Great Reversal it was transformed into a fearsome icon of slavery, misery, and defeat—or, at best, as a sign of release from this curse of existence, including the mandatory reincarnation of the soul or karmic rebirth.[5] In his book *Breaking the Circle: Death and the Afterlife in Buddhism* (1993), Carl Becker writes: "The Buddhist view is that this life is but one of millions of continuous lives of suffering, destined to continue indefinitely until the cycle is broken. This necessitates a path of selflessness and discipline that leads to enlightenment and freedom from the wheel of rebirth."[6]

What was true in the East was likewise true in the West. King Lear's fiery wheel of crucifixion was thus neither an idiosyncratic hallucinatory symptom of his personal madness, nor a pure creation of Shakespeare's sharp pen. It was a clear reference to the classical Greek myth of Ixion, who, Campbell reminds us, murdered his own father-in-law and attempted to seduce Zeus's perpetually put-upon wife, Hera, while he was Zeus's houseguest on Mt. Olympus. As punishment for his rank insensitivity to manners and family dynamics, Ixion was "bound by Zeus to a blazing wheel of eight spokes, to be sent whirling for all time through the air."[7]

And so, the sacred hoop became, for us, the cursed loop.

A Philosophical Illness

Our identification of the Great Reversal is a step in the right direction. But it is only a piece—if a key piece—of the larger puzzle. For one thing, it doesn't directly address the issue of time. Moreover, it tells us what happened, but not exactly why.

For example, suppose you're walking along one day, carefree and happy, whistling a familiar tune and soaking up the warm sunshine of a spring morning. Suddenly, your mood shifts into a dark cloud of dour pessimistic gloom. You find yourself helplessly shaking your fist at the sky, shouting at the heavens. Why?

One possible answer is that there is no logical reason for the change, only an underlying cause, like a chemical imbalance. You're suffering from a form of mental illness or brain dysfunction brought about by certain physiological processes. Your neurotransmitters are misfiring. It's Prozac time for you, old friend.

The problem with this kind of explanation in the "hoop-to-loop" scenario is that, as Campbell observes, people all over the world—in the East, as well as the West—simultaneously began experiencing the very same, or at least similar, "symptoms" during roughly the same time period. If everyone around you also starts running down the street cursing and wailing, it's not just you or something going wrong only inside of you. It's widespread, possibly contagious. This is an epidemic. Or even a pandemic.

Okay, so it must be something in the environment—an organism or chemical in the water, say, that's causing the problem. Or it could be the air. There's some sort of contaminant that's affecting a lot of people. Perhaps a germ that travels from person to person by casual contact. Uh, oh—you've caught the philosophical flu.

The problem with this analogy is that the "symptoms" of the Great Reversal were not just attitudinal mood swings, but also semiotic—that is to say, having to do with our understanding and interpretation of symbols, especially the circle. The responses themselves are meaningful and intelligent, not purely reflexive like a sneeze or a cough. It's as if we all turned toward the sky at the same moment, making the same gestures and speaking the same curse words in the same language. Get the picture? It's just far too coincidental to be merely accidental.

Wheels within Wheels

So it seems as if we're looking for reasons for this "event" rather than causes in the classically deterministic, mechanical, behavioral, or "scientific" sense. Or put another way: Our emotions are a function of our beliefs. A change in attitude thus hints at an underlying change in our belief patterns. And such beliefs don't change on a dime. Usually, we're most reluctant to give them up. When we do, we have to have a reason.

Let's return, then, to our earlier analogy.

There you are, strolling along, musing to yourself about how wonderful life is, when suddenly, out of nowhere, you encounter an obnoxious, foul-mouthed moron screaming epithets, smoking a smelly cigar, and walking a killer junkyard dog named "Spike"—and he's heading straight for you. "Sic 'em!" the moron gleefully yells to Spike, as the dog's heavy jaws clamp down tightly about your bleeding ankle.

Now how do you feel? It would be perfectly understandable if your paean to the universe became a dirge at this point, and it would not be surprising if you developed an aversion to dogs, cigars, and inconsiderate morons.

This little scenario is not far removed from what Campbell suggests may account for the onset of the Great Reversal: the invention of large-scale, conquering warfare and, specifically, its primary tool, the chariot. The chariot was thus the first doomsday machine, except that—unlike the runaway planet-smasher in *Star Trek*—its makers meant to use it. And they did, with relish, over and over.

What gave the chariot its unique power? Wheels. Campbell, in other words, blames the spoked wheel of the war chariot for the Great Reversal.

The chariot was invented by Indo-European, or so-called "Aryan," invaders from the area of Persia around 2000–1750 BCE. It appeared, he writes, "within the next three hundred years in almost every part of the ancient historic world,"[8] including Egypt, India, Greece, and China. By 500 BCE, the period of the Great Reversal, just about everyone who was anyone in the ancient world had experienced this new form of conflict and absorbed the lessons of life in the war zone. History may be the story of the vanquished as told by the victors, as they say, but the traumas of the defeated live on in the unhealed wounds of the collective psyche.

The victims—at least the ones who survived, for conquest now meant annihilating whole peoples and either leveling or occupying their cities and towns—soured on life. They came to associate an image they'd previously identified with joy and harmony—the circle or spoked wheel—with the terror and wanton destruction visited upon them by merciless invaders. As one of my favorite bumper stickers of years gone by proclaimed "Life sucks, then you die." Or worse yet, you die, but then you have to come back and do it all over again—and again, and again, and again . . .

In those cultures that didn't abandon the cyclical concept of time altogether, particularly in the East, it acquired a very different—decidedly negative—emotional "charge." For the Jain-Hindu-Buddhist traditions, the prime spiritual imperative of the individual becomes breaking the circle of life and death, or ending the perpetual cycle of reincarnation or rebirth in the world. Pass the course the first time around, and you won't have to repeat it. Life goes on, alas—but without me.

In the West, however, the circle was disconnected and hammered out of shape—smashed for all time, you might say. This was a mass event of violent destruction rather than an individual project of escape. The very idea of the repeating cycle/circle of cosmic and historical time was abolished in favor of a linear chronology. The clash of cultures that occurred when Black Elk's Sioux tribes met Custer's troops at the Little Big Horn was, at bottom, a cosmological and metaphysical conflict. What played out within the framework of reflexive racism and the political doctrine of Manifest Destiny was, at bottom, a philosophical war. Sitting Bull won the battle and the day, but the war was lost. The hoop lay broken.

Psychopomp

Yet, it's not entirely clear that Campbell's war-chariot explanation for the Great Reversal will suffice—at least, not completely.

Consider this: A chariot needs horses to pull it, does it not?

Nevertheless, the horse did not acquire the negative associations ostensibly projected onto the circle/wheel of terror. Indeed, for those "primitive" peoples who held on to their animistic respect for the circle, the horse was an especially potent symbol of spiritual freedom. Nor was this association easily erased or obscured.

As renowned Romanian scholar of shamanism Mircea Eliade notes, the horse was the symbol, *par excellence*, of the shaman's ecstatic soul flight— the freedom to leave her physical body and journey to the other world, the higher realms of spiritual reality.[9] Moreover, such decidedly positive associations were retained even in the very same classical Greek culture that concocted the horror story of Ixion's fiery wheel. Witness Pegasus, the white-winged steed that carries Zeus's thunderbolts as the symbolic bearer of divinely inspired power.

So it had to be more than the war chariot that did in the circle. War was undoubtedly a component of the Great Reversal, but it was only one contributing factor, not the primary cause. The Great Reversal was not just about the effects of war; war itself was only a symptom. The underlying disease is—so far—unnamed.

Gray in Gray

The great 19th-century German philosopher G. W. F. Hegel once wrote: "When philosophy paints its grey in grey, then has a shape of life grown old." Hegel was alluding here to a line spoken by Mephistopheles in Goethe's *Faust:*

> My worthy friend, grey are all the theories
> And green alone life's golden tree[11]

What Hegel meant is that, by the time we spin out our intellectual theories of life—or even, from Campbell's standpoint, mythologize our experience with sharp and clear symbolic images—life itself has moved on. What initially captured our attention or fancy has matured, or even completely passed us by.

Now, it may well be true that "objects in mirror are closer than they appear," as it says on my car's rearview mirror. But even if the perspective is skewed, in order for me to see those objects whole, they must be behind me. Understanding, not to mention wisdom, in other words, is retrospective. Hegel, quoting the poet, agreed: "The owl of Minerva spreads its wings only with the falling of the dusk."[12]

Thus we can see that the roots of the Great Reversal lay in a period prior to that of "the great axial sages." Their contribution—for better or for worse—was to distill and interpret the significance of earlier events, namely the advent of a new form of warfare. The Great Reversal was thus a reaction to the past. But just how far back must we go to find ground zero of this catastrophe?

We must journey much further backward in time, to a moment well before the invention of the war chariot—and certainly well before the 6th century BCE. Perhaps, along the way, we may find clues to our Myths of the Great Ending.

So, hop into our cozy little time machine. Sit back and relax, and I'll tell you a story as we go.

Once upon a Time

Once upon a time, a male child was born who would grow up to become a revered prophet, the founder of a great religion.

Then again, maybe he was born, and maybe not.

There is by no means universal agreement among scholars about whether this individual ever actually existed. Nor is there general agreement even among his followers about exactly where, or when, he was born—if indeed he was. However, a legend arose that several wise men were guided on their pilgrimage to the humble birthplace of this future great sage—a lowly farmer's stable—by the light of a brilliant star that shone brightly in the night sky.

By and by, the infant grew into a precocious young boy. Not much is known about his childhood, but apparently he became very critical of the religion in which he was raised. Despising the rampant corruption of the clergy, he questioned many of the doctrines and practices they taught.

When he got older, this brave youth went off alone to search for truth in solitude, apart from all human teachers. During this time of isolation, purification, and testing, he encountered, but successfully resisted, temptation by evil forces and then had a divine vision. Afterward, he returned to his people to teach his new way.

These teachings were eventually written down in sacred texts, although here there is controversy as well. Some believe that the original teachings of this master were distorted by later contributors, some of whom may have been keepers of the old ways who reintroduced elements thereof. However they came to be, there arose a set of metaphysical doctrines associated with this sage—a whole new view of the origin and destiny of the cosmos and the story of human history.

The story goes like this: In the beginning, the world was created by Goodness Then Evil intervened and corrupted the original pristine quality of the

Creation. There was, in other words, a failure—a catastrophic Fall—when elements of Evil got mixed in with the Good. The pattern became confused, twisted like a braided rope. Full-blown, open combat between Good and Evil and their respective angelic helpers broke out. Our mixed-up cosmos was at war with itself.

Good is destined to win this conflict and destroy Evil utterly, once and for all, thus purifying creation and making justice triumph. Each human being has a choice whether to accept the confusion of the world, or to fight on the side of the Good to help destroy Evil. The soul of each will be judged at death accordingly by the Good, who wants and needs human assistance for ultimate victory. Those who choose Good will get into Paradise; those who choose Evil will be sent to the Abyss; those whose deeds are balanced between the two will be sent to a holding area until the final judgment and the final battle between Good and Evil at the end of time.

The prophet of our story believed that his vision came from the Good, and that he alone was sent by the Good to lead humans to Goodness and thus usher in the new age, which has been delayed due to human weakness. This would be humanity's last chance to escape Evil and final judgment, which could be coming very soon—perhaps in the prophet's own lifetime. Toward the end of his life, however, the prophet came to believe he might have to return once more to secure this salvation.

Does the story sound familiar? You bet it does.

No, it's not Jesus and Christianity, but Zoroaster and Zoroastrianism— Zarathustra, in the prophet's native Persian (Zoroaster is the Greek version of his name). It is in Persia, not Palestine, that our time capsule has touched down, and our date-meter should read sometime between 1,800 and 1,000 years before Christ.

Right church, wrong pew—so to speak.

Don't be embarrassed. Remember that we were traveling *back* in time from our departure date of 500 BCE, not *forward* some 900 years to the time of the founding and codification of the Christian religion by the Church Fathers in league with the Byzantine emperors.

Christianity thus did not invent our linear conception of time and history—the familiar three-act drama of Creation, Fall, and Atonement that eventually leads to the End of Days. The scheme was borrowed—not directly or consciously, perhaps, but borrowed nonetheless—from Zoroastrianism, which became the chief religion of the Persian Empire. And just how did this appropriation come about?

Campbell suggests that it was through the actions of the Zoroastrian King of Persia, Cyrus the Great, who freed the Jews from their fifty-year exile and captivity in Babylon in 538 BCE and returned them to the Holy Land. It was under Cyrus's protection that the Great Temple in Jerusalem was rebuilt. The Zoroastrian timeline was assimilated by the Jews, and the anxious expectation of a Messiah bringing final redemption reached fever pitch in the years leading up to the birth of Jesus.

But it was Zoroaster, notes Campbell, who was the first to introduce this new "progressive view of cosmic history." He writes: "This is not the old, ever-revolving cycle of the archaic Bronze Age mythologies, but a sequence, once and for all, of creation, fall and progressive redemption, to culminate in a final, decisive, irrefragable victory of the One Eternal God of Righteousness and Truth."[13]

And who might that be? Why Ahura Mazda—the Zoroastrian Lord of Light and Goodness—of course. Who else?

Cosmic War

If the ancient Persians gave us both the wheeled war chariot and the concept of linear time capped by an apocalyptic battle between Good and Evil—virtually simultaneously—this suggests what we have already hypothesized, namely, that the ugly spoked wheel of war and the breaking of the harmonious circle are related, not as cause to effect, but rather as co-effects of some as-yet unnamed primary cause. Accordingly, the Great Reversal was already well under way at least 500 years, and maybe even 1,000 years, before the dates given by Campbell.

But is there any further evidence to support this hypothesis?

We could speculate that there was some reflection of Zoroaster's novel ideas concerning cosmic history in the imagery of the once-sacred circle itself. Well, it turns out there is a Zoroastrian symbol known as the Faravahar (or Farohar) that may hold the key. The carved image, which may have its origins in much earlier Egyptian designs of winged solar discs, depicts the profile of a hybrid man-bird with outstretched wings. The trunk of the figure's body is shown surrounded by—or perhaps emerging out of—a circle. In his hand(s), he holds a circular ring.

One esoteric interpretation maintains that the larger circle represents the eternal soul, while the ring symbolizes "the cycles of birth and rebirth, which the soul has to undergo to make progress on the path," leading to salvation and final release.[14]

The underlying message of the metaphorical image may also be that all that surrounds us, and from which we have apparently emerged, is in our hands. We are in control, in other words, of the world process—of nature, that is—through our decision to fight for Good and against Evil. We can therefore overcome and defeat nature by disentangling the mixed strands of darkness and light, just as we can overcome and defeat our own inner, evil nature.

Zoroaster thus gave us the End of the World, as well as the breaking of the circle, in two key senses: the Eastern sense, in which the individual escapes personally from the karmic repetitive cycle of life-death, and the Western sense, in which we are all subject to a linear temporal order. But wait—as the television infomercial pitchmen promise—there's more!

Alexander's Tutor

Now just hop back into the time capsule and we'll adjust the controls.

Let's take a brief detour to the home of one of Persia's archenemies, the ancient Greeks—Athens around 335 BCE, to be precise. It is here, hundreds of years after the time of Zoroaster, that we encounter Plato's great pupil and the able tutor of Alexander the Great: Aristotle.

Aristotle is often thought of as one of the first empirically minded Greek philosophers—a careful, plodding thinker and a true observer of nature—not as an otherworldly mystic like his master, Plato. He was certainly no self-anointed religious prophet like Zoroaster. Moreover, he was every bit as suspicious and critical of the old Olympian myths as Socrates, who thought that tales of fornicating, argumentative, petulant gods were ridiculous anthropomorphisms. Some regard Aristotle as the first scientist—or at least the first professor—dull, pedantic, boring.

Yet, in Aristotle's thought, and specifically in his later theory of art, we detect faint distant echoes of the Persian Zoroaster's gospel.

Most students of literature are taught that, in Aristotle's view, every important or serious story—by which he meant the tragic form—must have a beginning, a middle, and an end. This is because Aristotle believed that a true artist imitates nature. The coherent plot of any narrative that imitates the highest form of poetry, namely tragedy, must reflect the complete life cycle of an individual organism—which includes birth, aging, and death.[15]

But art does not merely mimic nature. What nature does blindly or unconsciously, the artist must do with full awareness, intent, and purpose.[16] The poet, in other words, is a kind of scientist whose aim is to reveal the underlying patterns in nature and bring them to controlled perfection in art, in and through the human mind.

Aristotle was thus adamant that the sequence of action in tragedy had to embody a *rational* presentation or order: crystal-clear, easily understandable, and totally satisfying. The narrative must leave no loose ends. It must be whole and complete. If we wonder what came before the beginning, what came after the end, or why the middle had to be just what it was, the poet has not done a good job.[17]

The Least We Can Do

Zoroaster's religious concept of linear time and his three-part sequence of cosmic history—Creation, Fall, Redemptive End—thus became, under Aristotle, the model for all significant stories. His achievement was to secularize the sacred.

Aristotle saw himself as an observer of "nature," and the artist as an imitator of it. What is interesting, however, is Aristotle's focus on the development of the isolated individual organism. In Aristotle's ethics, it is also the individual man—and he meant males only; no women need apply—who is perfected in a practical and intellectual virtue that is the moral ideal. Moreover, only a select few, a moral elite, qualify.

Older "archaic" or "primitive" cultures, on the other hand, focused on the overall cyclical process of nature—the larger community, or circle, of life— in which the individual organism was situated. Their emphasis was always on the unbroken continuity of the process. Endings become final, or at least seem to, when we perceive ourselves as detached from the larger field—as Aristotle, a city-dweller, did.

This sense of detachment is telling. Aristotle's is an intellectual and practical mastery of Mother Nature—we can do what She does, only better, because we can grasp, through the conscious rational intellect, the patterns that She blindly enacts only in her dumb, instinctive fashion. Breaking the circle is the least we can do.

Such an attitude of condescension is indeed the ideological forerunner of modern science. It complements and reinforces the moral and spiritual mastery of nature advocated by religious zealots like Zoroaster and his progeny, who see in nature's subtle, graceful complexities and darker shades of gray a challenge to their rigid, simplistic, black-and-white notions of purity and justice. Whereas the Omaha Chief allowed that death would always come out of season, for messianic and apocalyptic cults, the crooked must be made straight, soon—or else.

This is the contrast between what Campbell describes as "two completely different readings of the nature of the universe and of man"—namely, "a mystical affirmative" view of life as it is, "as against a moral corrective" of its presumed flaws.[18] It is the courage to affirm, versus the will to reform, the world. Or, should that general reform fail or prove too much, to flee altogether the pointless round of sorrow.

A Civilization of Our Discontents

The nascent transformation of our ideas, experience, and symbolic images of time thus predates Aristotle, the Great Reversal, the innovations of Zoroaster, and even the invention of the war chariot. All of these are but tributaries of a single common stream. To follow that main stream back to its source is to end up—where? Where and when did our sense of detachment and isolation begin?

"Man lived harmlessly on this planet for some three million years," writes Daniel Quinn in his novel *Ishmael*.[19] Then, around 8000 BCE, something rather drastic and unprecedented happened. Instead of feeling that they belonged to the world, people began to sense that the world belonged to them. It was theirs to do with as they liked. They could manage it, control it, and exploit it—whatever they chose.

Oddly, some humans got it into their heads that they were the masters of life rather than its servants. Ten thousand years ago, they revolted—the Agricultural Revolution—and the birth of what we call civilization followed: city-states, mass society, organized religions, the division of labor, mass warfare, famine, slavery, population explosion, pollution— in short, the works. "Archaic," "primitive," "tribal," "animist," "shaman" all became pejoratives—terms of derision applied by the newly "civilized" to their past.[20]

This implies that the Myth of the Great Ending is not at all what we think it is. It's not about the future at all, either real or imagined; it's about the past, and a consciously repressed trauma of catastrophic proportions. The world has already ended—and, for most of us, a long, long time ago at that. Nevertheless, the subterranean reverberations of that epochal, earth-shattering event are yet with us, still being sensed, but not quite appreciated for what they truly are: aftershocks.

We can't get the Myth of the Great Ending out of our collective heads for the very same reason that dreams may recur, over and over, with little or no real change in our individual dream-life: We just don't get it. "Like a movie rerun," writes Betty Bethards in her guide to dream analysis, *The Dream Book: Symbols for Self-Understanding*, "there is a message you're not seeing."[21]

What will happen if and when we do get the message? For some, it just may mean entering that seemingly lost world of nature and spirit from which we are exiled by thought and deed. As long as we believe in that exile and act accordingly, we are, indeed, exiled. The hoop, however, remains: We just can't believe our own experience of it. Properly understood, the Myth of the Great Ending is itself a gateway to that very experience.

The See-Er

The one who came closest to grasping this was the Paiute Indian seer Wovoka, the originator of the Ghost Dance movement that culminated in the ultimate act of hoop-shattering on the North American continent: the 1890 massacre of Sioux men, women, and children at Wounded Knee.

Wovoka is often dismissed as a failed, if well-intentioned, prophet who tried to give the indigenous tribes hope in a hopeless situation by cobbling together bits and pieces of the New Testament Apocalypse and Indian lore. What he actually did, in fact, was to intuit that the Christian promise of the future was really a disguised and distorted echo of the past, and that realizing this could alter present reality. Wovoka broke the code hidden deep within our Myth of the Great Ending.

Wovoka had a dream, or vision, that he related to the Native people: Come together. Make the sacred circle again. Do this dance. If you do this, and live in your hearts as we did before, and act as we did before, before will be now. The dead that were wiped away will come back to life—the two-leggeds, the four-leggeds, the winged ones, all of them. That world will live again, here and now.

When Black Elk performed the Ghost Dance, he left his physical body behind on the ground and went on a journey. He found himself soaring over a high ridge:

> On the other side of the ridge I could see a beautiful land where many, many people were camping in a great circle. I could see that they were happy and had plenty. Everywhere there were drying racks full of meat. The air was clear and beautiful with a living light that was everywhere.[22]

The Christian soldiers who murdered those who had assembled at Wounded Knee in an effort to mend the hoop probably told themselves that they were just trying to stop another Indian uprising. After all, what Wovoka taught was sheer nonsense, wasn't it? Or were they secretly afraid that what the Paiute said might be true, and that it was their hope for a miraculous deliverance from their own perfidy that was the true vanity of vanities? By keeping the circle broken, a straight and narrow line would lead to their final deliverance from evil, would it not?

"If there really is no End-Time," observes author Brad Steiger, "but only periodic transition times, the whole area of Apocalyptic revelation has little, or no, meaning."[23]

Yes, precisely.

The question is this: Would we kill to protect ourselves from the realization that our dearest beliefs are meaningless? Perhaps the only thing worse than this knowledge is the recognition that those beliefs do have some meaning after all, but it turns out to be the exact opposite of what it was originally supposed to be. In that case, we might want to distract ourselves as best we can to discourage any deeper investigation.

There are many forms this distraction can take. One of the most effective and entertaining is the prizefight, in which two muscular, well-matched combatants duke it out before cheering throngs that feel obliged to choose sides. What the betting audience doesn't know, of course, is that it's all a set-up, a clever ploy; the fix is already in. Both fighters, you see, work for the same boss.

We call this staged theatrical performance "the culture wars."

CHAPTER FOUR

FROM SACRED HOOPS
TO TIME LOOPS

There is nothing absolute and final. If everything were iron-clad, all the rules absolute and everything structured so no paradox or irony existed, you couldn't move. One could say that man sneaks through the crack where paradox exists.

ITZHAK BENTOV, *A Cosmic Book:*
On the Mechanics of Creation (1988)

Understanding the process of time brings a greater integration with the forces of destiny.

A. T. MANN, *The Elements of the Tarot* (1993)

So: Aristotle or Zoroaster? Whose side are you on?

Perhaps we should not be too surprised after all to find our culture wars still simmering away, occasionally reaching a roiling boil, decades, if not centuries, after the clash between science and religion supposedly was over and done with.

Yet the conflict between the empirically minded descendants of Aristotle on the one hand and the prophetically inspired minions of Zoroaster on the other rages on and shows no sign of resolution.

Our familiar controversies over abortion, stem-cell research, euthanasia, evolution versus creationism (or "intelligent design"), and the separation of church and state all testify to the robust endurance of an argument supposedly settled long, long ago. Just when we think they are dead and buried, once and for all, the old disputes rise from the cultural grave to haunt our every waking moment.

Is this a shocking turn of events? Not really. Most parents expect that siblings will fight in the backseat of the car on a long trip. And if our account thus far of the origin of the Myth of the Great Ending is accurate, then our two rough-and-tumble "opponents" are, at bottom, more alike than different. Which may help to explain why, like our bickering backseat brood, Aristotle and Zoroaster just don't get along. Nothing inspires conflict like common parentage.

What official science and religion share is a belief that things are progressing as they should, and must. In the end, the whole slate will be wiped clean anyway. The end may or may not be near, but it is inevitable.

Our would-be antagonists may disagree—violently, at times—over the proper interpretation of terms like "progress" and "end." But those are really relatively minor disputes in the scheme of things. These "enemies" embrace the same basic view of time, and they display the same basic mindset and temperament: narrow, dogmatic, and judgmental. The ride may be bumpy and contentious, but their destination is the same.

Not Aristotle *or* Zoroaster, then, but Aristotle *and* Zoroaster. Or—what? Is there a genuine alternative to our present seesaw cultural dynamic?

The answer, I believe, is yes.

Within some of the livelier precincts of science itself—and especially in the experiences of ordinary individuals who have somehow eluded indoctrination by the orthodoxy of both mainstream science and traditional religion—something has been pushing us toward a realization of another way, one that has more in common with the long-discredited adherents of the hoop.

How do we get off of the teeter-totter without falling flat on our faces? That's what we have to figure out. And that's what we'll begin exploring in this chapter.

The Haunting

The ghosts of Aristotle and Zoroaster haunt us still. Their shades were there at the birth of modernity, and have fed the push-me, pull-you dynamic all the way.

Modernity was born in revolution. The revolt, directed against the old medieval matriarch, Mother Church, was led on two quite separate fronts by the German ex-monk Martin Luther (1483–1546) and the French Catholic thinker René Descartes (1596–1650). Luther, who believed himself to be inspired by the Holy Spirit, created modern Protestantism; Descartes broke with his Jesuit teachers and founded modern philosophy. This he did both in his personal declaration to be his own teacher and in his philosophical first principle, known to every college freshman: "I think, therefore I am." Both the prophet and the philosopher rebelled against the Church's absolute moral, spiritual, and political authority. But there the resemblance stops—or does it?

Poisoned at the Source

Luther believed that the Church's great mistake had been in supposing that there was any part of the world that was good or redeemable. Only God is good. As far as he was concerned, the world is a stinking, rotten dung hole, and everything in it—including humankind, and even saintly Mother Church—is evil. Nature had not been merely corrupted by Adam and Eve's mishap in the Garden; it had been thoroughly, totally corrupted. Human nature is a cesspool, a toxic waste dump.

Thus our reason is completely useless, our will is utterly weak, and our desires are base, selfish, and perverse. To think that we can discover the truth as it is given to us in the Bible is an impious joke. In fact, the only reason that God gave Moses—and, by extension, all humanity—the moral law was to show him how incapable people were of following it. Only fools who don't get the joke think otherwise.[1]

Salvation from eternal torment in Hell is, therefore, a free gift given by God that we can never, ever earn on our own. We are powerless, and He is all-powerful. Between the two lies an absolute gulf. We can only hope for His mercy.

Divine justice and mercy will, of course, prevail in the End. Like Zoroaster before him, Luther believed in the ultimate triumph of Good over Evil and the destruction of the old, fallen world—all would come to pass, orchestrated from on high. The difference is that Luther believed the Great Conductor was also, in effect, playing all the instruments and singing all the parts, while the members of the orchestra only pretended to play their assigned roles. But this is an illusion. In effect, their parts are lip-synched and dubbed in by the Maestro, because they can never hope to get it right otherwise.

Effectively, all we can do is to hope that God will grant us a faith in Him that we can neither explain nor understand—nor, certainly, merit—and that we will be rescued thereby from our own iniquity. That He will do this for some is certain; that He will not do it for all is equally certain. But who will win the cosmic lottery, and why? This is a total mystery to us, but known even before Creation by Him. It's predestination.

Nothing So Far Distant

If, for Luther, the Church's mistake lay in trusting too much in human reason and humanity's innate potential, Descartes' diagnosis was the reverse: By placing too much emphasis on faith and blind trust in higher authority, the Church had stifled reason and human progress. Science would now show us the best way.

Descartes was one of those optimistic Enlightenment figures who believed that, when reason is used properly, there are virtually no limits to what we can know. There are no unsolvable holy mysteries before which we must bow down in mute adoration, only problems that remain temporarily unsolved. Ignorance is merely provisional. When our thinking is guided by the correct method, "there is nothing so far distant," he wrote, "that one cannot finally reach, nor so hidden that one cannot discover."[2]

What is the right method? Descartes took his cue from the physics of Newton, who held that physical matter can be broken down to basic building blocks called "atoms" (from the Greek, *atomos*, which means "indivisible"), a term borrowed from the ancient Greek philosopher Democritus. Once we understand how these basic components operate, we can predict and control events in the physical world.

Similarly, for Descartes, the path to truth lay in analytic-reductive thinking: breaking down large, unwieldy, and complex problems or questions into their smallest component parts—atoms of thought, you might say. And since the whole is but the sum of its parts—voila! Problem solved, question answered, case closed.

For example, "How do I graduate from college?" is a big question. Break it down: First, send some applications; then decide, based on your acceptances, where you want to go; then register for classes; then buy your books; then study hard and pass your courses; and so on. Before you know it, you will have graduated.

This grand optimism in the power of rational inquiry to lay bare the secrets of the universe had an eminently practical side, of course. The English philosopher Francis Bacon (1561–1626) supposedly declared that we should "put nature to the rack," if necessary, in order to torture those secrets out of her.[3] He also famously stated the fundamental equation of the scientific movement: "Knowledge is power."

Now couple Bacon's statement with the Cartesian faith in method, or the right use of reason. If all knowledge is possible, and knowledge is power, it follows that all power is possible. In other words, the qualities previously used to define the Deity—omniscience and omnipotence—are now employed as adjectives describing the human community of scientific inquiry over time, from the glorious present on to the future and the final curtain call.

The King—God—is dead; long live the King—us.

Frankenstein's Drive-In

There are virtually no limits to this form of psychological inflation, which is directed both outward to nature, and inward to the self—even to the one item that Descartes allowed might contain some genuine residual mystery: the soul, or what we call consciousness. For true believers in the materialist hypothesis of science, consciousness must ultimately be seen as reducible to the electrochemical processes of brain function, or as mere accidental by-products thereof.

As author Ronald Russell has astutely observed, there is a kind of giddy intellectual imperialism at work here. The spirit of conquest is plainly evident:

> What seems to have happened is that the problem of consciousness (where it comes from, what it is) has been interpreted as "science's last great frontier." It has come to be regarded as if it were one more territory that must be

conquered, mapped, and taken into control, using weapons and technologies that have proved themselves in other fields.[4]

These "other fields" include mastering the very process of evolution itself. Darwin gave us the theory, but now, thanks to our digital technology, we are going to rewrite the practice. In a recent article, science writer Michael Specter provides a fascinating (some might argue chilling) glimpse into the emerging discipline of synthetic biology, which is itself a synthesis of elements of such diverse fields as engineering, chemistry, computer science, and molecular biology. The avowed aim of this discipline is nothing less than the total "redesign [of] the living world."[5]

The holy grail of the synthetic biologists is not just to alter existing genes, but to manufacture brand-new ones from the ground up. "Eventually," writes Specter, these bold scientists "intend to construct genes—and new forms of life—from scratch," and are absolutely convinced that they will write computer programs that will enable "them not only [to] alter nature but guide human evolution as well."[6]

Yes, we can build you—better, faster, stronger, smarter, and healthier.

Jay Keasling, a professor of biochemical engineering at the University of California at Berkeley, sums up the ethos and credo—either grand or grandiose, depending upon your perspective—of the synthetic biologists' endeavor: "We have got to the point in human history," he opines, "where we simply do not have to accept what nature has given us."[7] In other words, it's the Great Ending of history as we have heretofore known it. To paraphrase the old Burger King motto: Special orders don't upset us. We can have it our way, after all.

Personality Disorder

So, are we omnipotent or impotent? Superman and Wonder Woman, or Super-worm and Doris Doormat? Well, what day is it today?

We suffer from this cultural bipolar disorder, swinging wildly from one moody extreme to the other: from the two warring camps of Jerry Falwell and Pat Robertson on the one side, to that of Isaac Asimov and Carl Sagan on the other. It turns out that megalomania and its opposite number—what a college professor of mine once dubbed "micromania"—are but two equivalent symptoms of a single philosophical/mythological disease after all.

For religion, nature is at best irrelevant, something to escape; at worst, it is evil, corrupt, sinful, and merits destruction. For science, nature is something "out there," a dynamic functioning machine to be studied objectively, analyzed, and used as humans see fit—exploited where feasible, preserved where necessary. Religion worships God as the controller (and ultimate destroyer) of nature, whereas science envisions humanity as the final controlling principle. In both instances, nature is seen as something apart that is or can be managed for human benefit.

Yet, even on the seemingly controversial issue of just who is in charge, the differences between science and religion may be less than meets the eye. For God can be seen as doing our dirty work for us. He may be our proxy, our surrogate, allowing us to sit back and enjoy his destruction of the evil world vicariously.

Even Saint Thomas Aquinas—perhaps the greatest philosopher of the Middle Ages—suggested that part of the joy of being in Heaven was gazing down into the dark abyss of Hell and enjoying the eternal torment of the damned. If "justice" is indeed just another name for "organized social revenge" as some have claimed, then God is our own ultimate Enforcer.

When "No" Means "Yes"

In his very first cinematic outing in *Dr. No* (1962), James Bond (Sean Connery, of course), striving to appear unimpressed with the eponymous villain's boasting, offers a curt dismissal of his adversary's grandiose ambitions. "World domination," Bond sighs laconically. "The same old dream."[8]

Yes, for some it has been the one and only dream for the last 10,000 years. And it's the prime cause of a recurring nightmare: the Myth of the Great Ending.

One way of looking at the drive to dominate nature that began with the Agricultural Revolution is that it is, at bottom, an attempt to control time—to force time to work for us and do our bidding. Cutting down a forest to plant corn or wheat is another way of saying: "I'm not going to just hang around to wait and see if some food happens to come my way. I'm going to make the future happen now."

Modern civilization has cut down on the wait time. We buy winter squash in summer, and summer squash in winter. We take wonder drugs to keep us awake, so we don't have to sleep and "lose" time.[9] We suck the fat out of our hips and pour it back into our lips to defeat the "ravages" of time. We freeze our own dead bodies in the hope that someday, somehow, somewhere, a cure will be found for the disease that "cut short" our time on earth. We prefer instant messaging to snail mail any day.

Go ahead, make a list of the familiar phrases: "Time is money." "Stop wasting time." "I want it yesterday." And so it goes, on and on.

Time is the ultimate commodity, and we "civilized" folk are the consummate commodity traders. And if it's true—as we're constantly telling ourselves—that free trade is the ultimate form of freedom, then we must be the freest people ever.

Aren't we? Isn't that the main story line of our progressive history?

The paradox is that time is like one of those multicolored straw tubes we used to call "Chinese finger puzzles": The harder you struggle to break free of its grip, the tighter that grip becomes. And so we become prisoners, not masters, of time. The solution, as we learn, is to loosen up and stop struggling.

When Wovoka told the people to dance their way back to sanity, he was urging them to reenter the natural cyclical rhythms of time and, in so doing, break through into that timeless dimension that annuls the felt distance between past, present, and future. The world ended, is ending, and will ever end—amen. Remember: Every point along the circumference of a circle is at once beginning, middle, and end, and all are equidistant from the center. It's just how you look at it, and what you're looking for, that determines when and where you are.

Taking the Measure

But you see, it's hard to measure progress if things are just going round and round in circles all the time. It's as if we're not really getting anywhere.

Measurement itself is another form of control. If, for instance, I can measure out the right amount of flour, set the proper temperature, and select the correct number of eggs, I can bake the same cake every time—provided, of course, that I follow the proper steps in their prescribed order. If I get something out of sequence—out of time, in other words—all bets are off. Putting the vanilla in after the cake has been baking for an hour, for example, just won't do.

This is the essence of our scientific method: step-by-step linear thinking. Controlled experience that yields a controlled result is what we call an experiment. In scientific experiments, wild experience is tamed and domesticated, carefully programmed to produce a certain repeatable outcome, like baking a cake. A centrally determined, common system of measurement is key to the process. Measurement is a prerequisite for understanding causes and effects. It is the ultimate, and most basic, tool of reason.

Class Project

We learn these lessons early. Back in the sixth grade, most of us were assigned a class project: the construction of a historical timeline.

In my case, my teacher marked off regular intervals in her neat handwriting on narrow rectangular pieces of yellow oak-tag and placed them at the top of the blackboard all around the room. She allowed each of us to choose a particular world historical event to study. (I chose the assassination of Julius Caesar, and drew some cartoons to illustrate the murder and its aftermath.) Then she wrote the dates of the events on the timeline so we could see how they all fit together.

My teacher, you see, was performing the role of God or nature in our religious and (pre-Einsteinian) scientific models of time. She was the cosmic controller. She set the common standard by providing the framework for events to unfold within a prescribed and determined field. Time is objectively real, a built-in feature of the physical universe having absolutely uniform units of measure, just like the oak-tag cards on the wall. The lesson: Time always moves at the same rate, and is the same for everyone and everything, everywhere—no matter what. The universe has an order, and we can figure out what it is, and somehow make it work for us.

Psychic Politics

Some observers associate the drive to control and gain mastery of time or nature with what they view as the historical development of the human ego, arguing that this was somehow a necessary evil, an inevitable step in the "evolution" of human consciousness. You can't make an omelet without breaking a few eggs, after all. This view is itself a manifestation of a faith in linear progress.

On the other hand, there are many spiritual teachers who maintain that the ego is just evil, the source of all our problems, and that we should strive to "erase" or "annihilate" our individual egos if we hope to make true spiritual progress and achieve lasting happiness and peace. Such ideas are even part of some religions.[10]

The problem, however, is not the ego itself, but rather our attitude toward it and our use of it. It is as if a member of a basketball team were to get the urge to play all the various positions—forward, center, guard. Or as if one member of a family suddenly decided to take over all the roles: mother, father, sister, brother, son, daughter. That would be madness, a kind of un-checked psychological imperialism. And make no mistake: World domina-tion is a delusion, not just a "stage" little Johnny has to pass through on his way to well-adjusted adulthood.

The ego is part of a family or team of the total self, just as the self is a part of larger and greater totalities, all the way on up to All That Is. Each must play its part cooperatively, as best it can, in concert with all the others doing the same. There is no evil, even of the necessary kind, in the ego and its functions—including and especially that of reason, which is an essential check against the very real dangers of uncritical awareness. Unquestioning acceptance is the ticket to Jonestown.

Thus, beware all self-proclaimed "spiritual teachers" who insist that their followers erase their egos in order to find bliss. You can rest assured that those "egoless" Ascended Masters are busily pocketing the ego-shavings of their flock and selling them at a hefty profit in order to grab their own fat piece of the pie. There is no surer sign of an imperialistic ego than the im-modest claims of its detractors.

But what is the imperialistic rational ego trying to conquer if not the very nonrational, intuitive, imaginative aspects of self that create and maintain those invisible bonds with its kin—the other group members "within," as well as the greater reality "without"? This bloated ego run amok is acid to the glue that holds our selves, and the world, together; it is this ego that seeks to control time at all costs.

Everything Old

Some years ago, the gifted psychic Jane Roberts declared that humanity was in dire need of a new "politics of the psyche"—that is, a new set of metaphors for depicting the inner and outer relationships of consciousness. What we need, she wrote, goes beyond the tired old image of "the ego ruling the self as God ruled man; man dominant over the planet and other species, as God was dominant over man."[11]

Happily, we already possess an example of this "new" psychic politics. It is provided by the very archaic peoples who never bought into—at least, not completely or with conviction—the absolute monarchism that is explicit in much religion, and implicit in science and its search for unbreakable, universal natural "laws." Indigenous peoples spurned the attempt to tame nature by reducing her to a rigid scheme of abstract theoretical concepts that served as a mechanism of intellectual control and practical management. They willingly yielded to nature's wildness—her seemingly chaotic patterns and the unplanned order that spontaneously emerges thereby.

In *Indian Givers*, anthropologist Jack Weatherford provides an example of this trust in the traditional Indian powwow. "No one is in control," he writes, which "seems to be typical of Indian community events."[12] Since no one is "in charge," the festivities never begin as scheduled. There is no master of ceremonies to order the dancers and drummers around. Some performers listed on the program never show up, while others not officially scheduled deliver impromptu performances.

All of this may seem chaotic to outsiders unfamiliar with and unaccustomed to Indian ways and their "peculiar" sense of time.

Yet, Weatherford insists, there is indeed an order, an organic flow, as each individual—freely doing his or her own thing—assists in the cocreation of a mass event that functions smoothly, like a flock of geese wheeling about in the air or a school of minnows turning in the water. "The event unfolds as a collective activity of all participants," he notes, "not as one mandated and controlled from the top. Each participant responds to the collective mentality and mood of the whole group but not to a single, directing voice."[13]

Magical Surrender

There is something profoundly magical in this kind of sensitivity to the "collective mentality," is there not? Whether we label it "instinct," "telepathy," or "the collective unconscious" tells us more about our own field of endeavor and its prejudices than it does about the phenomenon itself, which remains deeply mysterious, no matter what we say as biologists, psychologists, physicists, or parapsychologists.

By paying attention to the voice within, we are put in touch with larger forces and their dynamic. This move confounds linear thinking and measurement and the drive to manage and control our experience in a religious or scientific way. But it's the essence of the mentality for which the circle—rather than the straight line—is the key symbol.

Emil Sinclair, the youthful protagonist of Hermann Hesse's novel, *Demian*, is in search of his true self. As he stares into a blazing fire, he reclaims memories of certain lost childhood pleasures: gazing at natural phenomena like gnarled tree roots, clouds, smoke, and water. Not so much "observing them," says Sinclair, "as surrendering to their magic, their confused, deep language."[14] This reminiscence proves to be a fortuitous, but decisive, turning point in his quest for inner truth.

Not, you see, the detached observation of a scientist studying nature from without—and certainly not a religious indifference to, or condemnation of, the natural world—but rather a Tao-like yielding to the natural flow and going with it. This is what enables Sinclair to break through to a sense of connection to the timeless dimension: "The surrender to Nature's irrational, strangely confused formations produces in us a feeling of inner harmony with the force responsible for these phenomena,"[15] he adds.

This is the harmony we can all recollect when we arrive at the generative center of the hoop and sense the connection to all things. For such experiences are by no means the exclusive province of great artists, mystics, and shamans.

In *Visions of Innocence: Spiritual and Inspirational Experiences of Childhood*, psychologist Edward Hoffman documents numerous examples of this type of experience, drawn from the early lives of ordinary individuals, including a forty-seven-year-old woman named Yvonne who lives in Scotland and runs a small marketing business with her husband.

When she was a young girl, around eleven years old, Yvonne was lying on her stomach in the grass one afternoon in her parents' backyard garden, idly watching some ants struggling to move small pieces of leaf through the grass. Then, without warning, her perception shifted. She was no longer a mere outside observer, but a direct participant: "Suddenly my attention became so focused that I lost all sense of myself and my ordinary existence," she told Hoffman. "I felt as though I were that world of ants, the brown terrain under their black legs, the obstacles, the air enclosed by the green thickets reaching above them. Somehow I was fully merged with the ants' aliveness and purpose."[16]

Paradoxically, what is sensed or known in this state of connectedness—intuitively, instinctively, telepathically, clairvoyantly, mystically, or whatever term suits your fancy—may yet be a destructive influence when viewed from the standpoint of the circle's perimeter, the revolving cycles of life in the world. The End may not be at hand, but an ending may be. "The end of things is always hard," mused Joseph Campbell.

Well, no one said it would be easy.

The Voice Within

"Dreams," wrote the late Marie-Louise von Franz (echoing her mentor, Carl Jung), "are, as it were, the voice of nature within us."[17] Consequently, dreams—along with their kissing cousins, waking visions—are precisely the kind of "irrational, strangely confused formations" that wind up on the forbidden list of official science and religion.

This is particularly true of dreams and visions that wreak havoc on our established concepts of linear time—like those that seem to contain an awareness of future events, called by parapsychologists "precognitive," or, when a specific warning of imminent danger is sensed or involved, "premonitory." By our usual scientific standards, this is impossible, since the future by definition hasn't yet occurred. Thus the person reporting such an experience is either lying or deluded. In any case, it's bogus and best ignored, except as evidence of mental pathology.

While Eastern religions accept the reality of such psychic knowledge, they downplay its importance, calling it a distraction from the main "spiritual" aim of enlightened world-escape.

Western religions, on the other hand, accept that God may tell some people about the future—but only the special, holy ones, like prophets or saints. Otherwise, such experiences are likely to be demonic in origin and thus delusory. In short, it's either a bogey or it's bogus.

But what if it's not? And what if it's not select members of some spiritual elite prophesying the Great Ending, but completely ordinary, imperfect—even decidedly non-spiritual—types foreseeing events to come?

One of the most studied and gifted psychics, New York City artist Ingo Swann, insists that "Future seeing is not confined to famous psychics," or a special chosen few. "Momentous forthcoming events 'leak' into the consciousness of 'average' people," he writes, "and sometimes hundreds foresee bits and pieces of them," like a vast puzzle or mosaic that has to be assembled.[18]

British psychiatrist Dr. Peter Fenwick and his wife, Elizabeth, report a number of cases of ordinary individuals dreaming of major disasters—in very specific and concrete terms—before they happen. One such case was the Aberfan mine disaster of October 21, 1966, in which half a million tons of coal waste "slithered down a hillside above the small Welsh mining village of Aberfan, engulfing the school and obliterating a generation of schoolchildren." Researcher Dr. John Barker, after investigating seventy-five claims of precognition, concluded that at least thirty-five individuals had experienced genuine premonitions of the mining disaster, and that one man even "saw the name Aberfan in his dream."[19]

Moreover, public events foreseen need not be of a negative or disastrous kind, as Ingo Swann's own dramatic example attests—nor do they only occur in dreams.

Swann tells how he was invited to give a series of workshops and lectures on psychic matters at a conference in Detmold, (then) West Germany, in 1988. At the conclusion of his keynote address—which was simultaneously being translated into German for his listeners—someone from the audience stood up and asked him to make a prognostication. After all, he notes, he had been billed as a "super-psychic."

At first, Swann was irritated with the man's request. But as he tuned in to the audience, he felt his consciousness expanding, flowing outward, and becoming smooth and clear—like "liquid." Suddenly, he burst forth with a bold prediction: "The Berlin Wall will come down within eighteen to twenty-four months." It sounded so preposterous that his German translator simply stared at him in openmouthed astonishment. "Translate it," Swann snapped. "Translate it NOW!" And she did, to the thundering ovation and emotional outpouring of the assembled group.[20]

Of course, we know, in retrospect, that's exactly what did happen: The wall, and with it the entire Soviet empire, soon collapsed. But the most interesting thing about this incident is that Swann insists that his information came, not from inside himself, but from the unconscious perceptions of his audience: It was they who already knew, at a deeper level, what was to come. He simply articulated their unspoken inklings by assembling the pieces of the puzzle secreted in the minds of quite ordinary people. They were the source; he was merely the conduit.

I know that what Swann says about this is true simply because it's happened to me, and to people I've come to know. And none of us, I'd bravely affirm, are saints, fools, lunatics, or devils.

Shapes of Things to Come

During the second half of the year 2000, I began to have dreams and visions (during meditations) that seemed to suggest a major disaster was imminent.

On a number of occasions, a female guide figure I'd met in meditations met me inside a dark cave, where she warned me to "hurry," because there was "so little time" left. When I became concerned that this event was my own imminent death, she became impatient and snapped, "No, not *you*." Somehow, I knew by her response that many people would die in some sort of future event of a public nature.

In one dream, I was exploring a darkened chamber or cave when I came across an Egyptian sarcophagus. A disembodied voice shouted "Danger!" I awoke with a feeling of dread.

In another dream, I encountered a dark, swarthy, sinister-looking man of Middle-Eastern appearance who was filling capsules with poison. He told me with sadistic relish that just one capsule could annihilate an entire building full of people.

A third dream took place inside a large office building. Everyone was suddenly ordered to evacuate, as the entire structure was collapsing. As I tried to wake myself up out of this nightmare, I saw before my inner eye a map of the Eastern seaboard, with the caption, "Persian submarines" near New York City.

There were other dreams, including one about an airliner crashing near my college office in Brooklyn. All of them seem connected, and they were building up to some sort of crescendo, though I had no idea what it was.

Then, on September 11, 2001, I went to work as usual. I was teaching my 8:00 AM class, when suddenly I felt light-headed and weak. I sat down on the edge of the desk and glanced up at the clock: It read 8:45. I dismissed the class early, and went to my office to rest. An hour later, I discovered that at precisely the time I felt ill, the first of the planes had smashed into the World Trade Center. I wrote about these episodes in my first book, with the aim of encouraging others who'd had similar experiences not to think they were crazy and to come forth.

A few months after I submitted the manuscript to my publisher, I received a message from Matt, who worked in the publicity department. He admitted that both he and his wife, Leslie, a schoolteacher, had had premonitions of the attacks.

Leslie had suffered from a bout of recurring nightmares for a solid week before the event. Like one of my own "bad dreams," hers took place inside an office building. People were terrified, running down the hallways in a vain attempt to escape something that was chasing them, even though they seemed to know that they were doomed. Leslie woke up shaken. Her retelling of the dreams to Matt left him with an aftertaste of the horror she'd seen. He too began to sense something terrible was at hand and was filled with a kind of free-floating anxiety.

Mostly by word of mouth, using our respective networks of family, friends, and acquaintances, Matt and I collected dozens of similar stories, with the idea that we would write a book. Our respondents were overwhelmingly solid professional types, including psychologists, psychotherapists, college professors, school teachers, artists, nurses, and computer programmers, just to name a few. Many came forth only reluctantly, preferring to remain anonymous. They just wanted to tell their stories, to hear that they were not alone, and to have their perceptions validated.

Is such validation warranted? Consider the following sample report:

John, a middle-aged professor of political science who had earned his doctorate at Berkeley and has taught at well-regarded colleges and universities, was in the process of moving his family from Chicago to California early in 2001 in order to care for his aging parents. During this period, he dreamt that he was "falling, as if from some tower in the sky," and he awoke in terror.

The nightmares continued, and he began to experience symptoms of panic attacks—rapid heartbeat, cold sweats, the works. He thought he might be having a heart attack at one point, so he went for medical tests. When all the tests came back negative, he attributed his symptoms to the stress of moving.

Then one night—on the evening of September 1, 2001, to be exact—he had the following dream:

> I was in some enormous burning building. People were going crazy, desperate to escape, hoping for rescue. When the rescuers came, they were crazy, too. I tried to comfort people. It was no use. Somehow I escaped and expected to see the rural countryside where we live, but instead I was on an urban street. People were walking around dazed.

"When I recorded the dream," he added, "I wrote that they looked as if they were covered with 'thick pancake makeup from head to foot.'" But that was John's last nightmare. The panic attacks also suddenly ceased, for no apparent reason.

Ten days later, while watching TV, John saw the horrific events of his nightmare unfold in real time in all their gruesome details. There they were: The dazed people staggering through the streets of lower Manhattan, covered in ashes—or what surely resembled "thick pancake makeup."

Better Late?

Experiences like these are not new in the history of humankind, nor are they as uncommon as people may be led—or wish—to believe. This, in itself, tells us something important. If reality doesn't behave the way we think it should, we need to adjust our thinking. We need to find new theories of reality, and pronto.

The underlying problem is that the prospect of entering into nature's rhythms scares the pants off adherents of science and religion alike, who seek to keep nature at arm's length for fear of either intellectual or moral contamination.

From science's standpoint, any such identification suggests erasing the fixed boundary that divides the observer from what is being observed. This is very dangerous, for it compromises the investigator's neutrality and objectivity, two hallmarks of the scientific method. For example, in the past, physicians who became emotionally involved in their patients' plight were considered unprofessional and likely to err in their clinical judgment. Detachment is a virtue, empathy a vice.

As for religion, the medieval church condemned and forbade both dancing and dream interpretation, the former being associated with women and sexuality, the latter with divination and witchery (again, women and sex). Nor do any kind of religious authorities willingly or easily admit to error. For example, it took the Catholic Church a long time to acknowledge that the Inquisition that had prosecuted Galileo in 1633 for heresy had made a mistake, and to admit that, yes indeed, the earth does, after all, rotate daily upon its axis and orbit around the sun just as Galileo said it did. How long, you ask? Try 359 years.

Well, better late than never, I suppose.

Yet, of the two, it is science—physics, in particular—that has demonstrated significantly more flexibility in its ability to revise its ideas of reality, including and especially the old standard view of linear time and the division of observer and observed. It was Einstein, of course, who demonstrated, with his theory of relativity, that physical time is not absolutely uniform and universal as Newton and his successors had supposed. On the contrary, it varies according to the speed of the observer.

The late quantum physicist David Bohm began his long and distinguished career as Einstein's protégé. Yet, as Bohm noted, the relativity of physical time, while theoretically interesting, does not touch or alter our everyday lives or experience of time: "This variation is, however significant only as we approach the speed of light and is quite negligible in the domain of ordinary experience."[21]

So the obvious next question is: Are there variations in the measurement and conception of time that are indeed significant in the domain of ordinary experience—variations that may correlate with the kinds of experiences reported by those who say, for example, that they somehow glimpsed the future before it happened, or otherwise transcended the apparent limitations of linear time?

Dead Man Talking

Some years ago, I had a dream about meeting an individual who is dead in the waking physical world. I was excited because I'd never had the chance to meet this person while he was alive. What was unusual was that I was aware, in the dream, that this person was dead. So I asked for an explanation of how it was possible that I could be encountering a dead man in my dream—if he was something more than a figment of my imagination or a wish-fulfillment fantasy.

The answer I received seemed very convincing. After I awoke, however, the explanation that had been so crystal clear in the dream made no sense whatsoever. Nevertheless, I dutifully recorded the dream and the one phrase I could recall: "the plasticity of time loops." Having never heard of "time loops" before—and therefore having no idea how they could be "plastic"—I soon forgot all about them.

Occasionally, I was reminded of this phrase by something I came across by chance, or else dreamed. In one such dream, I saw the dead man I'd encountered in the "time loop" dream as the pilot of an old-fashioned biplane flying loop-de-loops. He delighted in playing the daredevil and relished grabbing my attention with his antics.

In the meantime, I came across a book while searching for another title by the same author that had been recommended to me by an acquaintance. The author was quantum physicist Fred Alan Wolf; the book was *Mind into*

Matter: A New Alchemy of Science and Spirit.[22] When I got to chapter 7, I was floored: The subject was time loops.

It turns out, you see, that time isn't a straight line at all. It's a loop. What does this mean? And how is a loop like a circle?

CHAPTER FIVE

CAN YOU "IN-SEE" THE END?

[Jesus's] disciples said to him, "When will the kingdom come?"

"It will not come by watching for it. It will not be said, 'Look, here!' or 'Look, there!' Rather, the Father's kingdom is spread out upon the earth, and people don't see it."

THE GNOSTIC GOSPEL OF THOMAS,
The Secret Teachings of Jesus (1986)

I'm saying there is "perception" or "insight" or "intelligence" which may not be part of the system.

DAVID BOHM, *Thought as a System* (1994)

The American Indian, with his simple, direct approach to the great verities of being, calls this valuable faculty "in-seeing," or "in-hearing," or "in-knowing."

J. ALLEN BOONE, *Kinship with All Life* (1976)

So, how do we get from the hoop to the loop? What sort of trek is this? If we pay close attention, we may discover that no effort at all is needed to make this journey. Indeed, quite the reverse: Just let go, and fall into the gap.

Everything Tries to Be Round

"The Power of the world always works in circles," observed Black Elk, "and everything tries to be round." What happens, however, when we blithely try to ignore or bend this great truth, and attempt to force a square peg into a round hole?

Well, we can expect two main results: gaps and breakage.

First, the breakage:

The damage was already evident to Black Elk in his own day, a scant forty years after the Sioux, their hoop smashed beyond repair, were coerced from their tepees into "square boxes"—the reservation's log cabins about which he complained so bitterly to a sympathetic John Neihardt.

"When we were living by the power of the circle in the way we should," Black Elk lamented, "boys were men at twelve or thirteen years of age. But now it takes them very much longer to mature."[1] Yes. Maybe never?

Just look around: It's not just our sports stars who act like crazed teenagers on steroids; it's our whole hyperaggressive culture. "Give me mine, now!" and "I'm so important and oh-so-busy!" are our mantras.

Our incessant drive for instant gratification infantilizes us as a matter of economic policy and social necessity. With daily transactions accomplished by the click of a mouse, few of us have the patience to—or see the point of—politely waiting our turn at a traffic intersection, or in line at the dry cleaners. Pushing, shoving, and cutting in front of others: these are the new rules of our uncivil society.

Bullies rule.

As Black Elk understood so well, emotional maturity and the capacity to achieve it are one of the first casualties of our flight from nature and truth. Living in "square boxes" has deranged us, stunting our psychological and spiritual growth, just as it did to the Indians in but a single generation. They were the canaries in the coal mine; we are the crazed mutants that have "adapted" to meta-dysfunction.

Now, as for the gaps—perhaps here, a parable is in order.

Once upon a time, a large group of people were standing around, watching intently as its two muscular leaders—tight-lipped, red-faced, grunting and groaning, sweating and cursing—tried their utmost to force a square peg into a round hole.

"Just a little more elbow grease, over this way," shouted one of the leaders. "Push harder!" yelled the other. Meanwhile, their loyal followers stood on the sidelines whistling and hooting, enjoying the unfolding drama and cheering them on.

After observing this exhausting and fruitless display, a brave soul stepped forth from the crowd. "It doesn't fit," she stated quietly. "Can't you all see that?"

The two leaders glared at her, slack-jawed and silent. The crowd turned toward the lone objector, fists clenched and eyes ablaze. "What do you mean it doesn't fit?" screamed one. "You dangerous lunatic!" shouted another. The crowd roared in unison as they stampeded over to the objector and trampled her to death.

Thus are all gaps sealed, and the forcing resumed—now uninterrupted.

You see, we need to talk more about the gaps, and the few who notice them.

Kinship with All Life

What we have been saying is that the Myth of the Great Ending in its current, popular forms is but the psychological residue of the unresolved trauma left by our creation of linear civilization and our rejection of nature's circular rhythms. As such, it is at once a chief symptom of the disease and the path to its cure. The wound is also the place of healing—another great mythological theme identified by Joseph Campbell.

Our disdain for the world's imperfection and our inability to make it over in our own image make us yearn in frustration for its destruction, or, at the very least, its abandonment. Yet, deep inside this hollow pining for the End, we may find the fertile seed of remembrance, along with the sharp pain of loss for what was and may yet still be—if, that is, we can find a way to shift our perspective, change our minds, and mend our hearts. It's never too late.

Consider: The octagonal red sign that says "STOP" is not a blanket prediction about everyone's future; it's an individual call to action in the here and now. Your own proper response to the sign is what makes its message "true."

For true believers, signs of the Great Ending are always plentiful—or so it is said. But what the myth seems to be and what it really is are two quite different things. As long as our thinking remains superficial, the nervous tic of the End Time drama will replay itself indefinitely. It will don ever-new costumes—cut from old cloth—just as soon as the old ones are retired to the wardrobe department.

To free ourselves from these destructive and obstructive patterns, we must teach ourselves to see through the gaps in appearances to the reality underneath. We must learn how to activate what Bohm calls our creative insight—our inner vision—so that, as J. Allen Boone, author of *Letters to Strongheart* and *Kinship with All Life*, says of the American Indian, we can actively "in-see" the End, instead of merely passively anticipating it and the final cosmic makeover.

You see, it's our own perception that needs correction, not the world.

In the 1930s, Boone (a descendant of Daniel) was a Hollywood film producer and former newspaper reporter who found himself saddled with the task of dog-sitting the Lassie of his day, the first great canine film star, a German shepherd named Strongheart. Boone was merely doing a favor for a friend.

In the process, however, he made an astonishing and ultimately life-changing discovery. Once he put aside his human arrogance and actually began to perceive his companion as he was instead of trying to order him around, he found that, behind the surface appearance of a "mere" dog lay a great intelligence and personality with whom he could communicate—nonverbally, but, we could say, telepathically. This realization utterly transformed his thinking and values.

"The great spiritual explorers who have searched for the real facts behind all appearances have told us that the universe is faultless in its conception, faultless in its purpose, and faultless in its operation," says Boone. "But they have pointed out," he adds tellingly, "that the average human has difficulty in seeing and experiencing this real universe because of his defective inner vision and his disinclination to correct it."[2]

Can we do this? Can we muster the gumption to look inward, beyond the shallows and into the dark depths, and reclaim our insight?

In a culture that worships cheap artifice—the glitzier the better—the blinding klieg lights of celebrity, and the polished, mass-produced images of corporate shills, are we even any longer capable of making the crucial distinction between what "seems" to be the case, and what, in fact, "is"?

Only time will tell.

Thought as a System

We shouldn't be too surprised if, when carrying around a rusty, old, worn-out, leaky bucket we find that it—well, leaks, now should we?

I'm afraid there's no kinder, gentler way to put this:

All our mainstream religions and philosophies are rusty, worn-out buckets. They are outdated containers of antiquated ideas about reality. Some, like Swiss cheese, sport huge, gaping, crater-sized holes. Others appear to be more solidly constructed, but are split along the seams of the structure. All are cultural vessels that are sinking fast: old systems of thought or ways of consciousness breaking apart and becoming useless, if not positively dangerous, in this perilous time.

What, then, is a "system"?

David Bohm defines a system as "a set of connected things or parts" that "are mutually interdependent."[3] These parts work together, depending on each other for their meaning and their very existence. Biological systems like our physical bodies and microorganisms, social systems like nation-states and classrooms, and ideological systems, including all of our philosophies and religions, all function in this broadly systemic way. A king without subjects is not a king; an argument without premises is not an argument. And so on.

Now, it is true that no system is ever absolutely waterproof or airtight. To be made up of parts is to have multiple points of attachment or entry. And that means having multiple points of vulnerability. There's a wise old saw: "The more you think up the plumbing, the easier it is to stop up the drain." A highly complex system is, therefore, more easily divided or altered, given that its parts typically enjoy some "play" in their interconnections.

For example, my hand is attached to my arm at the wrist by a flexible joint. Without this internal flexibility, my hand would be far less useful. But it is precisely at this point that stress, fatigue, or even breakage may occur.

Systems must also enjoy some degree of external "play"—that is, they are susceptible, to one degree or another, to outside influences. We catch the flu because our bodies are open to infection from the air that passes through our nostrils. Similarly, to the extent that our minds remain open, we can also catch contagious emotions or ideas—what some call "memes." This may be something as innocent as the latest clothing fashions and office buzzwords, or it may be something malignant, like a totalitarian ideology—or perhaps even apocalypse mania.

All systems are thus open to change, both internally and externally. However, most systems, in order to preserve their sense of identity, if not their very existence, usually fight change tooth and nail. As Bohm dryly notes, a system "tends to sustain and maintain its structure, so that when something from the outside comes in it reacts in such a way as to avoid basic change."[4] Resistance may ultimately be futile, but that doesn't matter to the system.

Thought systems typically don't question their own most basic assumptions, including those that gave rise to the questions they were meant to answer. For example, Christianity envisioned and presented itself as the answer to this burning question: "How can we humans escape the sentence of eternal torment in Hell for committing the Original Sin?" But if there is no Hell, and there was no Original Sin, then there is no problem to which Christianity is the only possible solution. Inside the system, however, such questions would be heretical—or merely crazy.

Bohm points out that the very tense of the word "thought"—past, as opposed to the present tense of think*ing*—betrays its tendency to fly on autopilot, as if all the outstanding issues have already been settled and no major course adjustments are in the offing. It's a done deal. Thought acts as if it has all the answers, the total picture: the truth, the whole truth, and nothing but the truth. Outsiders (rival thought systems) are threats to that claim and are either expelled or co-opted.

Just as a healthy body fights off viral or bacterial infection, new or foreign ideas are absorbed and transformed into something more palatable to the host system. This is what Christianity did when it channeled pagan goddess worship into reverence for Mother Mary. Islamic fundamentalists who abhor the West still use their cell phones and laptop computers to wage "holy war." Paganism may yet enjoy the last laugh over Christianity, and technomodernity may swallow the retro-medieval fantasies of a new caliphate. But in the meantime, the system fights on.

Wordplay, Seriously

This process of self-preservation leaves traces in our ordinary language, although we're usually not aware of it. There is significant "play" in words, too.

I had a vivid reminder of this truth some years back. I was lecturing on the political and social conflicts in ancient Athens when I made a passing reference to our own Civil War. Instantly, the hand of a female student sitting in the back row shot up. "You mean," she chided in her soft, native South Carolina drawl, "The War between the States, don't you?" Well, that comment inaugurated a lively discussion.

In the case of the Civil War, the phrase or name we use to describe that series of events is determined by—or, in turn, helps to determine or shape— our point of view. The system of thought and action we inhabit influences how we read its history. Conflicting ideas of justice, sovereignty, revolution, and democracy are at stake.

Whether we consciously realize it or not, words embody and reflect rival theories, concepts, worldviews, and even metaphysical beliefs. A close look at language often reveals yawning gaps and dangerous blind spots in the system.

This is particularly true of the word "religion."

In his televised interviews with Joseph Campbell, journalist Bill Moyers asked the great mythologist for his definition of "religion." Campbell's reply is significant—and perhaps unintentionally misleading:

> Well, the word "religion" means [in its Latin root] *religio*, linking back, linking back the phenomenal person to a source. If we say it is the one life in both of us, then my separate life has been linked to the one life, *religio*, linked back. And this becomes symbolized in the images of religion, which represent that connecting link.[5]

Now, only things that are already or inherently separate can be linked—or relinked. If they are relinked, the presumption is that these things were once joined together, then severed, and now at least have the capacity to be reconnected. But what if they were never really disconnected to begin with? Then "religion" represents a false reunification predicated on an illusion of separation. You can't truly have a reunion if there never was a lack of unity.

Campbell was critical of biblical traditions in general, and Christianity in particular, for their separation of nature and the divine. All the more curious then that his account of "religion" silently gives a nod to the Christian metaphysical scheme, which assumes that separateness is a built-in, primary feature of reality. Just as a sculptor is a separate being from the sculpture she makes, so the biblical Creator God is viewed as separate from His creation. The world, although the product of divine acts, is not itself divine, and has fallen even further away from God into sin. Yet God, in His mercy, sent Christ, His Son, as a kind of family court mediator, to help his human "children" reestablish a healthy connection to their Heavenly Father.

Was Campbell unaware of this parallel, or was he merely simplifying complex matters of language for a TV audience? That is unclear. What is clear is that his etymology would have been rejected by one of his own chief mentors, Carl Jung.

In his 1949 foreword to the Taoist book of wisdom, the *I Ching*, Jung relays that the Latin root of *religio* is *relegere*, which means "a careful observation and taking account of . . . the numinous." The "numinous" is that which is mysterious, sacred, or holy. In a footnote, however, Jung notes that the early Church Fathers settled on a very different derivation of *religio*: not from *relegere* (the "classical"—that is, pre-Christian or pagan—etymology), but from *religare*, which means to "reconnect" or "link back." *Relegere* and *religare*, so close in spelling, are yet far apart in meaning.[6]

The reasons behind this subtle but significant semantic switch become clearer in Robert Graves's book, *The White Goddess* (1948). Graves notes that the pagan Roman philosopher Cicero derived *religio* from *relegere*, which means, "to read duly," or to "pore upon or study." Saint Augustine, writing hundreds of years later, says Graves, derived it from *religare*, meaning 'to bind back' and supposed that it implied a pious obligation to obey divine law."[7]

Do you see what is going on here with this "mere" wordplay?

What was it that "pagans" were at pains to read so closely? Not the Bible, which was written by mere humans, but the Great Book of Nature, which was not. "Knowledge was inherent in all things," observed the Oglala Sioux chief, Luther Standing Bear (1868–1939). "The world was a library and its books were the stones, leaves, grass, brooks, and the birds and animals that shared, alike with us, the storms and blessings of earth."[8] Thus the shamans paid close attention to particular signs and auguries—*this* dream; *that* flock of birds; *this* rock; *that* stream; and so forth. Everything was significant. Nature spoke to us, and we were wise to listen to her and heed her messages.[9]

But in Christian thinking, nature is fallen: corrupt, evil, and sinful. Our own nature has betrayed us—first in Eve's impetuous act of fruit theft, and subsequently in every spontaneous impulse and desire. It cannot, therefore, serve as the guide or standard for anything. Above all, we must not pay attention to it or yield to it. God is against nature, and so must we be. There is no meaning in nature—except a negative one.

Moreover, God's moral laws, directed against human nature, are general in form: "Thou shalt do this kind of thing" and "Thou shalt not do that kind of thing." Pagan reverence for the particular features of a landscape, animal, or plant, and careful attention paid to particular circumstances and subtle aspects of things have been replaced by an abstracting mentality that simplistically categorizes, classifies, and legalizes—slicing and dicing reality into "good" versus "evil."[10]

Thus, with a couple of minor change in vowels—from *relegere* to *religare*—the entire archaic metaphysic and epistemology was annexed and annihilated.

Minority Reports

And yet, as we have seen, because a system's resistance to change is never absolute, we should always expect to find occasional bleed-throughs, minor leaks, and breakdowns, if only at the periphery of our control-happy civilization, which has sought to manage, destroy, or—if all else fails—abandon nature. And so we do.

Among the so-called "higher" religions, Taoism is virtually unique in having preserved its vital links to the archaic sensibility and the cyclical view of nature and time. This can be seen in the dynamic interplay of Yin and Yang, and in the ideal of a sage who paradoxically acts by "not acting"—that is, by not trying to force nature to do our bidding and instead "going with the flow," as opposed to pushing the river.

This is what is meant by the Taoist phrase *wu wei*, the concept that Chang Chung-yuan translates as "noninterference."[11] What does it mean, then, not to interfere, but to harmonize with the functioning of nature? The Taoist sage Chuang Tzu replies: "Forget the passage of time (life and death) and forget the distinction of right and wrong. Relax in the realm of the infinite and thus abide in the realm of the infinite."[12]

The Tao thus calls for an immersion in the infinite as expressed in and through the places, inhabitants, and rhythms of the natural world, and not a moral corrective to the world or the waging of a holy war against evil. Like the indigenous shaman, the Taoist sage seeks company with, and the wisdom of, all creatures: "In the days of perfect nature," says Tzu, "men were quiet in their movements and serene in their looks. They lived together with the birds and beasts without distinction of kind."[13] That is to say, not with a condescending air of superiority, but with a humble sense of living among equals blessed with equal insight and dignity.

Compare this all with the words of the Sioux chief, Luther Standing Bear: "The character of the Indian's emotion left little room in his heart for antagonism toward his fellow creatures," Standing Bear recalls, adding:

> For the Lakota, mountains, lakes, rivers, springs, valleys, and woods were all finished beauty. Winds, rain, snow, sunshine, day, night, and change of seasons were endlessly fascinating. Birds, insects, and animals filled the world with knowledge that defied the comprehension of man.[14]

To experience the world as "finished beauty"—perfect, just as it—is the key shift of perception.

Adherents of the ancient Greek Mystery cults and some Gnostic Christians—as evidenced by the quote from the Thomas Gospel cited in the epigraph—had a view of the Great Ending that has more in common with Wovoka than St. Augustine: "The kingdom of the Father is spread out on the earth, but people do not see it." The peaceable kingdom exists *on the earth*, here and now, and is not an event to be brought about in the future, somewhere else—in heaven, for instance. The trick is to "in-see" it.

But these few dissident voices—like the Native cultures we systematically exterminated—have always existed at, or been squeezed to, the cultural margins. The system maintains its integrity by expelling invaders and co-opting critics. This has been true in philosophy, as well. Outliers need not apply.

Fortune's Wheel

Harvard physician and philosopher William James (1842–1910) lived during the post-Civil War period when both medicine and philosophy (among other disciplines) were becoming rigorously professionalized fields. Candidates increasingly were required to satisfy common standards as set by academic programs, advanced degrees, standardized tests, and new licensing processes.

In theory, this sounds like progress. In practice, however, the "new rigor" signaled the triumph of the mechanistic ideology of Newtonian science, which forced out dissenting views in the "hard" or natural sciences, in the "soft" or social sciences, and even in the humanities.

A key part of this story is told in sociologist Paul Starr's book, *The Social Transformation of American Medicine.* Starr explains how the allopathic approach in medicine, which reduces the human being to the status of a complex physical mechanism composed of divisible parts and separable subsystems, successfully squeezed out its more holistically oriented rivals—including osteopathy, homeopathy, and chiropractics—to achieve prestige, respectability, financial reward, and, in the process, a virtual monopoly of social power. The white lab coat became a signal mantle of cultural authority, even more potent than the judge's black robes.[15]

James, however, decried what he termed the theory of "medical materialism." He did not agree with de la Mettrie that man is just a machine. Moreover, he had the sheer audacity to suggest that actual human experience should trump our intellectual concepts and theories about reality—even if those abstractions belong to something as seemingly solid and sound as science. "In my belief," James opined, "a large acquaintance with particulars often makes us wiser than the possession of abstract formulas"[16]—a statement that would have had Standing Bear's hearty assent.

James, you see, did not limit "experience" to "sense experience," or what can be perceived by our physical senses in three-dimensional space and through linear time. Accordingly, he did not rule out the possibility of widely reported, but much-maligned experiences like telepathy, precognition, and contact with spirits of the dead that seemed to violate the metaphysical dogma that only physical matter is real. James became a committed investigator of such "psychic" phenomena, even serving as president of the British Society for Psychical Research (1894–1895).[17]

In my student years, I heard James's name mentioned by my professors only on rare occasion, and only derisively. No works of his ever made it to our reading lists. It was as if he'd never existed—or, worse yet, as if he'd been the loony old uncle locked in the attic that no one ever spoke about in polite company. Henry James was okay, at least for those snooty literary types in the English Department. But in academic philosophy, his brother William was *persona non grata*.

In retrospect, the reason for this avoidance is clear. James became an outcast not simply because he took seriously particular experiences like precognition or telepathy that dogmatic philosophical materialists dismiss as fraudulent or delusory, but because he took *personal* experience seriously. He saw the gaps. He discerned the lack of fit between square peg and round hole—and said so: "Weight, movement, velocity, direction, position, what thin, pallid, uninteresting ideas!"[18] James decries the ideal that science had enshrined as its idol.

For James, then, the scientific quest for an absolutely impersonal ideal of pure objectivity serves chiefly to distort rather than to clarify, or to conceal rather than to reveal, the ultimate truth of things: "How could the richer animistic aspects of Nature," he asks incredulously, "the peculiarities and oddities that make phenomena picturesquely striking or expressive fail to have been singled out and followed by philosophy as the more promising avenue to the knowledge of Nature's life?"[19] Philosophy, in following science's lead, has likewise betrayed its calling.

Nevertheless, that failure, as James well understood, lies at the heart of the classical scientific approach, which has no use for that which is "merely" subjective—what James dubbed the "egotistic" elements—including the feelings, attitudes, intimations, intuitions, and all the unquantifiable subtleties of consciousness that make us precisely and uniquely who and what we are:

> That unsharable feeling which each one of us has of the pinch of his individual destiny as he privately feels it rolling out on fortune's wheel may be disparaged for its egotism, may be sneered at as unscientific, but it is the one thing that fills up the measure of our concrete actuality, and any would-be existent that should lack such a feeling, or its analogue, would be a piece of reality only half made up.

"If this be true," he concludes, "it is absurd for science to say that the egotistic elements of experience should be suppressed. The axis of reality runs solely through the egotistic places—they are strung upon it like so many beads."[20]

For James, our subjectivity is not antagonistic to truth, nor is it dispensable, nor is it even the superficial, incidental icing on the cake of reality; rather, it is the chief ingredient, without which there would be no cake at all. Without it, you may as well hang up your apron and close the bakery for good.

Holomovement

James was no physicist, mind you, but his view of the contributing role of the subject in creating the objective world was a brilliant anticipation of much that was to come in the revolution of quantum physics that lay on the cultural horizon.

In his epochal book, *Wholeness and the Implicate Order*, David Bohm developed his own interpretation of quantum theory. He reminds the reader that it was his onetime mentor, Einstein, who demonstrated the limitations of the classical Newtonian notion that physical time "is absolute and does not depend on conditions," by showing that "physical time is in fact relative, in the sense that it may vary according to the speed of the observer." And yet, as we noted earlier, Bohm acknowledges that, despite its importance as a scientific theory, the relativity of physical time does not touch our everyday lives or affect our direct experience of time.[21]

However, Bohm's own startling view of the relativity of time goes far beyond anything his mentor Einstein would ever have countenanced. Let me explain.

For Einstein, you will recall, space and time are a continuum. That is to say, at bottom—no matter how hard it may be for us to grasp or form a mental image of this—they are the same thing. And they—or it—are basic structures of the universal order.

For Bohm, on the other hand, it is not just space and time, but all of reality that is an unbroken whole. Space and time are both mere abstractions out of the larger totality—mere partial truths at best, at least when they are not erroneously mistaken for the literal, complete, and total truth, which is always beyond our ken.

Bohm was fond of quoting the early 20th-century American philosopher of science Alfred Korzybski to the effect that—and I'm paraphrasing here—

things are always something more and other than what we think they are. Even a simple analogy can mislead us if we ignore its limitations. For to say that one thing is *like* another tacitly implies that they are also *un*like each other—that, in other words, they are not absolutely identical. For example, a pencil is like a pen (they are both writing instruments, etc.), but also unlike a pen—as we may discover, much to our chagrin, when we try to erase our pen markings. For Bohm, all thought is analogical and is, thus, never an exact representation of reality, which is ultimately mysterious.[22]

This mystery goes beyond, even as it incorporates, mind and matter. On Bohm's interpretation of quantum theory, while consciousness is as real as physical matter and its conditions, space and time, both consciousness and the physical world are understood to be projections of a hidden, vast primary source that transcends, but informs, both. As he explained to philosopher Renée Weber in an interview:

> This is not to say that I equate mind and matter, or reduce the one to the other. They are, rather, two parallel streams of development which arise from a common ground that is beyond both, and cannot be described at this stage.

Bohm emphasized that, while this "common ground" exhausts our analogical modes of thinking, we may yet have some direct experience of it: "Perhaps that 'beyond' is where the mystic experiences transcendence and immanence together as one whole," he added tellingly.[23]

The primary ground of existence, or the hidden source projector, is what Bohm calls the "implicate" or enfolded order, as opposed to the "explicate" or projected order, which is the unfolding or manifesting of what is merely implicit. As he notes, "the word 'manifest' means that which is recurrent, stable and separable."[24] These adjectives nicely describe the law-like material world we perceive through our senses, and slice, dice, and triangulate with our minds.

Mind or consciousness itself, on the other hand, says Bohm, is "more subtle" than matter—you can't pin it down. As William James pointed out, you can't weigh and measure a thought or feeling—or determine its location with a GPS device. So, in this sense, mind's qualities bring it closer to the implicate order.

Yet, Bohm adds, echoing the Native Americans and shamans of old, "we do not have any knowledge of mind without matter, or matter dissociated from mind or life." The matter and energy of a seed come from its environment, while the subtle intelligence of the seed continually provides new information to create the living plant. Did life miraculously arise from lifeless matter? Not so, answers Bohm:

> Who is to say that life was not immanent, even before the seed was planted? In the same way, it is held that the more complex an animal, the greater its display of intelligence, but the intelligence must also be immanent in the matter that constitutes the animal. If the immanence is pursued more and more deeply in matter, I believe we may eventually reach the stream which we also experience as mind, so that mind and matter fuse.[25]

This fusion of gross matter and subtle mind is itself an aspect of the melding of the greater implicate and explicate orders, between which there is a constant mutual exchange, back and forth, both ways. Thus what we perceive and think always affects, and is affected by, that which we do not sense and cannot grasp. Reality is thus an undivided, dynamic whole, a continuous stream simultaneously flowing in both directions. This is what Bohm called the "holomovement," in which absolutely nothing is ultimately separate, or separable, from anything else.

What does this theory do to our usual notions of linear time? It upends them.

One implication of Bohm's view is that physical time is not, as classical physics and common sense tell us, "a primary, independent, and universally applicable order, perhaps the most fundamental one known to us."[26] Rather time, with its seemingly uniform standards and measurable units, is merely a secondary projection of a non- or trans-temporal reality that is itself beyond measure.

Therefore, when we carve reality up like some galaxy-sized salami into certain standardized measurable bits—seconds, minutes, hours, etc.—we are artificially separating things (moments) that are not really separate. But, since reality is one whole salami, after all, there is nothing that says it must be cut up in one-inch slices, or quarter-inch, or whatever. It's up to us to decide how to slice it; and it can be cut in literally an infinite number of ways. I'll give you an illustration.

Back in the 1970s, when I was a college student in Boston, I took up jogging to get some exercise and de-stress. Part of my regular route took me across the Harvard Bridge that spans the Charles River and links Boston to Cambridge near the famed Massachusetts Institute of Technology (MIT). One day, I happened to notice something odd: Every so often on the sidewalk spanning the bridge was the word "Smoots" with a number attached to it—1 Smoot, 10 Smoots, 20 Smoots, 30 Smoots, and so on— painted in bright red lettering. What on earth is this? I wondered.

Eventually, I asked a friend who had lived in the city for a long time and knew its history, lore, and architecture. He laughed. "Well, the story I heard is that some guy named Smoots, who was a member of an MIT fraternity, got so drunk one night that he passed out. As a prank, his frat brothers laid him end-to-end across the bridge, marking out the length of his body. 'One Smoot' equals his height. They repaint the lettering every year. It's an initiation."

The length of the bridge is approximately 364 Smoots. Or is it?

What Bohm is suggesting, you see, is that we could just as easily use "Smith," "Jones," or anyone else as the standard of measurement. It's no more, nor less, silly really than "feet," "meters," or "inches." The ancient Greek philosopher Protagoras (c. 500 BCE) declared that "Man is the measure of all things." But it turns out that not man, or even all humans, but everyone—all loci of consciousness, including rocks, plants, animals, and the subatomic particles—are the measures. For there is no one absolute time sequence. Thus the myriad temporal fluctuations and glitches "subjectively" experienced by individuals are just as significant and real as the "objective" sequence of units registered by a mechanical or electronic clock. Or, as James said, "the axis of reality runs solely through the egotistic places."

Psychological time as we experience it is, of course, variable or relative as a rule—it moves like a tortoise when we're bored, speeds by like a hare when we're having fun, and may stop altogether if we're stoned or meditating. "Studies on such mind-affecting drugs as cannabis, LSD, etc., indicate that time distortions occur," notes engineer and consciousness researcher Itzhak Bentov:

> When a person has been trained by biofeedback to produce theta waves or can put himself into a deep meditative state and at the same time is able to watch the second hand of a clock in front of him, he will be surprised to find that the second hand has come to a stop.[27]

Having experienced this odd effect myself, I can attest to its subjective reality. But the question is, are these variations, properly speaking, *distortions* of the One True Time, or are they—as Bohm's revolutionary view clearly implies—alternate, but nonetheless equally valid, perceptions produced when we regularly transcend the limits of linear time "in our heads," and not merely in the extraordinary cases in which matter approaches the speed of light? Are there, in other words, different, but equally valid, alternate time sequences?

Bohm gives the example of two people who haven't seen each other for a long time. When they meet again, they find themselves picking up their relationship, or perhaps even the thread of their last conversation, "as if no time has passed." Now this is not, he says, a mere manner of speaking; it is a fact. "What we are proposing here," he states, "is that sequences of moments that 'skip' intervening spaces are just as allowable forms of time as those which seem continuous."[28]

And, for Bohm, "allowable" clearly means "real."

Thus the Myth of the Great Ending, with its notion of a single End to time, once and for all—for one and all—is beginning to smell conspicuously out of date.

Loops, Qwiffs, and Toothpaste Tubes

Which brings us to quantum physicist Fred Alan Wolf and the concept of time loops. Our point of departure here is the standard interpretation of quantum mechanics, which holds that the mind-consciousness of the observer creates the observed reality of space, time, and matter. The question is, how? How does an amorphous, ghostly blob of sheer quantum possibility—a virtually limitless field of infinite potential, or what Bohm called the implicate order—coalesce into an actual, limited world "out there" that we perceive, experience, and measure? The short answer is: all at once. And this is where the concept of time loops comes into play.

What's a time loop?

Years ago, someone gave me a piece of exercise equipment. It was a simple loop of flexible metal, a spring cable, with a plastic handle at each end. The idea was that, by pulling outward on each handle and thereby stretching the cable, I would increase the size and strength of my upper arms, shoulders, and chest.

That, in a nutshell, is a time loop.

To have time, you first need tension—pull between two opposite poles. Without that pull, there is no experience of space-time-matter, all of which are codependent aspects of reality—meaning that one can't exist without the other.

According to Wolf's metaphor of choice, the field of mind-stuff, or infinite possibility, squeezes itself into space-time like toothpaste oozing from an invisible tube—punctured at both ends—onto a toothbrush. There are two surging streams of metaphysical possibilities—quantum wave functions, or *qwiffs*—a double flow, one from the past gushing forward into the future, the other from the future flowing backward into the past. Where these two streams converge, a time loop is created, and, as he says, "the world we commonly and uncommonly experience as 'out there' arises both in our minds and in what we believe is objectively shared reality."[29]

Thus, the plastic handles of my old exerciser are the two holes in the cosmic toothpaste tube—the twin metaphysical portals through which the unlimited quantum potential is squeezed, and thereby limited. These are the essential end or boundary points, linked together in a closed loop. Events unfold in what seems to our human brains—programmed by nature to help us survive as a species in the physical world—as a simple linear chain of cause and effect that moves only ever forward. In truth, however, past, present, and future arise simultaneously, all at once, as equidistant points radiating from a central point. Just like a circle.

The old shamans were right after all, you see.

Everything within the time loop is thus the cause of everything else—and so the future also creates the past.

Strange to the Strange

This is perhaps one of the most difficult concepts to grasp, for it challenges just about everything we think we know about time—and, indeed, about ourselves—not to mention the specific subject at hand, the Myth of the Great Ending.

Consider, then, two examples that illustrate this phenomenon.

The first comes from the writings of the famed out-of-body explorer and consciousness researcher, Robert Monroe, whose experiences and work we will examine at greater length in later chapters. Monroe was the author of a classic study of out-of-body experiences (OBEs), *Journeys Out of the Body* (1971), and two more important volumes, *Far Journeys* (1985) and *Ultimate Journey* (1994). He is also the founder of the educational and research institute in rural Virginia that bears his name.

At one point in his out-of-body explorations, Monroe encountered a wise and witty entity he dubbed simply "Inspec"—an acronym (and Monroe loved acronyms) for intelligent species, which Monroe tacitly suggests human beings are not. The Inspec, which initially appeared as a powerful, brilliant white light before which Monroe nearly prostrated himself in awe, became an ally, advisor, and guide in his nonphysical adventures. Above all, the Inspec was his trusted friend.

In *Ultimate Journey*, Monroe describes how, one day, without any prior warning or further explanation, the Inspec informed Monroe that he would no longer be able to meet with him as before. Monroe was dumbfounded and crestfallen. "The feeling of abandonment and lack of direction was overwhelming," he confesses, as he found it nearly impossible to get over the loss of his nonphysical companion.[30]

Later, however, Monroe discovered the reason behind his friend's sudden departure. It turned out that the Inspec was none other than himself—or rather, himself as he would be in the future. A future version of himself had been slipping back into the past to lend assistance, perhaps even as the catalyst behind his initial forays beyond the physical body. But as the Monroe from the past/present slowly caught up, in experience, knowledge, and wisdom, to what he had only potentially been, the Inspec had less and less guidance to offer, until his role reached the point of redundancy.

The second example comes from the writings of Sue Watkins, friend and biographer of the late Jane Roberts. Roberts, one of the great psychics of the 20th century, spoke for the nonphysical entity, Seth. Like Monroe, Roberts was a metaphysical explorer of the first rank, as well as an original and insightful thinker. We will examine her work in subsequent chapters.

Watkins had attended many of the ESP classes that Roberts ran out of her home in Upstate New York back in the early to mid-1970s. In one class, Seth made an appearance, as he often did, to comment on the proceedings. Watkins took the occasion to ask Seth if he could enlighten her about a strange incident that had occurred when she was only fourteen or fifteen years old. She and her friend had been out walking along the road near her house when, astonished, they glimpsed a huge, egg-shaped object cruising slowly and silently over the tops of the tall pine trees. It was no airplane, no weather balloon—they were sure it was a UFO.

At first, Seth told Watkins merely that the shape of the object would change. Watkins was perplexed by this response. Seth seemed to be talking about the future, when she'd asked about an incident from her past. Then Seth—adding fuel to the fire of the mystery—declared:

> It has a connection—before you ask anything else—with an event in what you think of as the future, and some of your future comprehension had to do with the way you perceived that particular event in your past . . . and, in a way, it was a sign sent from a future self into the past.[31]

Move forward in time to 1994, twenty years after the above exchange, and a decade after the death of Roberts. Watkins was sitting at her desk, glancing through a beaten-up copy of an old book on UFOs that she'd recently picked up, by chance, at a garage sale. The descriptions of the UFO sightings and the attendant abduction experiences—the sensations of flying through the air, of leaving the physical body, of being gifted with startling glimpses into the nature of reality—reminded Watkins of Roberts's vivid account of her own earliest psychic episode.

So she went over to her bookshelf to look at her old autographed copy of *The Seth Material,* one of Roberts's early books. As she touched the spine of the book, a bright yellow ball of light "ballooned up out of the space directly above the book's position on the shelf." The brilliant round orb "expanded like a burnished soap bubble in the air in front of my face," stated Watkins, "glowing brighter and brighter until suddenly, abruptly . . . it vanished."[32] Poof! The miniature UFO was gone.

A light went on in Watkins's brain, however. She recalled Seth's comment from two decades earlier, about the strange object she'd glimpsed above the trees when she was a teenager, how it would change shape one day, and how her future self had been sending messages back into her past. The circle had now been closed. Suddenly, it dawned on her: She would write a memoir of her friend, Jane Roberts.

Blinking Off, Turning On

What these anecdotal examples bring home is a key point made by Wolf: that there exists an intimate relationship between the idea of a time loop— as well as our usual experience of time—and story, which, of course, also links it to myth, the shared stories of our collective imagination.

A time loop cannot arise without specified boundaries or end points—a start and a finish. The middle is what happens in between: "All stories," says Wolf (echoing Aristotle), "must have beginnings and ends together with a connection between them."[33] Our minds need to connect these two dots. Otherwise, we literally draw a blank. Nothing, as it were, has happened.

Wolf cites neurophysiologist Benjamin Libet's work on perception to support his contention that to perceive or recall events, either in our own minds or "out there" in the world, we must construct a narrative about them—a history, either actual or merely imagined, that connects the beginning state to the end state in a logical sequence of cause and effect. The story may be about a pig falling down in the mud, or about the explosive birth, expansion, and final contraction of the universe. But the tale must somehow be plausible. "We usually don't remember bizarre things as really happening to us," observes Wolf. "We remember what we call a 'classical' world, a rational world of cause and effect."[34]

David Bohm would say that is because memory is basically a kind of tape recording that replays our sensory impressions of the physical environment. We usually only recall the "manifest" content of the explicate order, or "that which is recurrent, stable, and separable."[35] In other words, we tend to focus our attention on the crudest, most superficial, and relatively unchanging expressions of the deeper implicate order—the seemingly "solid" objects of space-time—even as we ignore the subtle, underlying dynamic that creates, sustains, and reabsorbs them in a never-ending cycle of enfolding-unfolding. We see the dots, but don't notice their interconnections. We value product over process, which is invisible to us.

What Bohm is saying can be illustrated by the following analogy. Imagine you are standing on the seashore, totally mesmerized by the clumps of green seaweed, pieces of driftwood, and shell fragments lying about in the sand at the edge of the water. To you, they're just there; and you're so taken with your treasures that you don't notice where they came from. You are utterly oblivious to the fact that all this detritus is being washed in and out by the rhythmic motion of the ocean tides. That's the funny trance we're in when we mistake surface appearances for the sole reality.

If we were to speed up the movement of the waves exponentially, we would, in effect, have what engineer Itzhak Bentov dubs "the oscillating universe": a cosmos that blinks on and off at an incredibly high rate of speed, namely, about fourteen times per second. According to Bentov's hypothesis, "The atoms of our bodies are such oscillators; they vibrate at a rate of about 10^{15} Hz," or cycles per second. This, as he notes, is very, very fast indeed:

> It is possible that our bodies blink on and off at this very high rate. There is no way of knowing whether this is so since presently we have no way of registering such rapid phenomena. However, we cannot assume that all the atoms in our bodies beat synchronously or coherently. We have to visualize our bodies blinking on and off gradually, different areas disappearing, others appearing. *In other words, we are partially "out" all the time* [italics mine].[36]

That is to say, we are partially out of our bodies all the time. Another way of putting it is that our consciousness is never exclusively focused in physical-matter reality, or the explicate order, as we may suppose. We don't usually recall these "side trips," or what happens when we are "out"—in other words, what we are experiencing all the time at the implicate level—because, as Bohm says, we are "so habituated to the explicate order."[37]

Habituated? Now this is indeed a telling choice of words.

Habits are certainly hard to break. Yet we refer to them as "second nature" to distinguish them from "first nature," or true automatisms and mere reflexes like belching, blushing, or digesting our food. These reflexive responses are hardwired in us by Mother Nature to ensure or enhance our survival, or as effects of larger bio-system functions. Habits, by definition, are software; they are learned behaviors. We can *stop* smoking or cracking our knuckles just because, at some (perhaps distant) point in the past, we chose to *start* puffing and cracking. We loaded the program.

Now, it's true that there are some individuals who apparently can control the autonomic responses of their nervous and other bodily systems—temperature, heart rate, digestion, pupil dilation, and so forth—through the use of techniques like meditation, biofeedback, hypnosis, or even through sheer belief (or what religious people call "faith"). Much evidence suggests that this is so. These too, then, may be habits of a kind—albeit more tangible and measurable than the habits of thought, perception, and memory that lock our attention onto the explicate order.

When, pray tell, did these mental habits begin?

Bohm finds a key clue in the work of child psychologist Jean Piaget, who discovered that infants are initially more interested in things that move— say, people making funny faces or mobiles spinning above their cribs— than things that stay still. Babies naturally tend to be process- rather than product-oriented. They're far more sensitive to the dynamic qualities associated with the implicate order than the static qualities of the explicate order. "Recalling that movement is sensed primarily in the implicate order," says Bohm, "we see that Piaget's work supports the notion that the experiencing of the implicate order is fundamentally much more immediate and direct than is that of the explicate order, which . . . requires a complex construction that has to be learned."[38] Initially, then, our minds are quite supple; we have to work hard to become stiffs.

Can we unlearn what we have worked so assiduously to learn? For one thing, if the world is already ending some fourteen times per second, isn't all the fuss about "the End of the World" much ado about nothing?

Moreover, the sheer possibility of breaking old habits of awareness and training ourselves to recall what we have been teaching ourselves to forget implies that we have a great deal more flexibility—in other words, freedom—than we may care to admit, or perhaps even to use. But maybe—just maybe—out of the corner of our (third) eyes, we can catch a fleeting glimpse of the universe as it pulsates, in and out: the diastolic and systolic rhythm of the vibratory cosmos.

This happened to me. A year before I stumbled across Bentov's ideas, I had a direct experience of the oscillating universe. In 1978, I was still a college student. One Saturday night, a friend insisted that I try his girlfriend's hash brownies. I choked down the brownie, which tasted awful, like chocolate-flavored straw. At first, I felt only slightly more relaxed than usual, and a bit giddy. So when my friend suggested we all take a subway ride to the local science museum, I did not object.

By the time we arrived at the museum, however, things began to get—well, strange. Colors were much clearer and sharper than usual, as were sounds. In fact, all of my senses were more acute, to the point of overload. The sensitivity became almost excruciating. Most irritating of all was that some idiot was playing a bizarre prank, flicking the exhibit hall lights on and off very rapidly, like a strobe light. It was so disorienting that it made me dizzy and more than a little nauseous.

With a creeping sense of dread, however, I suddenly realized that it wasn't the room lights that were blinking on and off; it was the entire universe— with me in it. And it was doing so at a mind-blowing clip. Here, gone; here, gone; here, gone.

But gone where? Where was it? More to the point: Where was I?

I was terrified. At least, part of me was. But I was also intrigued. It was as if I'd been afforded a peek behind the wizard's curtain. Intuitively, I knew that this was no mere "hallucination." Things are definitely not what they ordinarily seem.

This singular experience subsequently proved to be what famed author Joseph Chilton Pearce called the first crack in my cosmic egg. "Our cosmic egg," he writes, "is the sum total of our notions of what the world is, notions which define what reality can be for us." But these notions are not necessarily fixed; they can be quite fluid—if we let them: "The crack, then, is a mode of thinking through which imagination can escape the mundane shell and create a new cosmic egg."[39]

This flexibility is tied in with that mysterious phrase I recalled from my strange dream, namely the "plasticity" of time loops. How are time loops plastic? Wolf answered this question as well.

"The important point here," he writes, "is that the end points [of the time loop] emerge into space and time because of our *desire* to have a story."[40] To be more precise, not any old story, to be sure, but rather, *this particular story*, whatever it is. Focused intent is what thrusts the narrative out of the realm of sheer possibility into actuality. We choose the story line and thereby create our reality—our past, present, and future. We are not passive victims of impersonal forces or cosmic puppets of higher powers. A wiser version of us may give the less wise a swift kick in the pants, or perhaps a helpful nudge in the ribs, as a reminder. But we are free to ignore such imprecations and sleep on in our numb ignorance if we so choose.

And yet, of course, we *do* remember "bizarre" events like dreams, UFO sightings, out-of-body experiences, and other anomalies, as accounts like Monroe's and Watkins's—along with many, many thousands of others—suggest. All these episodes confound our "classical" views of the cause-and-effect universe of three-dimensional space and linear time that our physical brains, hardwired for survival in a dog-eat-dog world, compel us to believe—but not quite, or always and everywhere, completely. This is called reading the fine metaphysical print of our life contract, which is always recommended.

You see, the "plasticity" of time loops mitigates their mandatory conformity to the classical narrative form. Even if the Aristotelian model of beginning-middle-end is hardwired into the neurophysiology of our gray matter and its evolutionary imperatives, our consciousness (which is not so restricted) can choose to rewrite the software program to suit itself. Thus, endings can be perceived or created "hard," like the rigid, forceful, explosively apocalyptic conclusions favored by the proponents of linear time, or "soft," like the kinder, gentler, never-ending cycles of change embraced by the adherents of the hoop.

More and more, then, it is beginning to look as if the very idea of "The" end of "The" world is an idea whose time has come—and long gone. It's a museum piece, an antique, not a living, breathing myth.

Whose ending is it? Which world are we talking about?

These are the real questions we must now ask.

CHAPTER SIX

TO THINE OWN SELF

> I wanted only to try to live in accord with the promptings
> which came from my true self. Why was that so very difficult?
> HERMANN HESSE, *Demian* (1970)

N ot *the* world, but *a* world—my world, to be precise. What ends my world? Ah, me and mine: That one, tiny little word "my" is a philosophically loaded term, after all, heavily freighted with significance. For "my" implies "I"—to wit, the self. What, in truth, am I? Who am I? If I don't already know, how can I find out?

Demons, Gadflies, and Days of Doom

According to Joseph Campbell, only a small minority of wise men and women the world over have never interpreted the Myth of the Great Ending in the literal sense of "a day to come of terminal doom."[1] The End is not a mass public event to come, a metaphysical coda to be awaited passively with either trembling hope or hysterical fear. Rather these mystical sages— echoing, consciously or not, the old tribal shamans—have understood world annihilation symbolically, as a coded call to an individual experience of radical self-transformation in the present moment.

What is thus invited is the sudden, but not, therefore, any less profound awakening of a greater quality of consciousness—an increased depth and breadth of awareness—and thus a brand-new way of perceiving the world. These illuminating flashes of intuitive vision are what Bohm called "insight," and what Boone dubbed "in-seeing." To view the world in this way, says Campbell, is to behold it as a radiant whole that we affirm as it is, in all its paradoxical terror and glory, rather than as an error to be corrected or a lost cause to be abandoned.

In this overtly visionary reading, the only "world" to be destroyed is the individual's own antiquated worldview: those rotted-out belief systems, ingrained habits of mind, and socially conditioned automatisms of consciousness that have led to stagnation and misery, both for the individual and for others.

By default, we operate primarily on autopilot, thinking and doing what we've been taught to think and do, or what others have thought and done in the past. We are creatures of custom, habit, and tradition—what Colin Wilson aptly terms "the robot."[2] Then, when things go wrong—as they inevitably will—we find ourselves scratching our heads, utterly perplexed. Why? Because the robot is in the driver's seat, and we're just going along for the ride.

This problem, of course, is nothing new. It came with the birth of civilization, the agriculturalist revolt against animistic tribal society, and the need to simplify the learning of increasingly complex tasks brought about by the division of labor. Mindlessly repeating past performances perfected by trial and error does indeed save time and energy, as anyone who has ever learned to drive a car or speak a foreign language can attest. Rote memorization has its place.

But it can become a demon. When the spontaneous response of our creative intelligence is eclipsed by conditioned patterns of sheer habit and routine, it may be painful—or even impossible—to alter course, even when the situation calls for new solutions. Socrates compared himself to an annoying fly waking up a reluctant sleeper from an afternoon's snooze. When he questioned the decrepit received wisdom of his Athenian contemporaries, however, he provoked an angry response—they swatted him dead. We're asleep at the switch, the bridge is out, and the train is careening toward disaster. And on we sleep.

This is why Monroe (whose exploits we'll discuss in later chapters) emphasized the importance of acquiring what he called a "different overview."[3] By this, he meant a coherent perception of reality based, not on secondhand mass beliefs passively absorbed from our environment or inherited from our forebears, but rather on hard-won, firsthand knowledge acquired through our own direct personal experience, including and especially those experiences—like out-of-body experiences—that are dismissed, denied, or denigrated by the officials of our authoritative traditions. In fact, it's precisely what isn't on the cultural menu that we most need to eat.

Peeping Inward and Outward

Happily, the symbolic reading of the mythic End as a metaphor for a certain type of self-transformation may no longer be the exclusive turf of the esoteric elite. Indeed, the idea of the radical relativity of time championed by quantum physicists and psychics alike has rendered the old literal views, not merely obsolete, but also clearly nonsensical.

Seth, the entity for whom Jane Roberts spoke in trance, employed the term "Psychological Time" to describe a capacity of the nonphysical, or "inner," senses to perceive alternate time sequences in the physical world. "From within its framework you will see that physical time is as dreamlike as you once thought inner time was," says Seth. "You will discover your whole selves, peeping inward and outward at the same 'time,' and find that all time is one time, and all divisions, illusions."[4]

What Seth says basically echoes the views of Bohm, who suggests that the phenomenon of picking up a conversation "as if no time has passed" by two individuals who haven't seen each other for years is not a mere illusion, but an expression of the real plasticity of time. Ordinarily, when we bend or shift time in seemingly impossible ways in sleep—for example, when I dream that I'm in Boston one moment and in Chicago the next—we don't allow the seeming illogic of it to trouble us when we awake, because we say, "Well, it was only a dream."

However, if the classical Newtonian idea of absolute time is at best limited in scope, and our differing subjective perceptions of time, awake or asleep, are equally valid and real—in effect, if there are as many alternate time sequences as there are possible psychological ways of experiencing time—then the notion of a single end to time and history, Once and For All, is as passé as slide rules and analog TV.

Many times or time sequences imply the existence of the quantum physicists' many worlds, or what Seth dubbed "probabilities," as well as the "probable selves" or alternate versions of those who inhabit them. Not "The End," but rather, which end? To wit, whose end? There are as many possible "ends" as there are selves to experience or create them—and that may well be infinite.

Moving the Boggle Threshold

So what ends my world?

The mind reels. We approach that tender psychological barrier that my late friend, parapsychologist Rhea White, referred to as the "boggle threshold." We just can't believe it. But is this threshold a fixed barrier or a moveable bar?

One major hurdle is that those who read the Myth of the Great Ending in a more literal fashion have long dominated our cultural discourse. Their belief systems have skewed our ideas of reality and tainted our sense of our own possibilities. By believing that we are separate from nature, we have created conditions like global warming and overpopulation that shore up the literal belief in doomsday. This is the foolish dog chasing his own tail while congratulating himself for having cornered his prey—the idiocy of self-fulfilling prophecy carried to the extreme.

Theoretical misunderstandings thus have practical effects. By attempting to subjugate and deny nature, we have tacitly undermined our ability to trust in our own nature. We're not sure we can know ourselves. We may even doubt whether there is such a thing as a self to be known. At best, such a notion may be tolerated as a quaint, if sometimes useful, fiction; at worst, it may be despised as a cruelly ironic joke, or dismissed as altogether too much sound and fury, signifying . . . nothing.

In the opening epigraph to this chapter, Emil Sinclair, Hesse's youthful protagonist, poses the question asked by all young people learning to make their way in the world—the question Hesse asked of himself his entire life—namely, why is it so difficult to live in accord with the promptings that come from our own true selves? To which the custodians of what passes for wisdom in our age reply: "Hey buddy, are you, nuts?"

How, indeed, did we manage to get to this sad point? And how can we learn to move past it? To address such questions, we must return to the beginning.

The Myth of the Great Beginning, that is.

Back to the Garden

"In the beginning, God created the heavens and the earth." These, of course, are the familiar words of the very first verse of the very first chapter of the very first book of the Bible, Genesis: our religious story of how all things came to be.

According to Genesis, God created the world, meaning everything—physical and nonphysical reality—that is not God. Not just the earth, but all the planets, galaxies, universes, astral planes, heavens, etc., and the entities within them. Actually, He created the world twice. Or rather, to be more precise, there are two very different accounts of creation in Genesis, written at two different times—the older account recorded in chapter 2, and the newer version found in chapter 1. These were cobbled together by editors who either couldn't or wouldn't deal with the evident discrepancies in the order and manner of divine creation.

These well-known complications aside, most biblical theologians settled on the idea that God created the world from the ground—that is to say, from the subatomic particles—on up. In Latin, the term is *ex nihilo*, meaning, "from nothing." Everything that exists is dependent for its existence and its continued being on God, whereas God, in turn, is dependent upon nothing but Himself. God is the all-powerful, totally self-sufficient source. In fact, He is the only truly self-sufficient entity there is. His creation, totally separate from Himself, is His (and only His) artifact. That world is His handiwork, but it does not share His essential powers.

That God is omniscient and all-knowing follows logically from His nature. God is all-powerful; knowing is a power; QED, God must possess all knowledge. But the world God made is neither omnipotent nor omniscient. It is not eternal and invulnerable. Whereas the Creator's powers are unlimited, the world of His making is a strictly limited, finite creation.

Thus, God knows His work from the inside out in a way that work can never know itself. And that work includes us humans. In other words, Our Heavenly Father Knows Best. He knows us better than we can ever know ourselves. After all, He made us—not to mention everything else that exists—from absolutely nothing. And He knows absolutely everything. Is that not crystal clear?

Genesis tells us we were made in God's "image." Yet, given that God has no physical form, it's not clear what this means. If it means that we are somehow "like" God—say, in our capacity for free will or intelligent thought—that still does not erase the yawning metaphysical gap between infinite creator and finite creature, or between divine and human capacities. As we have seen, for one thing to be "like" another tacitly implies a degree of unlikeness—that they are not identical.

Moreover, the premise that we are not the ultimate interpreters of ourselves, and that we are truly known only from without by a Know-It-All Authority, is further underscored by the oft-told tale of Adam and Eve and the Tree of Knowledge. Straight off the divine assembly line, neither Adam nor Eve evince the self-awareness possessed by even three-year-old toddlers who recognize the distinction between male and female genitalia. Adam and Eve cavort naked in the Garden, not knowing the difference between male and female, but "cleaving" to each other, as the text says, as man and wife. Ignorance is (or at least can be) bliss—at least if you're prelapsarian Adam and Eve.

God clearly created Adam and Eve in a state of ignorance. Thus knowledge—including self-knowledge—is something that has to be pumped in from without. It is, shall we say, an optional software package to be purchased later at very great cost and not part of the original human operating system. Nor is its acquisition part of our inherent birthright, since Adam and Eve were specifically forbidden to get it for themselves.

When Eve follows her impulse of curiosity and eats the fruit of that forbidden tree—heeding what Hesse might call the promptings of her true self—all hell breaks loose, as "the eyes of both were opened and they knew that they were naked." In the Christian view, it's literally Hell for them when God finds out about their transgression.

In the specifically Christian reading of this myth, it's not merely that Adam and Eve commit the Original Sin by disobeying God's explicit order not to eat from the Tree, but that in the very act of seeking self-knowledge they bar themselves—along with the rest of us, for "in Adam's Fall, we sinned all"—from ever attaining it. They stole the fruit that God might have given them as a free gift had He chosen to. Yet, as a result, they can't really use it. That's the awful paradox.

Not only is nature in general cursed by God as a result of the first couple's transgression, but human nature as well. That means that human consciousness is corrupted. Our basic wants and desires, our capacity to think and reason, and our ability to choose freely and act effectively are all rendered untrustworthy and liable to malfunction—in a word, to be and to produce only evil. "The impulses of nature and the impulses of the spirit are at war with one another," declared St. Augustine (quoting St. Paul, Gal. 5:17).[5] And we must do our utmost to fight on the side of spirit (good) as against nature (evil).

Thus the medium of human perception—our awareness, the very instrument of self-knowledge—has been contaminated, perhaps even fatally infected, by the virus of Original Sin. By analogy, we can't trust the self-images we behold any more than we can trust the images seen through a microscope or telescope whose lenses are marred by serious optical defects. Consciousness is a distorting lens.

We are mental and moral prisoners of sin, captivated by bizarre fun-house mirrors of self-deception in a charnel house of terror and lies. Our only hope is to await rescue by the higher powers of truth, justice, and the righteous way.

Religious texts are notoriously open to alternative interpretations, and the Myth of the Great Beginning is no exception. So everything I've said thus far about the meaning of these stories is doubtless contestable. And it will be contested, both by orthodox religious apologists and by occultists and mystics who find in such texts hidden, esoteric meanings meant only for some wise spiritual elite—meanings that conflict with the standard, exoteric readings favored by orthodoxy.

Nevertheless, I think it fair to say that, these considerations notwithstanding, there is a certain core message that the culture has taken away from this myth—a kind of unconscious mental patterning that has grown and hardened over the millennia, irrespective of our consciously held beliefs or ideological allegiances. Stripped of all specifically religious associations and references to Revelation, Original Sin, God, Creation, etc., this core message may be summarized as follows:

Human consciousness is a radically imperfect, untrustworthy instrument. Human beings can't really know themselves subjectively, from the inside; genuine self-knowledge is impossible.

The only reliable self-knowledge must come to us from an external Authority, who knows us better than we can ever know ourselves.

The Secret Sharers

Religion and science are ostensibly mortal enemies in the ongoing slugfest of our culture wars. Ironically, however, once you get past all the propaganda, it turns out that mainstream science essentially accepts these same three premises. The vocabulary is quite different, yet the ideas are remarkably similar.

Mainstream scientists, by and large, adhere to the metaphysical assumptions of 17th-century philosophical materialism, supplemented by the idea of a constantly changing universe suggested by Darwin's biology (life evolving from simple to more complex forms through chance adaptation) and Hubble's cosmology (the universe seen as expanding outward from the origin point of the Big Bang).

Science famously claims that it has no need of any supernatural "God hypothesis" to explain these natural processes. The only true reality is physical matter, namely atoms, in constant motion, the predictable movements of which are governed by the deterministic laws of physics, chemistry, and biology, all of which are expressible in the dispassionate and precise language of science: mathematics.

Basically, then, the universe is a vast nuts-and-bolts machine, selfregulating and self-producing. At some point, in some aspects, this mechanism— inexplicably— became aware, and even self-aware. Nonetheless, mind or consciousness is a mere accidental by-product of physical processes. Just as the kidneys produce urine, so the nervous system excretes mind. Consciousness, in other words, is just brain piss.

"For seeing life is but a motion of limbs," wrote 17th-century English philosopher Thomas Hobbes (1588–1679), "why may we not say that all *automata* (engines that move themselves by springs and wheels, as does a watch) have an artificial life? For what is the *heart* but a *spring*, and the *nerves* but so many *strings*, and the *joints* but so many *wheels* giving motion to the whole body . . ."[6] Unfortunately, we have a tendency to develop a Pinocchio complex. We're puppets who imagine that we're somehow "free," exempt from the grinding gears of ironclad physical necessity, even as our strings are pulled by the laws of nature.

As odd as it may sound, then, consciousness is an obstacle in the search for true knowledge, including self-knowledge. If we really want to know what moves us and how we move, we must discount consciousness and its peculiarities as much as possible. As Carl Jung observed:

> [M]ost of the natural sciences try to represent the results of their investigations as though these had come into existence without man's intervention, in such a way that the collaboration of the psyche—an indispensable factor—remains invisible . . . [Thus] science conveys a picture of the world from which a real human psyche appears to be excluded.[7]

This is the paradox of classical mainstream science: it is a quest for knowledge without a knower, a purely objective account scrubbed of all subjective colorings (that is, distortions), including our wishes, wants, feelings, desires, beliefs, values, hopes, fears, the limitations of our perceptions, and subjectivity itself. As Jane Roberts once wryly observed, it's "as if you could explain an orgasm better and more scientifically if you'd never had one yourself."[8] We're just "things": mere physical objects to be observed, weighed, measured, and catalogued, just like all other objects, from subatomic particles to stars—and everything in-between.

It follows that we are imperfect observers of ourselves, and that others know us from the outside, at a distance, better than we can ever know ourselves up close, from the inside. This is why we rely on experts—presumed authorities—to tell us what's wrong (or right) with us. Standardized tests measure our intelligence and capabilities. For the most part, doctors ask patients about their symptoms mainly to humor them. Laboratory tests and results, not subjective anecdotal evidence—that is, descriptions of our personal experience—are the only reliable guides to truth.

This principle also applies when the disease is of the mind rather than the body. According to Freud, for example, psychoanalysts grasp the true meaning of their patients' dreams far better than the patients do, as, on his view, the conscious mind censors the emotionally charged content of the unconscious dream message, which always appears in a disguised form. Thus a pencil is really a phallus; a door is really the womb; fear is really desire. Psychoanalysts see through all the mental flimflam and can decode the dream symbols; whereas we poor, benighted dreamers cannot, and we suffer accordingly from that ignorance through the symptoms of neurosis. It is the task of the analytical Authority to—ever-so-gently— guide us to a truer understanding of our own dream experiences.

Not I

Thus, despite the apparent wide gap between mainstream materialistic science and biblical religion, the basic core message of the Myth of the Great Beginning is endorsed by science in all the core essentials affirmed by religion:

Human consciousness is a radically imperfect, untrustworthy instrument.

Human beings can't really know themselves subjectively, from the inside; genuine self-knowledge is impossible.

The only reliable self-knowledge must come to us from an external Authority, who knows us better than we can ever know ourselves.

There is, of course, one—or at least one—key difference between science and religion. Whereas for religion, the external Authority who knows us better than we can ever know ourselves is God—or duly authorized earthly representatives like priests, ministers, pastors, rabbis, mullahs, cardinals, or popes—for science, it is the dispassionate researcher/practitioner in the white lab coat. The costumes may be different, but the function remains much the same.

There are some scientists and scientifically minded philosophers who would venture even further, however. Self-knowledge and the quest for one's "true self" are not at all what they're cracked up to be anyway, they insist, because there really is no such thing as a "self"—no continuous sense of personal identity, no individual ego, no mind or consciousness that survives bodily changes, let alone the ultimate change of death. And by extension, to be sure, there is no such wildly exotic fauna as an eternal "soul." In short, bye-bye to the very concept of an "I."

This was the conclusion reached, for example, by 18th-century Scottish philosopher David Hume (1711-1776). Hume was an "empiricist," meaning that he believed knowledge must be based strictly on the actual data of our five physical senses. No "extra"-sensory perceptions need apply! Any extrapolation beyond these data is, from Hume's perspective, totally unwarranted, an artificial construction of our own imaginings, a conceptual flight of fancy.

Not surprisingly, this sensory data reflects the matter-in-motion universe of constant change that science posits. What Hume called our sense perceptions or impressions exist in perpetual flux. Look within and what do you find? Yourself? No, says Hume, only particular perceptions of something or other: of heat or cold, hunger or satiety, happiness or sadness, fear or desire, pain or pleasure.

What's more, he notes, these perceptions turn, and turn into each other, on a dime. If I move my eyes in their sockets one way, I see a patch of gold in my visual field; if I move them the opposite way, I see blue. Happiness is followed by sadness as surely as satiety is replaced by hunger. As the ancient Greek philosopher Heraclitus stated more than a millennium before Hume: Nothing abides; all is change.

What "I" am, then, is merely the sum total of sense impressions at any given moment—what Hume dubbed a "heap or bundle of different perceptions." And since these are constantly changing from moment to moment depending upon the environmental stimuli, "I" am merely the response to those stimuli, which is, in effect, constantly changing as well. We tell a story about some single, enduring, cohesive "self" that exists beyond all such random fluctuations; but we never really experience this "self." All we actually know is the sum of the various impressions.[9]

While some commentators have compared Hume's views to those found in the Buddhists' doctrine of "no-self" (in Sanskrit, *anatta* or *anatman*), there is, I think, an important underlying difference that transcends the surface agreement.

It is true that Buddhism also stresses the impermanence of worldly existence. According to Buddhist teachings, our attempt to deny this by attaching ourselves to things that change and will inevitably pass away—possessions, prestige, power, family, even our hair and teeth—is the cause of all human suffering.

The difference is that, for Hume, there is, in the end, only the discon-nected dots of our various fluctuating sense data. For Buddhists, the idea of "no-self" is taken to mean that there is no separate self, no one unchanging identity or individuated self apart from all else, because, ultimately, every-thing is inseparably connected with everything else in what yoga teachers and scholars Joel Kramer and Diana Alstad, in their important book *The Guru Papers*, call a perfectly "seamless web of existence."[10]

Hume denied the self on the grounds that disunity is all we can know. The Buddhist doctrine of "no-self," on the other hand, is embedded in a metaphysical conclusion Hume could never accept or rationally justify: that only unity is ultimately real. Indeed, according to Kramer and Alstad, "The Buddhist Void [the source of the phenomenal world of our experience] posits ultimate reality as devoid of differentiation and is structurally identical to the [Hindu] concept of Oneness [in which the individual drop of water melts into the sea]."[11] The many are the illusion; only the One is real.

This metaphysical ideal of pure undifferentiated Oneness common to both the Hindu and Buddhist traditions is the justification for the spiritual practice of total submission to the authority of the guru, as well as for adher-ence to what Alstad and Kramer dub "renunciate" moralities—that is, ethical systems that require the individual to renounce all self-interest with the aim of becoming "perfectly egoless."[12]

Joseph Campbell condemns the guru model, with its requirements of total relinquishment of personal freedom and responsibility for one's life choices, as at once improper and dangerous—a recipe for the kind of psychologi-cal and moral disaster seen in 1970s cults like Jonestown and the Rajneesh group in Oregon.[13]

Kramer and Alstad see this call for surrender of personal autonomy as a form of rank authoritarianism: a malignant dictatorship of the few ex-ploiting the many. They rightly argue that a certain degree of self-interest and self-regard—egoism, in other words—is both healthy and necessary. You can't have sympathy, compassion, or love for others unless there is a "you" present to experience and become the vehicle of these fine qualities. Moreover, since it is therefore impossible actually to get rid of our egos, the failure to live up to the ideal creates guilt and fear in us, which then become the levers by which the gurus—none of whom are perfectly selfless either, of course—manipulate their minions.

They likewise point to the role of apocalyptic thinking, the literal belief in End Time scenarios, in providing a kind of psychological amplification system that increases fear and guilt over our own imperfections, while at the same time offering the hopeful possibility of a final purification. This "apocalyptic paranoia," as they call it, rallies the troops and reinforces group solidarity with the "us versus them" mentality. "Although the guru usually preaches the unity of all humanity," they write, "he becomes increasingly more separate" and paranoid, mistreating followers and counseling violence toward outsiders.[14]

Is Authenticity Overrated?

The deeply skeptical Hume basically wanted to get rid of the idea of a knowable ultimate reality altogether. Doubt was his god, or at least his devil's best advocate. His morality was basically "utilitarian," meaning that he believed that humans typically are, and properly ought to be, motivated solely by a reasoned calculation of what is most useful to them, which is to maximize their own pleasure and minimize their own pain. He would have had no truck with the Hindu-Buddhist ideals of renouncing self-interest or submission to a guru. Religion, to him, was bunk, sheer hokum that could not be rationally justified.

Far closer to Hume's sensibility are the views of certain postmodern thinkers like the late American philosopher Richard Rorty.

Like Hume, Rorty believes that the "self" is no more than a yarn we spin, a tall tale. There is no one fiction that is truer, or any more "real," than another. It's an issue of free choice—essentially an aesthetic question of taste—and, as the old saying goes, there's no disputing about matters of taste. It's not that someone who prefers anchovies on their pizza is right or more reasonable, or that the person who prefers pizza plain is wrong; it's just that different people like different things. "Whatever floats your boat," as the saying goes. There's no meaning "out there," no "true destiny" to discover (and follow), and certainly no heroic quest for "Truth."

For Rorty, the best that philosophy can do is to offer ironic commentary on the frenzied attempt of the foolish to obtain what used to be called knowledge—either self-knowledge or knowledge of the world—that has some sort of timeless or metaphysical significance. All we have are our "descriptions of descriptions"—meta-talk about talk. We're trapped in the hall of mirrors called language, culture, and history, so the very notion of breaking through to a truth that is not made by "us"—considered as animals who use words to get what they want—is sheer illusion.

It is thus no accident that Rorty mocks the search for one's true identity as a kind of party game, useful for entertainment purposes perhaps, but not much else. He suggests it's high time that we "give up what [fellow philosopher] Stanley Cavell calls the 'possibility that one among endless true descriptions of me tells me who I am.'" The hope of separating the wheat from the chaff, and finding one's true self, is a fool's errand that

> drives the youth to read their way through libraries, cranks to claim that they have found The Secret which makes all things plain, and sound scientists and scholars, toward the ends of their lives, to hope that their work has 'philosophical implications' and 'universal human significance.'[15]

Authenticity, in short, is vastly overrated.

These poor, deluded Emil Sinclair types are wild-goose chasing what the great suspense film director Alfred Hitchcock used to refer to as a "MacGuffin": an arbitrary plot device—like a stolen secret formula or a codebreaking machine—that's used to drive the action. It's what the characters always seem to be after. But it is really the chase itself that counts and not the "MacGuffin"—a theatrical mechanical rabbit meant to spur the greyhounds to run around the track.

The postmodern idea of the infinite plasticity of the self—which is a denial of the very idea of nature or an objective metaphysical reality—is often celebrated as an ideal of ultimate personal freedom: We can make ourselves into whomever or whatever we want ourselves to be, and then put it on YouTube. And just who are the popular icons of this postmodernism? One biographer of the late Jackson dubbed him a "post-modern shape-shifter."[16]

But what is this "freedom" except the rigid mask of an increasingly desperate, compulsive, fear-driven attempt at self-control? This is simply the same old drive to dominate nature that began with the Agricultural Revolution, dressed up in a brand-new, garishly outlandish costume. Michael Jackson could not accept his race, his gender, his age, or his sexuality. As a result, he turned himself into a grotesque, pitiful self-caricature. His face literally became a mask, and this was no accident. By constructing a self-image straight out of a page in a plastic surgeon's catalogue, he hadn't so much found his individuality as he had erased all evidentiary traces of it.

This is not to say that we don't have significant choices in our lives, or that our beliefs about ourselves and our potentialities don't matter, or don't influence our reality. They most certainly do. But acceptance of ourselves as we are must be the point of departure for any meaningful effort at self-transformation.

What is more, a truly transformative perspective would upend, rather than reinforce, our standard—and clearly dysfunctional—cultural beliefs and values. It would challenge rather than reinforce our feverish obsession with external appearances, the lurid cult of celebrity—to be is to be adulated, or at least noticed by an audience—our distracting absorption in trivia and gossip, and the entire entertainment circus. Celebrities who specialize in reinventing themselves at the drop of a hat are not postmodern freedom fighters; they're prisoners of tired old clichés.

The most challenging perspective of all would be one that questions what we have seen as the widespread, virtually universal—if not quite unanimous—rejection of the notion that we can and must discern the underlying natural patterns of our lives and character, and thereby discover the essential true selves that we are, and are trying to become, more or less consciously (with any luck, more rather than less).

What am I, really? Am I more than my physical body? More than measurable, if fluctuating, biochemical states? Am I my soul? My oversoul? Am I my ego? Is there an ego? Is the ego a demon? An angel? Both? How can I know?

Our attention has been focused on answers to these questions. But maybe these are the wrong questions to ask. Not exactly wrong, perhaps, but slightly misleading. Perhaps we should be asking: Why do we find ourselves asking these questions in the first place? Could the very act of asking itself be a symptom of having inadvertently wandered—or been deliberately led—down the wrong path?

Questions about Questions

British philosopher R. G. Collingwood also had the distinction of being a practicing archaeologist and historian. In fact, he held dual chairs of philosophy and history at Oxford University. He was precociously brilliant, and, like most brilliant thinkers, far ahead of his time. Decades before philosophers like the late Thomas Kuhn (who coined the term "paradigm shift"[17]) developed insights into the fundamental ways in which our worldviews change and thereby alter our perceptions of what is "scientific" or "real," Collingwood questioned certain widely held assumptions. Instead of trying to make history into a "science" as many did and still do, he saw that science was actually a kind of history.

What Collingwood learned from his fieldwork in archaeology, as well as his absorption in the ancient history of the Roman occupation of Britain, is that the standard empiricist model of knowledge favored by the scientists and philosophers of his, and even our own, day, which claimed that knowledge is the patient yet progressive accumulation of hard facts and solidly verified new data, is deeply flawed. He came to doubt that any fact was ever as hard or solid as we may suppose. For there is no such thing as a fact apart from its interpretation. And interpretations—including the best scientific theories—are contestable and open to change. Even a small pottery shard or a dagger can be controversial.

Gaining knowledge, then, is not like building a house, brick by brick, from the foundation up. It's more like an archaeological excavation, in which we must dig down deep within ourselves to find and reconstruct the basic underpinnings—the underlying context—of our beliefs. All knowledge is thus ultimately self-knowledge; for we must get beyond the mere "facts" to the reasons why we view them in one way rather than another. We must, in other words, become the archaeologists of our own minds or consciousness, which is itself a window on the mass consciousness of our culture. To look inward is, at one and the same time, to look outward—and vice versa. "Man does not struggle with either his intellectual or his moral problems in solitude," Collingwood observed. "He receives each alike from his environment, and in solving them he is doing other people's work as well as his own."[18]

Collingwood worked all this out in what he called his "logic of question and answer,"[19] which was not really "logic" in the formal sense at all, but rather a theory of inquiry.[20] Boiled down to its essentials, what he was saying is that the meaning of a statement is tied to the question it is intended to answer. And it may not always be obvious what that question is or what is, in turn, the context of its arising at all. This kind of inquiry requires some serious "digging."

For example, take the simple statement "The grass is green." This seems to be a rather straightforward factual assertion, either true or false, made in answer to the question "What color is the grass?" Answer: Green. Check. Now let's move on.

But wait a minute. Suppose A and B, who are longtime friends, are engaged in conversation. A is explaining to B how depressed he is of late—he's suffered some serious losses and setbacks. He's grieving. At one point, A says reassuringly, "The grass is green." B sighs and nods his head in agreement.

Are they really talking about the color of the grass?

Or suppose a husband and wife who have a contentious relationship are having a familiar type of disagreement. He's purchased a pair of slacks to match a sports coat, but his wife takes issue with the color combination. "They're green," he insists. "The grass is green," she sniffs, her voice dripping with cold condescension.

Are they really just talking about the color of the grass?

In the first instance, "The grass is green" signifies something like "Life goes on; things are sure to improve," while in the second case it has the flavor of "You're an idiot, as usual." What is the point of suffering? Why can't we ever agree, even (or especially) on the smallest matters? These are the respective questions being asked.

The contexts of both utterances are thus long-standing relationships (and continuing conversations or arguments) that have a certain history. To interpret and grasp the meaning of those seemingly identical and isolated factual statements with any accuracy requires an understanding of their place in that history. To abstract them from that context, as Collingwood insists, would be to falsify them.

Entering the Rhythm

When we shift our perspective to the historical context of the debate about the self, certain common themes emerge.

One striking theme is the widespread denial and derision that greet the ideals of self and self-knowledge, as expressed by mainstream philosophy, science, and religion. It is eerily reminiscent of the ridicule and scorn once heaped on "outlier" phenomena like sightings of UFOs and psychic functions like precognitive knowledge of the future and clairvoyant perceptions of distant objects, people, and places. Even as government authorities and members of the scientific-academic establishment mock these things in public, these same agencies and officials are engaged in private high-level research into UFOs and ESP, and even make use of trained clairvoyants in secret military intelligence-gathering programs. What is the common link?

In a word: Fear—what Robert Monroe identified as "the great barrier to human growth."[21]

When individuals are very afraid, when they experience something they can't explain or understand and may not be able to handle, they may dissociate from their own experience. They pretend it isn't happening to them, that it isn't real.

We may not know what UFOs are, or be able to explain how we acquire information by means other than the intellectual processing of data gathered by the five physical senses, but reasonable people have experiences of such things all the time.

Similarly, we may not be able to offer a precise definition for or provide a detailed sketch of the contours of the self. Yet we all experience a distinct sense of personal identity that may nevertheless be flexible or porous enough to include, or meld with—at least on occasion—other entities and life-forms, including loved ones, plants, animals, minerals, persons living in other times and/or places, other (nonphysical) aspects of our selves, and even so-called mystical experiences of the divine or the whole of existence. I am bounded, yet unbounded. Odd—but true.

What we are all seeking, says Joseph Campbell, is not the *meaning* of life—that is, verbal definitions, explanations, concepts, or theories—so much as an *experience* of being alive, in which the life we live on the purely physical plane has resonances of our deeper, innermost being and its connection to Source. In other words, to our true self.[22] This echoes Nietzsche's pungent quip that what really counts is "Not eternal life, but eternal vivacity."[23] What good is it being alive after you're dead, if you're not alive while you're alive?

Because they are naturally vivacious, young children often spontaneously enjoy experiences of this kind—even ones that closely resemble those relayed by the great mystics and shamans. This is particularly true before the heavy draperies of civilization's cultures, or what the poet William Wordsworth dubbed "the shades of the prison house," descend and threaten to suffocate tender minds and hearts.[24]

In his marvelous book *Visions of Innocence*, psychologist Edward Hoffman records hundreds of such memorable experiences, remembered in convincing, pristine detail by individuals well into their adulthood and even old age. In many instances, these fondly recalled episodes proved to be absolutely pivotal in the person's development, determining career paths for people as diverse as anthropologists, artists, and forest rangers, and shaping both sensibilities and outlook.

For example, a seventy-one-year-old anthropology professor recalled a childhood visit to the seashore when she was four. "Breathing with the waves," she said, "I entered their rhythm." Suddenly, she recalls, it was as if, "a door opened,"

> and I became the sun, the wind, and the sea. There was no 'I' anymore. 'I' had merged with everything else. All sensory perceptions became one. Sound, smell, taste, touch, and shape—all melted into a brilliant light. The pulsating energy went right through me, and I was part of this energy.[25]

There was no "I" anymore. This marks not the dissolution of the self, but rather the dissolution of our false ideas about the self. As "part of this energy," Helga remained distinct, yet bonded, a mystical surfer riding the cosmic waves. In the web of existence, you see, there are seams, after all: we ourselves. Individuality is not reduced to a meaningless aggregate of data, or annihilated in a featureless void. It is enhanced in its quality through its encounter with the rhythm of the hoop.

Helga became an anthropologist in order to study comparative religion. "The surge of energy that swept through me sixty-seven years ago has continued to carry me," she told Hoffman. "It reminds me that I will always be in the middle of the stream as long as I keep the memory alive."[26]

Writer Philip K. Dick once defined reality as "that which, when you stop believing in it, doesn't go away"—no matter how much you wish it would.[27] This, I suggest, is the primacy of nature asserting itself against artifice; it is the stubborn and resourceful weed poking through the cracks in the cement sidewalk.It is, as Helga the anthropology professor indicated, the rule of following the great rhythm of the waves, the natural energies that drive and inform the universe.

Civilization is the great artifice: the hysterical, cracked sidewalk desperately trying, with all its might, to hold itself together against the reasserting power of nature, which promises to end its world. Each of us is, at least potentially, that weed of truth, instinctively moving out of the darkness of ignorance and inching toward the light: a heliotropism of epic proportions. We are slowly winding our way toward a flash of insight. Some of us may even be lucky enough to get hit by lightning.

Now I mean, quite literally, hit by a bolt of lightning, right out of the proverbial blue. Would that be sufficient to "end my world"?

As we'll see in the next chapter, the answer to this question is: Absolutely, yes.

CHAPTER SEVEN

INTO A DARK FOREST

Midway life's journey I was made aware
That I had strayed into a dark forest,
And the right path appeared not anywhere.

DANTE ALIGHIERI, *The Divine Comedy, Inferno,* I, 1–3

There is and can be no self-knowledge based on theoretical
assumptions, for the object of self-knowledge is an individual—a relative exception and an irregular phenomenon.
Hence it is not the universal and the regular that character-
ize the individual, but rather the unique.

C. G. JUNG, *The Undiscovered Self* (1958)

A few years back, I attended a conference where I gave a talk on the Myth
of the Great Ending. At the conclusion of my lecture, a balding, distin-
guished-looking middle-aged man who was standing in the rear of the hall
raised his hand to ask a question.

"Didn't we create and perpetuate this myth because of our awareness of
our own approaching death?" he offered sincerely.

No, but we tend to think this way. Maybe, in part, we just can't help it. We're
so accustomed or conditioned to thinking along Aristotelian lines—every
story has a beginning, a middle, and an end—that, as soon as we think we're
halfway through, we become anxious and fidgety, wondering just how and

when the whole thing is going to wind up. This holds true for individuals as well as civilizations. Today, it's built into the digitized way we live our lives, and thus just about everything we do.

For example, my computer is so smart now that it monitors my printer to let me know precisely how much ink is left in the printing cartridges. As long as the blue line on the indicator bar shows more than 50 percent, I feel safe and secure. But once it crosses that magic number, I become antsy. I know I'm running out of ink and that I'll have to make a visit to the office supplies store soon to buy another cartridge.

From this standpoint, the much-ballyhooed midlife crisis is about death. "I've seen the light at the end of the tunnel, and it's the oncoming train," goes the refrain. That's the funeral train—the Grim Reaper express—and it's headed straight for you. Look out! You're running out of time. You're about to be depleted and discarded.

Carl Jung, for one, believed otherwise. Jung suggested that the midlife crisis was about life, not death—not about what we've used up or how little we have left, but about that reserve tank we haven't touched at all. Specifically, it's about the greater life in us that we haven't lived out. "Many—far too many—aspects of life which should also have been experienced lie in the lumber-room among dusty memories," he says. "Sometimes, even," he adds, "they are glowing coals under grey ashes."[1]

What Jung is getting at, I venture, is this: At some point, the jig is up. The carefully constructed social mask that civilization has forced us to create and don—often at gunpoint, literally or figuratively—begins to crack and tear; the nuts and bolts start to loosen, and our natural selves—the original faces behind our disguises—yearn to express themselves and be seen in public. As the poet Robert Bly puts it, the mask starts to "rattle."[2] It doesn't quite fit anymore. Now what do we do?

At this point, we face a rather stark, and perhaps irreversible, choice: We can either heed the call of nature by allowing the impulses of our true selves to assert themselves, or we can turn our backs on that call by siding with civilization and its process of enculturation. That is, we can elect to repair the mask with tape and glue so that it stays rigidly fixed in place until we die. By so doing, we remain complicit in our own disfigurement, even as we revel in our "success" and various "accomplishments"—our academic degrees, trophies and trinkets, and other material signs of social prestige. The victims identify with the oppressor.

Sometimes, however, that call of nature is so insistent and overpowering that it may seem as though we have no choice but to heed its demands—no matter what the cost. By taking a look at these special cases, we may learn something important—and perhaps indispensable—about what it means to end our worlds.

Struck by Lightning

On a summer's day in 1994, the world of Dr. Tony Cicoria, then a 42-year-old, successful orthopedic surgeon from Upstate New York, abruptly ended.

Dr. Cicoria was taking time out from a family picnic to phone his mother from a public telephone booth when he was struck by lightning—literally "enlightened." That's when this very nuts-and-bolts, scientifically minded clinician—he has both a medical degree and a Ph.D. in physiology and cellular biophysics, and was not, on his own view, a particularly spiritual or religious person—had what researchers call a near-death experience (NDE) that changed his life.

What is an NDE? The term was coined by yet another physician, Raymond Moody, a psychiatrist who also holds a Ph.D. in philosophy. Although Moody first used the term in the 1970s, the phenomenon has been recorded down through the ages, both in oral traditions by the shamans and in ancient literary texts like Plato's *Republic*. Moody's book, *Life After Life*, went on to become a bestseller, spurring interest among both academic researchers and ordinary folk. Individuals who had had NDEs went on TV shows like *Oprah* and *Phil Donahue* to tell their stories, while books by NDErs became staples on the bestseller lists.

Individuals who have had an NDE have either been pronounced clinically dead with no measurable brain activity, or, in the absence of medical monitoring, been in dire physical circumstances like a car accident or a heart attack that bring them to the precipice of earthly existence. What they describe happening to them varies somewhat from case to case. Yet there are certain commonly reported features that veteran researchers like Moody and psychologist Kenneth Ring have used in order to construct a working model of the so-called "core" or prototypical NDE.[3]

Typically, NDErs describe exiting their bodies and being able to view and identify it from an external vantage point. They then report making a kind of transit through a dark area—often described as a tunnel, but sometimes as a forest or other place—and entering a transcendent realm of peace and bliss. There, they may encounter what they call a loving being or energy of brilliant white light, deceased friends or relatives, or other entities. Certain information may be imparted to them about themselves or about their future. Sometimes, this communication takes the form of a so-called "life-review," in which the individuals experience, in a three-dimensional display, every single event from their past, as well as their results, good and bad, for themselves and others. At some point, they are either told they must "go back"—that it is not their time to die physically—or else they are given a choice whether to stay in the realm of bliss or return to earth. Many choose to return to physical life either because of "unfinished business" or obligations to others like spouses or children who would suffer in their absence.

Tony Cicoria's account of his NDE shares a number of these "core" features. He saw his physical body from outside it and above the ground. He watched, unconcerned, as relatives frantically administering CPR tried to revive him. Floating above the fray, he no longer felt any connection to the events unfolding below: "My consciousness came with me . . . I was surrounded by a bluish-white light . . . [I felt a sense of pure] well-being . . . peace. The highest and lowest points of my life raced by me . . . pure thought . . . pure ecstasy . . . . Then—slam! I was back [in my body]."[4]

Break on Through

Die-hard skeptics may be tempted to explain away exceptional experiences like Tony Cicoria's as mere hallucinatory fantasies of a trauma-shocked nervous system. But it becomes difficult to be so dismissive when there are measurable results arising from such episodes. These are chiefly of two general types.

In the first, NDErs may return from their voyages to "the other side" with verifiable information that they likely did not get, or could not have obtained, from "normal" channels—i.e., sensory input combined with conscious reasoning or unconscious inference. Frequently, cases reported in the literature go like this: Two friends, A and B, suffer a car crash and are rushed by separate ambulances to a local hospital. Unbeknownst to B, who is unconscious and in cardiac arrest, A dies en route to the hospital. However, B has an NDE in which she encounters A, who informs B of her passing, and of the necessity of B's return to the physical. B, who returns to her body and is revived by medical personnel, is not told of A's passing, in order not to upset her in her precarious state. However, B already knows of A's death from her NDE and speaks of it matter-of-factly to stunned hospital personnel.

The second kind of evidence that supports the reality of NDEs is more indirect—the aftereffects of the episode on the experiencer, not simply as felt by them. It is, of course, expected that the scientifically minded will pooh-pooh "subjective" self-reporting, but many of these reports have been confirmed by outside observers, including family, friends, and coworkers, and even measured by standard personality tests and responses to tailored questionnaires and other examinations.

It's this second type of evidence that is so strongly presented by Cicoria's case—strongly enough to have caught the attention of no less than famed neurologist and best-selling author, Oliver Sacks, who made Cicoria the subject of a chapter in his most recent book, *Musicophilia: Tales of Music and the Brain.*[5]

"Musicophilia" is the Greek word for "the love of music." It was this sudden, passionate, and all-consuming love—specifically of piano music—with which Cicoria was inflamed following his close brush with death, courtesy of the literal "bolt from the blue" that knocked him back thirty feet and into brief cardiac arrest. A former rock-and-roll devotee, he became virtually obsessed with listening to classical piano music. Chopin was a particular favorite.

Despite his lack of musical background, knowledge, or skills, Cicoria taught himself to play the piano that, serendipitously, had been stored in his home. Like Mozart, he also began to hear musical tunes in his head—and, like the shamans, especially in his dreams. Although he didn't know musical notation or composition, he did his best to record his inspirations. One night, he even had a dream of himself giving a concert of his own music on stage—seemingly a highly improbable turn of events. Yet, even as he continued to practice medicine, piano music became his one true love. And, he notes, he was becoming "very spiritual."[6]

Of course, none of the profound aftereffects of Cicoria's NDE prove, beyond any doubt, that he really visited the "afterlife." But surely, the cause must be proportional to the effect. *Something* of a profound nature occurred as a result of that lightning strike; something radically transformed a previously materialistic scientist's beliefs, values, and behavior, and opened him up to a wider, truer view of reality, as well as a more fulfilling range of experience and activity. This is not the kind of result typically seen after hallucinations, nor is it evidence of pathology—indeed, quite the reverse. It smacks of health in the literal sense of the term: wholeness.

In the process of becoming more complete, Cicoria learned to take the nonrational side of life—including his intuitions, impulses, and especially his dreams and creativity—far more seriously than before. What he called his "gift dream" of giving a concert of his own music was literally fulfilled (with the help of Sacks) when he performed his *Lightning Sonata* on stage in January 2008.

Cicoria was recently asked by an interviewer to speculate on the role of experiences like NDEs in altering human consciousness. His reply sheds much light, not only on Hermann Hesse's conundrum (Why is it so very difficult to live in accord with the promptings that come from our true selves?), but also on Carl Jung's view of the midlife crisis. In fact, it reveals the crucial link between the two. His remarks—chock-full of genuine insight—are worth citing here:

> Part of the human condition is that if you're aware someone else is doing something differently from you, you're likely to conform. You're instructed out of your uniqueness very rapidly by friends, family, society. If you have a particular gift, or your own special awareness, it may be suppressed to the point that it either isn't expressed, or it's suppressed until a later point in life when you discover: I have this gift; I can use it!

He added, tellingly:

> Nothing is black and white to me anymore; everything is
> gray. I've tried to teach all my kids this lesson: Whatever
> you're passionate about, whatever you like, explore it.[7]

Joseph Campbell's favorite formula for this was succinct: Follow your bliss.

Despite being a driven, successful, middle-aged physician, seemingly comfortably ensconced in his career, Cicoria followed his newfound bliss, and, as a result, he realized his "gift dream" of giving a concert performance of his own piano music. He even made a CD of his *Lightning Sonata*. At present, he's writing a book that he hopes will reconcile his more mystical and scientific interests.

None of this would have been possible unless he had followed the urgings of what he terms the "life force," or the subtle "pressure to do certain things" to which he learned to become sensitive following his accident and NDE. Yet all this, important as it became to him, was not part of his original life program. Or was it?

We are all meant to follow our bliss. That's why we chose to come into this world to begin with—to develop our own special awareness; to live out of, and express, our uniqueness; to give our particular gifts. We all do this naturally and spontaneously when we begin. Instinct and intuition are meant to be our guides.

But we get sidetracked, particularly in civilized cultures that are either hostile (as in the West) or indifferent (as in the East) to nature. Civilization forces us to fit into systems that teach us to be indifferent or hostile to our uniqueness, and even our own bliss. We learn to hate our true selves. We learn, as Cicoria says, from family, friends, and society that it is far more important to fit in than to stand out.

The question is: Do we have the power to resist the pressure to conform? Why don't we have it when we are younger? And if we don't, how can we acquire it? What does it take to develop the power to end my world?

You Can Get It (Do You Really Want It?)

What, after all, is "power"?

Presidents of the United States have it. Generals, corporate CEOs, media celebrities, and Nobel Prize-winning scientists have it. Gurus and prophets have it, too. But what is it?

In the most general sense, power is simply causal efficacy: the capacity to get things done, the ability of causes to have significant effects. And, of course, since there are many different kinds of "things" to do, or "ends" to reach, as well as varying skills or means to achieve those ends, there are many different kinds of power—political, financial, military, intellectual, and personal. There are also more subtle forms of power, like the power to meditate or to connect with other realities. But this, too, is an ability that enables us to achieve our aims. Spiritual power is still power. Whether and how we value it depends on us.

By its nature, power fluctuates; it tends to wax and wane. You can have it one minute and lose it the next. Jimmy Carter and Richard Nixon had it; when the Iran hostage crisis and Watergate intervened, they lost it. Michael Jackson had it, as did Johnny Carson. Jackson noisily imploded; Carson—without a great deal of fanfare—quietly retired.

We also speak of the power of natural energies like storms or explosions. Hurricane Katrina had great power—the power nearly to destroy an entire city. And so, of course, did the Big Bang, which got quite a bit done in its day.

This contrasting set of examples points up the distinction we usually make between creative and destructive power. The power to make and the power to break are really just two sides of the same coin—alternative, but ultimately complementary, ways of expressing or channeling one and the same energy.

When the Sioux holy man Black Elk was only nine years old, he had his Great Vision. As he told his biographer, he was taken up to the Sky Lodge, where he met the Six Grandfathers, whom he recognized as the six Powers of the World in human form. These were the powers of the six directions—North, South, East, West, Above (the power of the sky) and Below (the power of the earth)—who acted as Black Elk's teachers.

The first Grandfather to address Black Elk, the power of the West, gave him two gifts. The first was a wooden cup, "full of water and in the water was the sky." Then the West Power—the wise old man—spoke directly to him:

"Take this," he said. "It is the power to make live, and it is yours." Now he had a bow in his hands. "Take this," he said. "It is the power to destroy, and it is yours."[8]

Of course, in our ordinary modern, "civilized" way of thinking—which we can stick to, for the moment—we make a fundamental distinction between the power of impersonal forces like Katrina and the Big Bang, and the power of personal agents like ourselves. We are alive, conscious, and purposive; they are not. They are nonconscious energy systems. Hence, from this "mature" or "enlightened" perspective, it would be a mistake to say that Katrina "meant" to destroy New Orleans, or that the Big Bang "intended" to produce the universe. To talk in this shamanistic or archaic way—as Black Elk did—would be either mere poetic license or a symptom of mental confusion. To think otherwise would invite charges of relapsing into primitive superstition and childish personification. We resist all such talk and congratulate ourselves on our intellectual sophistication.

By decoupling our notion of human power from that of natural power, we distance ourselves from nature, and nature from us. What nature does is "merely accidental"—the universe produced by the Big Bang is dubbed "the fortunate accident"—and is, therefore, regarded as something that, at least potentially, ought to be managed and controlled. By us, of course, the ones who act deliberately. Katrina was an accidental by-product of a chance concatenation of atmospheric conditions and weather patterns. The bolt of lightning that struck Tony Cicoria from out of the blue was, on this view, surely no less of an accident, as judged by the usual, if no less banal, standards employed by insurance companies and "common sense" alike.

This same condescending attitude is then extended to everything that is spontaneous and unplanned, including our own impulses and instincts, which must be tamed, held in check, and submitted to the bureaucratic planning department of our rational intellects for the official stamp of approval. Get in line, wait your turn.

At the same time, we distance ourselves from the old truth, expressed by the Grandfather of the West, that every use of power has both creative and destructive results. This makes it easier to ignore the negative side, and to accentuate the positive—in other words, to remain ignorant and shortsighted.

Thus our idea of human power is reduced to a rather simplistic formula—namely, the ability to get what we want. That's how we usually define "power." And if you ask most people what it is they want, they won't have any trouble telling you: faster Internet service; more channels on their cable television; harder bodies; jobs that pay more money; bigger houses; more powerful and prestigious cars; younger, better-looking faces; the latest cell phone gadget; and so on. Make your own list.

This overly narrow, sadly circumscribed, exclusively anthropocentric—not to mention quite shallow and materialistic—notion of power, of course, begs the crucial question: How do you know who "you" really are, or what "you" really want?

The problem is that our concepts, as well as our senses of power, self, and self-knowledge, are all intimately connected. They are developed simultaneously in the course of the very socialization process that demands the surrender of our uniqueness. For example, a young girl who discovers that she has a talent for mathematics will be rewarded and encouraged to develop that ability as a path to social and economic success—even if she does not enjoy math, and would prefer to be writing short stories or reading poetry instead. We tend to follow the applause.

The imperative to fit in determines the trajectory of the learning process, including the cultivation of certain skills and abilities, and the benign neglect or deliberate downplaying of others. This is what makes it so difficult to mount an adequate defense against the pressure cooker of conformism. We are swimming inside the belly of the very beast upon whose protection and largesse we must rely. If we slay the beast, we may kill ourselves in the bargain. At least, that is the fear.

Our self-image thus becomes skewed and distorted. We are like an octopus that believes, and acts as if, it has only one appendage instead of eight. Its dismemberment may only be illusory, but if the octopus thinks it cannot swim, defend itself, or find food, this belief has real effects. Thus even illusions can have great power—if, that is, we allow them to.

We think we know who we are, what we want, and how to get it. Then, cruising merrily along at a brisk 90-mile-per-hour clip—wham! We slam headlong into a brick wall. We never know what hit us—or rather, what we hit. In midlife, we may well find ourselves crushed, apparently by circumstances completely out of our control. If we're lucky, however, a bolt of lightning may strike us, simultaneously illuminating our predicament and opening us to insight: a new vision of the radiant world around us, its multiple dimensions hitherto unnoticed and unsuspected.

And what if we're not so fortunate? What, then?

Power Failure

Not long ago, a professor friend I'll call Dan dropped by our lake house in Maine for a brief summer visit. Actually, we'd never met before in person. A psychologist by training and a longtime college teacher, Dan was the friend of yet another friend who had introduced me to Dan because he knew that we shared an interest in out-of-body and near-death experiences. Dan had even done research in this area. He and I had kept in touch mostly by e-mail, and occasionally by phone. This would be our first face-to-face meeting.

Dan arrived on a sunny Friday afternoon in July. We shook hands warmly. He said he was anxious to see the lake, but as we ventured toward the water, he seemed somewhat edgy and preoccupied, as if he were only half paying attention to what I was saying or what he was seeing. Later that evening (perhaps to account for his earlier distraction), he remarked how little he had been reading lately. He was having eye trouble and complained that none of his glasses any longer corrected his vision. Still, he said with a sigh, he hadn't taken the trouble to have an examination.

By Saturday morning, an unstable front had moved in from the mountains. A storm ensued, bringing with it much rain and cooler temperatures—cool enough for me to throw a few logs in the fireplace and make us a couple of mugs of hot tea. Nursing our drinks, we sat before the crackling fire, chatting amiably about our mutual interests in what some would call the "paranormal," and what others might describe as "consciousness studies."

As our discussion veered toward academic life and the demands of teaching and research—particularly after many years in the classroom—Dan's demeanor visibly changed. His face sagged as he talked of his writing projects.

"I promised a couple of editors I'd do these book reviews," he offered languidly, "but I don't know if I'll do them. I just can't push myself to do them."

I nodded sympathetically.

"I think I'm beginning to understand that great nostalgia for the 'other side' that some of those near-death people talk about," Dan mused wistfully. "Not that I've ever thought of suicide," he continued. "But I just can't seem to sustain the energy for these projects." Dan looked dejected as he stared down at the floor, his fatigue clearly in evidence.

The fire began to crackle and sputter. "Must be damp wood," I grumbled as I moved the logs around with the poker in hopes of igniting a spark.

Just then, Dan perked up noticeably and steered the conversation to what was clearly his one true passion: acting. He'd performed in some local community groups and had even starred in a regional dinner-theater production that went on to garner some favorable reviews. Yet that "one big break" always managed to elude him. So he turned, instead, to writing plays, hoping to score a breakthrough. He'd shopped his manuscripts around the fringes of Broadway—friends of friends who knew producers, that sort of thing. But so far, his efforts had not borne fruit.

Once again, Dan's face took on that hangdog look. His fatigue was palpable. He was clearly tired of his present world, yet he seemed to lack the power to end it. Why? Was this simply a run of bad luck? Or was there more to it than that?

On the positive side, Dan knew that reality is a much richer and deeper affair than the shallow materialism of those whose idea of happiness is simply more and better consumption of purchasable luxury goods. His interest in and acceptance of the reality of phenomena like out-of-body and near-death experiences testified to his wider, deeper perspective. He also had some degree of awareness of his "true(r) self" and its requirements for nourishment.

So what was the missing ingredient? Was it that Dan's knowledge was "merely" intellectual, stuck at the level of pure theory? If so, what could make it more visceral and immediate—and perhaps, thereby, more practical and transformational? What would close the gap? Do we literally have to get struck by lightning? Or are there slightly less painful—and less physically dangerous—alternatives?

Perhaps we can address these questions, and even learn a thing or two in the process, by studying the cases of two brave souls who cracked the hard, thin shell of conventionality and its pseudo-wisdom, to venture off into the vast unknown—Jane Roberts and Robert Monroe.

CHAPTER EIGHT

THE WOMB OF MYTH

In a manner of speaking, your factual world rises on a bed of fantasy, myth, and imagination. . . . Myth is not a distortion of fact, but the womb through which fact must come.

SETH, IN JANE ROBERTS,
The Individual and the Nature of Mass Events (1981)

The majority of accepted beliefs—religious, scientific, and cultural—have tended to stress a sense of powerlessness, impotence, and impending doom.

SETH, IN JANE ROBERTS,
The Individual and the Nature of Mass Events (1981)

I do not believe that there are any more dangers facing us in the interior universe than there are in the physical one. We should explore each world with common sense and courage. The interior universe is the source of the exterior one, however, and traveling through it we will encounter our own hopes, fears and beliefs in their ever-changing form.

JANE ROBERTS, *Seth, Dreams and
Projections of Consciousness* (1987)

The world of Jane Roberts ended abruptly on September 9, 1963. At least, that was the beginning of the end. Or was it the end of the beginning?

Although Roberts didn't quite realize it at the time, she had been wandering aimlessly in the thicket of her own dark forest when she serendipitously tumbled into a seemingly bottomless metaphysical rabbit hole—and nothing, including herself, was ever quite the same again. And who could blame her?

A Fantastic Avalanche

In 1963, Jane Roberts was an ambitious aspiring author of short stories and poetry with one recent novel to her credit. In her mid-thirties, she was still angling to "make it" in the literary world, when everything suddenly and irrevocably changed. Up until this point in her career, success had been defined by her self-described youthful "hopes for recognition or good reviews from *The Saturday Review* or *The New York Times* book section."[1] That was not to be.

Feeling restless and having difficulty finding inspiration, her mood turned sour. Her poetry became crowded with dark, oppressive images of death and decay, some seemingly triggered by a "small household tragedy" like the death of her pet cat.

Yet, as she later admitted, the real culprit was "the growing sense of panic with which I viewed the passing years."[2] The crisis of midlife, in other words, had stolen upon her. Beneath the surface pursuit of her professional goals and artistic excellence, the tectonic plates of her deeper, unknown self were shifting.

The earthquake arrived on that fateful autumn evening in 1963, as Roberts settled down at her writing table in the living room of her apartment. Her husband, Rob Butts, who was also an artist, was working on his painting in the rear studio three doors away. What happened next is best told in her own words, as she described it in *The Seth Material* (1970):

> What happened next was like a "trip" without drugs. If someone had slipped me an LSD cube on the sly, the experience couldn't have been more bizarre. Between one normal minute and the next, a fantastic avalanche of radical, new ideas burst into my head with tremendous force,

as if my skull were some sort of receiving station, turned up to unbearable volume. Not only ideas came through this channel, but sensations, intensified and pulsating. I was tuned in, turned on—whatever you want to call it— connected to some incredible source of energy. I didn't even have time to call out to Rob.[3]

The revelatory aspect of this fantastic "trip," or what she herself described as an "intuitive breakthrough," clearly illustrates the "insight" experience as described by David Bohm: the sudden, dramatic shift to a creative new perspective that overturns or surpasses old beliefs and ideas, and initiates a new, unified way of thinking and understanding.

But it didn't stop there. As Roberts continues her account, it is clear that what happened to her next was equivalent to the shaman's soul-flight—what the ancient Greeks termed "ecstasy," from the Greek word *ecstasis* (or *ekstasis*), literally, to be outside of or beside oneself—or what, back in the 1970s, the veteran consciousness researcher Charles Tart, in concert with Robert Monroe, christened simply but elegantly, out-of-body experiences, or OBEs.

It was as if the physical world were really tissue-paper thin, hiding infinite dimensions of reality, and I was suddenly flung through the tissue paper with a huge ripping sound. My body sat at the table, my hands furiously scribbling down the words and ideas that flashed through my head. Yet I seemed to be somewhere else, at the same time, traveling through things. I went plummeting through a leaf, to find a whole universe open up; and then out again, drawn into new perspectives.[4]

In *Seth, Dreams and Projections of Consciousness* (1986), which was written around the same time as *The Seth Material*, but published only posthumously, Roberts expands on her account of this initial, mind-blowing episode:

One moment I sat at my desk with my paper and pen beside me. The next instant, my consciousness rushed out of my body, yet it was itself body-less, taking up no space at all; it seemed to be merging with the air outside the window, plunging through the treetops, resting, curled with a single leaf. Exultation and comprehension, new ideas, sensations, novel groupings of images and words rushed through me so quickly there was no time to call out. There was no present, past or future: I knew this, suddenly, irrevocably. . . . Then, gradually, I became aware that my consciousness was settling back in my body again, but slowly, like dust motes descending through the evening air down to where my body sat upright at the table, head bent, fingers furiously scribbling notes about what was happening as if they had a mind of their own.[5]

And, as if to answer our lingering question about my professor friend, Dan, and the insufficiency of his "purely theoretical" nature to support his wider knowledge of reality, Roberts concludes:

I felt as if knowledge was being implanted in the very cells of my body so that I couldn't forget it—a gut knowing, a biological spirituality. It was feeling and knowing, rather than intellectual knowledge.[6]

"Spirituality" was not then even a word in her vocabulary—indeed, it may well have been the furthest thing from her mind. The dozen-page manuscript, titled "The Physical Universe as Idea Construction," that Roberts discovered her hand had scrawled out when she returned to her physical body from her cosmic voyage contained metaphysical concepts that were foreign to her way of thinking. These ideas sharply challenged some of her most dearly held—and, quite frankly, dark and pessimistic—assumptions about the utterly futile, fleeting, trivial, and meaningless nature of human existence. "My intellect just could not get beyond certain points," she candidly admitted, "and I knew it."[7] She had reached an impasse.

What was the "Idea Construction" manuscript implied—or, in some cases, just flat-out stated—is basically what the great shamans have always known and said: That everything that exists is alive, conscious, purposive, and interconnected; that our world is therefore a meaningful and creative process in which consciousness, including human consciousness, plays a formative role, helping to make and shape our experienced reality; that we are much more than we think we are, our larger true identity being profoundly greater than our religious and scientific beliefs credit. We are neither passive victims of an indifferent, accidental universe, nor cosmic puppets whose strings are pulled by some vengeful, judgmental deity.

At a deeper-than-conscious level, Roberts well understood that all the old mainstream traditions, scientific and religious, were moribund; the cultural egg was cracked wide open and could not be put together again. "I believe that I had gone as far as my intellect and normal creativity could take me," she wrote, "and that new channels were opened when I needed them the most," adding quite tellingly: "Generally, I think, these other channels open when we have ceased to rely upon most of the answers that have been given to us by others and found wanting."[8] As she would soon discover, her dramatic out-of-body episode opened those very channels.

The rejection of pat answers creates an opening for genuine inquiry. For Roberts, this took the form of research triggered by the acceptance of a proposal she had sent to her publisher outlining a practical book on how to develop intuitive or psychic modes of perception. These are the "other channels" she is referring to here, and which—much to her own surprise—she subsequently found herself easily able to access: clairvoyance, telepathy, and precognition. She herself, in the heyday of what came to be called the New Age, was labeled a "channeler"—though, for reasons we will discuss, she abhorred that term.

What opened were the floodgates of consciousness, unleashing a virtual torrent of psychic phenomena. In addition to her experiences with "extra-sensory perception" (or, more properly, extra-physical sensory perception), there were numerous out-of-body experiences, meetings with aspects of herself she came to accept, more or less, as reincarnations from the past (and future), as well as with alternate or "probable selves" in what quantum physicists called "parallel worlds."

But the prime locus of all these mind-blowing experiences was her ongoing encounters with the self-described "'energy essence personality' no longer focused in physical form,"[9] named Seth, for whom she eventually spoke in trance for many thousands of hours over the course of the next twenty years, right up until her death in 1984.

This psychic torrent was accompanied by a creative tsunami whose ripple effects continue unabated. Roberts published over twenty books during a twenty-year span, including ones dictated by Seth (in virtually complete form) while Roberts was in trance. They also include several volumes of poetry, the trilogy of *Oversoul Seven* novels, and three very important "aspect psychology" books in which Roberts develops her own highly original ideas concerning the many alterations of consciousness she experienced and speculates on their cultural and metaphysical implications. Since her death, much previously unpublished material has appeared in print and is still being released.

Much of this vast material, both published and unpublished, as well as the voluminous correspondence carried on over the years by Roberts and her husband with physicists, psychologists, parapsychologists, and ordinary readers, is archived at Yale University's Sterling Memorial Library. It is one of the library's most frequently visited special collections—an eloquent testimony to the enduring power of a genuine world-ender's ability to inspire others. The academic establishment cannot contain or co-opt that inspiration, any more than the henhouse can remain safe once the fox is inside.

The "Me" of Me

The Seth development occurred as part of Roberts's research for her original book on extrasensory perception.[10] Several months after her initial out-of-body episode, she and her husband were casually experimenting with a Ouija board. At first, they obtained mostly gibberish and fragmentary responses. Then suddenly, without any warning, the answers took on a degree of intelligence and clarity—along with a wry sense of humor—that was at once surprising and intriguing. In response to a request for a message, the planchette spelled out: "Consciousness is like a flower with many petals." Rob, sensing the shift, asked who was there. "You may call me whatever you choose," came the reply.

> I call myself Seth. It fits the me of me, the personality most
> clearly approximating the whole self I am, or am trying to
> be. Joseph is your whole self more or less, the image of the
> sum of your various personalities in the past and future.[11]

Now, not only was there a distinct personality coming through; it was con-
veying challenging ideas about the nature of reality and the self that neatly
dovetailed with the provocative notions Roberts had received during her explosive OBE, which she had recorded, in an altered state of consciousness, as
the "Idea Construction" manuscript. Nor did it take long for her to realize
that she knew what the planchette was going to "say," even before it moved.
In fact, she experienced a kind of inner pressure to speak the words aloud,
instead of going through the painstaking process of waiting for the plastic
pointer to spell them out slowly, letter by letter.

> The pointer paused. I felt as if I were standing, shivering, on
> the top of a high diving board, trying to make myself jump
> while all kinds of people were waiting impatiently behind
> me. Actually it was the words that pushed at me—they
> seemed to rush through my mind. In some crazy fashion I
> felt as if they'd back up, piles of nouns and verbs in my head
> until they closed everything else off if I didn't speak them.
> And without really knowing how or why, I opened up my
> mouth and let them out. For the first time I began to speak
> for Seth, continuing the sentences the board had spelled
> out only a moment before.[12]

This proved to be a disconcerting—if undeniably exhilarating—turning
point in the Seth development. Additional physical phenomena gradually
manifested. Rich Kendall, who attended the ESP classes that Roberts gave
for a time out of her Elmira, New York apartment during the 1970s, describes the profound unforgettable impact of witnessing this dramatic transformation—from Jane to Seth—firsthand:

Jane took off her glasses, placed them on the nearby coffee table, and began speaking in a loud deep masculine voice. Her eyes seemed to take on a darker cast, while her facial structure in a subtle but definite way had changed; as if the muscles themselves were somehow more alert, more focused. The most striking change however was within the eyes. There is an intangible quality within the eyes of every person, reflecting the uniqueness of their identity, and thus distinguishing them from all others. For all intents and purposes the personality that was now gazing out from behind Jane's eyes was not Jane.[13]

Was Seth a split-off fragment of Roberts's own subconscious personality? Or was he a fully independent entity, the disembodied spirit of someone who had once walked the earth and might even have known her and Rob in a "previous life," as Seth himself seemed to claim? Roberts wrestled not only with the profoundly challenging metaphysical messages that were coming through, but also with the nature and identity of the apparent messenger. Indeed, these issues were inseparable. She remained, throughout the process, intensely skeptical, always questioning herself and Seth, and yet, at the same time, open to experiencing these altered states of consciousness and whatever insights into the human condition they could offer.

Radio, Radio

"Channeling," wrote psychologist Kathryn Ridall at the very height of the channeling vogue in the late 1980s, "is the ability to connect with other beings and other levels of consciousness and to express their reality through our body." A channel acts as an "intermediary," bridging the physical world and nonphysical worlds or dimensions of reality. "You could think of a channel as a living transmitter of subtle energies," she adds, "much like a telephone or a radio station."[14]

This definition, of course, describes in technological language familiar to our scientifically trained ears a phenomenon that has probably been around since the beginning of the human adventure. The ancient shamans were also acting as intermediaries, for example, when they invited the spirits of animals like birds and bears to make temporary homes in their bodies, as expressed through their physical movements and vocalizations.

Nor was this kind of "intermediation" limited to what civilized folks condescendingly think of as "superstitious" or "ignorant" primitives. No one was more rational than Socrates, who once boasted that he was "at all times . . . the kind of man who listens only to the argument that on reflection seems best to me."[15] But he didn't listen *only* to rational argument; for there was the *daimon,* the inner voice or guardian spirit that had guided him since childhood, and that warned him of possible danger.

Some skeptical commentators, like the scientifically minded British philosopher Bertrand Russell, have tried to interpret the *daimon* metaphorically, as "the voice of conscience."[16] But this tortures beyond recognition the plain meaning of what Socrates says about it. And while Socrates seemed to deny that the *daimon* supplied him with any paranormally acquired information—he took pains, at one point, to distance himself from "those prophets"—if he heeded the advice of the *daimon* about impending dangers, he was, in effect, acting on premonitory warnings about the future. Socrates, in short, was a channel—an individual who, according to Ridall's definition, "acts as an intermediary between our physical world and the unseen dimensions of the universe."

The problem with the term "channel," as far as Roberts was concerned, was that it was far too mechanical a metaphor. If interpreted literally rather than symbolically, she claimed, it could be misleading. She didn't feel like a passive receptacle or mere "transmitter," but rather like an active cocreator of the Seth material. It was, she maintained, a mutually shared blending of distinct, though closely related, consciousnesses that resulted in the production of the Seth sessions. The gestures, the words, and the ideas were Seth's, but they wouldn't have been what they were without Jane's body and mind to provide the forms of expression.

Thus, whenever she felt that Seth was "around," Roberts had to give an inner form of permission that enabled the transformation to take place. She never felt "taken over" or "possessed" by Seth, which is one key reason why she hated the term "control," used by earlier trance-mediums to describe the entities that served as their chief guides to the yonder shores of reality once referred to as "the spirit realm." She always retained some rudimentary level of awareness of what Seth was saying to others, though she often was off on her own, on some out-of-body excursion that—not coincidentally—might be illustrating some aspect of the message Seth was delivering at the time. But even when she later had to be apprised of what he had said, she did not feel like a mere bystander or conduit. There was an intimate, creative exchange that made the relationship unique—and workable.

Changing Channels

At first only reluctantly, hesitantly, and somewhat grudgingly, Roberts released her original literary ambitions for another, arguably more profound, aspiration: the philosophical mystic's quest for ultimate truth, knowledge, and wisdom. Sensing the inadequacy of the answers to life's questions provided by conventional science and religion was just the first, if most painful, step. Gradually, she came to appreciate the paradoxical nature of reality, including the process of inquiry itself. As she acutely observed, answers only generate further questions, making it impossible to arrive at a total explanation—what religion claims to provide—or a final theory of everything—what many scientists still yearn for and hope to achieve. Reality, she noted, was simply too vast, too richly complex, and, frankly, just too darned interesting for that kind of ultimate closure:

> Yet ultimately it seems that answers to the most important questions only lead to more meaningful questions in which terms like "yes" or "no," "true" or "false," "real" or "unreal" finally vanish in a greater context of experience large enough to contain the incongruities, eccentricities and seeming contradictions in which our greater reality happens.[17]

Thus, the farther she ventured into the inner realms of awareness, the more she came to understand what the ancient Greek philosopher Heraclitus had described as the depth without bottom that is the human soul. Yet, even within this dizzying, mind-boggling infinity of selves and worlds, we somehow retain a distinct identity, or what she often referred to as an "inviolate" individuality that neither can be nor ought to be surrendered. This is the view of the self developed in her non-Seth-dictated "Jane" books—*Adventures in Consciousness*, *Psychic Politics*, and *The God of Jane*. Here, Roberts sets out her reflections on her trance and other non-ordinary experiences—views that may be found in embryo in that world-shattering "Idea Construction" manuscript.

Who or what, then, was Seth? Was he merely a split-off fragment of Jane's own unconscious mind? Or was he an all-knowing spirit guide? Like the great Irish-American medium Eileen Garrett before her, Roberts steadfastly refused to accept pat scientific or spiritualist answers to this question.[18]

Since Roberts recognized her own creative role in giving Seth a voice, she accepted the responsibility for resisting—and emphasized the ever-present dangers of accepting—the kind of simplistic and often far too literal reading of psychic messages (not to mention the adulation of the psychic messenger) to which naïve admirers and skeptical critics are equally prone.

Moreover, her literary background made her supersensitive to the subtle nuances of language, including and especially the often oblique signs and symbols in which psychic data is transmitted and received. "[W]e must stop automatically taking such information at face value," she demanded, "translating it automatically through ancient beliefs."[19] For when we gaze through the psychic portal, she opined, we are confronted with many different kinds of data—the inner equivalents of television newscasts, fictional dramas, fact-based docudramas, soap operas, and game shows. To accept what we perceive through this window at face value would be equivalent to, say, checking into Princeton Plainsboro Hospital in order to be treated by Dr. Gregory House, or—the opposite error—to think that Hurricane Katrina is merely the latest made-for-television disaster movie.

More and more, Roberts came to view Seth as both a genuinely independent entity and, paradoxically, part of herself—her greater self, that is. Seth himself became, for her, a kind of philosophical window, offering a new perspective not merely on other realities, but also on a highly original and insightful concept of multidimensional selfhood that she dubbed "Aspect Psychology"—a concept she developed at length, particularly in *Adventures in Consciousness* and *Psychic Politics*.

At the same time that quantum physicists like David Bohm began to talk about the universe as a kind of vast hologram in which each part, at least in some adumbrated form, contains the whole, Roberts, quite independently, set out an essentially holographic vision of the self.

In her vision, each aspect of the larger entity or "Source" self—that is, each human incarnation in linear time, non-embodied selves outside of time and space, and alternate selves in parallel worlds or "probable" reality systems— may be seen as a unique assemblage, in varying selected permutations and combinations, of a rich bank of characteristics shared by the whole. While she thus would not deny that Seth was an aspect of herself, she felt it no less true to say that she was an aspect of him.

She and Seth can thus be seen as distinct, coequal branches of an entire family tree of consciousness sharing a single root source. The branches are distinguishable extensions of the same tree, but ultimately not separable from it or from each other. Moreover, there are an infinite number of trees whose roots grow in the same soil, all in constant underground communication with one another. Thus all information transfer between different parts of the self, as well as between the various "Source" selves, is primarily telepathic and virtually instantaneous. Language comes on the scene as the mere tip of a vast data-interchange iceberg. If we weren't in constant telepathic touch with each other—and everything else—human language would not even be possible.

Robert Monroe, as we shall see, came to a remarkably similar conclusion in what he called "nonverbal communication" (NVC), which he claimed is the primary mode in nonphysical reality and is unconsciously employed by us even in physical-matter reality. Monroe would have called Jane's seminal "Idea Construction" revelation a super-concentrated "thought-ball" or ROTE (related, organized, thought-energy that is instantly and totally transferred), which can be gradually "unrolled" at length and over time.

The prime purpose of all of this subterranean psychic chatter, however, is not idle chitchat or gossip, but rather the cocreation of reality. We are not the passive victims of an accidental universe or helpless children begging for mercy before an angry, vengeful God. We are integral elements of All That Is, active co-participants in the grand scheme of creation, sharing, in equal measure, both the responsibility and the joy of cosmic creativity. We are responsible for shaping our own lives, from moment to moment, both on levels perceivable by our physical senses and those far beyond them.

No Ending, No Beginning

This creation is not, however, something that happened a long time ago, in a galaxy far, far away. Creation takes place in an eternal present, or what Seth/Jane termed a "spacious present." This is the same circle of time/eternity known well by the shamans. As Roberts understood—and as Seth continually emphasized—this amounts to saying that all aspects of the greater self exist at the same distance from the center. Therefore, no single personality or aspect thereof is "higher" or "lower," metaphysically speaking, than any other; no event is "more" or "less" real than any other or exists, in any ultimate sense, "before" or "after" any other. It's all happening Now. And everything that could possibly be, Is.

As Seth explained one day to the members of Roberts's ESP class, while our physical senses are made to parcel out discrete chunks of time in a linear sequence of past, present, and future, reality itself is not limited. Thus, there is, in the ultimate sense of things, no past, present, or future, but only an "eternal now":

> But everything in the universe exists at one time, simultaneously, and the first words ever spoken still ring throughout the universe; and in your terms, the last words ever spoken have been said time and time again, for there is no ending and no beginning. It is only your perception that is limited.[20]

The boundless nature of reality is precisely what Black Elk emphasized when he recalled his Great Vision. This was the ecstatic experience he had when he was only nine years old and was taken up to the Great Lodge in the sky—the spirit world—to be instructed by the Six Grandfathers, the Powers of the Six Directions of the universe.

At the climactic moment of his visionary quest, Black Elk saw himself taken to the center of the world hoop: the top of the sacred mountain in the Black Hills of South Dakota that the whites had named Harney Peak (after General William S. Harney, a notorious Indian-killer). "I was standing on the highest mountain of them all, and round about beneath me was the whole hoop of the world," Black Elk recalled. There he saw "in a sacred manner the shapes of all things in the spirit, and the shape of all shapes as they must live together like one being." There was, in his vision, but "one circle"—and yet, paradoxically, also "many hoops" of which the One is composed. In this mystical unity, however, he saw not a pure, undifferentiated oneness, but an infinitely rich multiplicity. For immediately after he gave his account to Neihardt, he added: "But anywhere is the center of the world."[21]

If anywhere is the center, so everywhere is the center, and thus nothing is absolutely circumscribed. All places, all beings—and all moments—are equally holy. No great endings, no great beginnings. Or rather, each and every moment is both, yet paradoxically neither.

As Seth's comments on simultaneous time indicate, this is the very same principle that Roberts was rediscovering for herself, through her own psychic explorations. It's what we may call a visionary eruption of the indigenous sensibility. This nonlinear, nonhierarchical attitude reverberates throughout her writings and her emerging, radically democratic ideas of multiple self-hood.

As we saw in chapter 5, with Sue Watkins's odd experience of her future altering her past, what we think of as our "future selves"—in either this life, or, in terms of a traditional notion of reincarnation, a "future" life—can just as easily influence our "past" selves, and vice versa. In Roberts's view, it is every bit as possible that, say, my Civil War self elected to be a soldier during that "earlier" period because the self that I am in this present life chose to be a pacifist.

This view flies in the face of certain conventional notions that unresolved "past-life" traumas are the cause of present problems—or, if one is inclined to be more optimistic, provide opportunities for personal growth. The former, of course, is the Freudian view of the role of unresolved childhood frustrations and conflicts in shaping adult neurotic misery, while the latter is what Jungian Roger Woolger, practitioner of past-life therapy and author of *Other Lives, Other Selves* (1988), dubs the popular Western myth of reincarnation.

According to Woolger, this myth—widely accepted in the New Age movement—is derived from French occultists of the 19th century and Mrs. H. P. Blavatsky (1831–1891), the famous Russian-born medium and cofounder of the Theosophical Society. The dominant metaphor of this myth, he observes, is that life is like a classroom, with an ascending sequence of grades, and we either get promoted or demoted to a good or bad future life, or graduate altogether and rest in one of the heavenly astral realms. "It strikes me as essentially linear," observes Woolger, "with an obvious appeal to the progressive and optimistic spirit of the American psyche."[22]

On the more pessimistic side, however, is the traditional Eastern picture, which—as we have already noted—plays down the notion of an evolving soul. This is particularly true of Buddhism, which doesn't even believe in the existence of an enduring individual self or soul. The aim, in such a view, is to get off the wheel of rebirth altogether, and thereby to escape the ceaseless, pointless round of incarnations and break the circle of cosmic pain and misery once and for all.

Woolger acknowledges that Roberts's view of reincarnation, which he calls the myth of the Multiple Self, is distinctive and original. Neither viciously cyclical, like the standard Eastern myth, nor straightforwardly linear and progressive, like the standard Western version, it is thoroughly holographic:

> This myth maintains that the total personality is an agglomerate of conscious and unconscious personality fragments or selves, held together by a kind of transcendent core Self and directed by the ego self. Each personality fragment has its own karmic history from other lives and these underlie and predispose persistent complexes in the current life. Like an unstable chemical formula this agglomeration of selves may undergo all kinds of transmutations, which irradiate throughout the total self and change its overall character.[23]

The one word that Roberts would have objected to in the above characterization is "karmic." In Woolger's terms, each fragment is a unique "agglomerate" of the whole, and, as such, may be liable to change or be considered "unstable."[24] But this is just another way of saying that it is *free*: free to influence, not only itself, but also the whole. Hence your current life—namely, whichever one you happen to choose or focus on—is just as much an effect of your future life (or lives) as it is a cause. The vectors of force run in all directions, all at once.

The circle, you see, knows no bounds.

Roberts plainly had no use for standard esoteric doctrines of reincarnation, which envision a sequence of lives and a moral-spiritual progression of the soul based on some cosmic accounting of deeds and misdeeds. She possessed an almost instinctive revulsion toward the Hindu-Buddhist idea of karma—an antiquated ideal of crime and punishment that struck her as a more abstract and impersonal version of the Catholicism in which she had been raised but had long ago rejected, with its bombastic, self-righteous, and unforgiving (yet supposedly "all-loving") personal God dishing out damnation and bliss to sinners and saints. She rejected the idea that we are "forced" to return to earth as punishment or to "burn off" bad karma, or that being emotionally attached to the things of this world is a kind of vice. Nor did she believe that our fate lies in the hands of a justifiably angry God. Rather, she insisted that we freely choose our life circumstances, with all their challenges and opportunities, as well as the responses we make to them.

Probably So

As her trance work with Seth and her own independent psychic experiences continued, Roberts was confronted with yet further complications of her notions of self—not to mention time and reality—and still further elaborations and elucidations of her/Seth's holographic vision that went beyond the concepts of reincarnation.

Even more spooky to ponder is that aspects of us existing in other times and places—including those alternate versions of the present time sequence, parallel worlds, and other realities that Seth dubbed "probabilities"—may, with justice, regard *us* as mere dream characters or surrogate versions of themselves. And who is to say that they would be wrong? Such encounters took place in what Roberts referred to as psychic "bleed-throughs."

These breakthroughs may be triggered quite accidentally by some physical or psychological trauma, or else occur naturally and spontaneously during dreams, out-of-body episodes, or even daydreams. In such cases, these other aspects of ourselves may perceive us as their alternates, while their life histories and identities could be experienced as ours. In one of the trance sessions discussing probable selves recorded in *The Seth Material*, Seth comments on this phenomenon:

These other probable events become just as "real" within other dimensions. As a sideline, there are some interesting episodes when a severe psychological shock or deep sense of futility causes a short circuit so that one portion of the self begins to experience one of its other probable realities. I am thinking in particular of some cases where the victim ends up suddenly in a different town with another name, occupation, and no memory of his own past. In some, the event, it is only one of all the other probable events, but he must experience it, you see, within his own time system.[25]

This may also hold true for multiple simultaneous incarnations—that is, alternate versions of the same Source self, living in different places on earth in the same overall—or even an overlapping—time period.

This is the concept Seth named "counterparts," which he announced in the sessions recorded in Volume 2 of The "Unknown Reality" (1979). "Many people realize intuitively that the self is multitudinous and not singular," says Seth. If we are open to such impressions, we are likely to think in reincarnational terms, "so that the self is seen as traveling through the centuries, moving through doors of death and life into other times and places." But Seth insists that this is a vast oversimplification:

Quite literally, you live more than one life at a time. You do not experience your century from one separate vantage point, and the individuals alive in any given century have far deeper connections [biologically and spiritually] than you realize.[26]

Counterparts may belong to different races, genders, and nations, as well as quite different economic and social classes—rich, if you're poor; female, if you're male, etc.

In other words, if I dream (or fantasize) of Jeannie with the long blond hair, it's perfectly possible, not only that she really exists (somewhere, somewhen), but that I *am* Jeannie in some ontologically real sense, and not in the trivial or "merely psychological" sense in which we usually think of such fancies. Now this is not the same thing as saying that Jeannie is my "soul mate," my soul's "other half," or my one true destined love. For there may be numerous counterparts alive at any given time—many kindred personality chips off the same old block of the Source self, so to speak.

The counterpart concept was brand-new to Jane Roberts and her husband. It isn't too difficult to tell from their reactions to Seth's statements that it further stretched their credulity, if not outright scandalized them—though it also helped to explain a recent dream of Rob's in which he had vividly experienced himself as a black woman.

Yet, the counterpart idea was not new to the Native Americans who had long ago accepted it, because—as with psychic perceptions of telepathy, precognition, and clairvoyance (and reincarnation, for that matter)—they had known of its reality and refused to fudge the data of their own experience.

"In formulating their understanding of the world," writes Lakota Sioux philosopher Vine Deloria Jr., "Indians did not discard any experience. Everything had to be included in the spectrum of knowledge and related to what was already known." This comprehensive inventory included "individual and communal experiences in daily life," the "keen observation of the environment," and "interpretive messages that they received from spirits in ceremonies, visions and dreams."[27] In other words, the Indians relied upon psychic data typically discounted by both skeptical scientific materialists and religious dogmatists.

Thus Ohiyesa matter-of-factly states that the Indians accepted the reality of psychic powers. He cites many examples, including a Sioux prophet who foresaw the coming of the whites fifty years before the event and his own grandmother, whose intuitive sense correctly discounted a reliable report of the death of Ohiyesa's uncle: "While our clan were wailing and mourning," he recalls, "my grandmother calmly bade them cease, saying that her son was approaching, and that they would see him shortly."[28] And they did—two days later, when he rode into camp.

"Many of us believe that one may be born more than once," relates Ohiyesa, "and there are some who claim to have full knowledge of a former incarnation." Furthermore, he adds, "There are also those who believe in a 'twin spirit' born into another tribe or race"—essentially Seth's counterpart idea. He then tells a story of a Sioux war-prophet who became convinced that he had a spirit brother among the Ojibwe—the ancestral enemies of the Sioux. He named the particular band to which his twin belonged and gave precise details of his life.

By and by, the two bands, Sioux and Ojibwe, met and established peaceable relations. As the Sioux war-prophet had predicted, the Ojibwe band was led by a war-prophet who turned out, not only to closely resemble his Sioux brother in bearing and physical features, but also to sing "the very [same sacred] song that he himself was wont to sing."[29] Twins—physically and spiritually—indeed!

An Indian Sensibility

It was, then, her "Indian sensibility"—that is to say, a scrupulous, near reverential fidelity to actual life in all its rich diversity, complexity, and mysteriousness—that characterized Jane Roberts's inner explorations and marked her out as one who would not conform to any set ideology, theory, religion, or worldview. The revolutionary ideas she heard from Seth and formulated on her own were a far cry from both the traditional Catholicism of her youth and the bohemian world-disdaining (almost Buddhistic) sensibility of the beat-generation artists with which she later flirted.

These ideas did not arise from theoretical speculations on problems in physics or out of a need to fill out some metaphysical system that she had merely read about, secondhand, in books. They grew directly out of her need to make sense of her own immediate experience, which, she emphasized over and over, had to become the benchmark for us all. She asked all of us to end our world—to end our reliance on anything other than nature viewed without prejudice or guile, or anything perceived through the distorting filters of science or religion.

> We must look at our own experience again—and learn to trust it. We must be our own psychic naturalists, combining reason and intuition. We must refuse to let old theories define our realities for us, limiting and distorting the very scope of our lives.[30]

Psychic naturalism, this magnificently elegant ideal, is both a showstopper and a world-ender. It blasts the human imagination wide open, freeing it from the decaying rusty shackles of all the prevailing shopworn myths of the past, including and especially the Myth of the Great Ending in its more literal, stupefying versions.

Allow me to explain.

David Bohm points out that, after Galileo effectively won the war with the Catholic Church over who could better explain such celestial phenomena as the motion of planetary bodies (one can lose battles, as Galileo apparently did at the Inquisition, but still emerge victorious in the overall campaign), science slowly but surely took over the old role of religion in trying to provide an explanation for everything. Religion, of course, said that God made everything, or that God willed everything. But when these explanations ceased to be satisfying, people looked to science for answers. As many still do.

Science then decided it could do what religion tried, but failed, to do: provide a totally comprehensive account of existence, down to the last subatomic particle. Many scientists today still yearn for a grand, final Theory of Everything that will surpass even the Unified Field Theory, which says that electromagnetism, gravity, and both weak and strong nuclear forces are merely alternative expressions of the same energy system.

In essence, then, science took over a prime function of religion, and thereby began to resemble it. That is why many religious people quite rightly fear science as a competitor trying to encroach on religion's territory. These suspicions are justified.

There is also, as we have seen, another way in which science became a kind of ersatz religion, or at least an alternative to religion—that is, in the efforts of many mainstream scientists to cling religiously (that is, dogmatically and tenaciously) to the philosophy of mechanistic materialism, which says that only physical matter is real, and that reality as a whole is constructed as a kind of super-machine, operating according to certain deterministic causal laws.

This kind of militant dogmatism that passes for rationality is what some call "scientism," to distinguish it from true science, which is a method of inquiry and an attitude, not a fixed ideology. Scientism leads to such peculiar episodes as a group of prominent Nobel Prize–winning scientists signing a public manifesto against astrology as a form of irrational nonsense, even though some of the very same signatories later privately admitted that they'd never read anything even remotely connected to astrology or bothered to examine any evidence for it.[31]

True philosophers, like all good scientists, are supposed to be open-minded and willing to examine evidence and arguments, including counter-evidence and counterarguments. Doubt is good. But then there are others, like arch-skeptic and professional paranormal debunker Paul Kurtz, who unequivocally declares in his *Humanist Manifesto II,* that "Modern science discredits such historic concepts as the 'ghost in the machine' and the 'separable soul.'"[32] No doubts there! This is just another, newer version of the same old sanctimonious religious certitude.

The scientific hope for the End of Knowledge as expressed in the drive for a Final Theory of Everything is really just a secularized, gussied-up version of old religious nostrums: Everything we need to know is contained in the Bible, which is the complete and final Revelation of God to Man. This is the Myth of the Great Ending all over again, dressed up in a slightly different costume.

Roberts's worthy ideal of "psychic naturalism" offers a vaccine against both virulent scientism and the messianic apocalypticism that afflicts End of Knowledge cultists. Against the latter, she implored us to remain open to the possibility that, at any moment, we could well have a surprising experience that may upend even the most widely and strongly held, most well-confirmed and well-established theory—which, after all, is only a model that is more or less useful for working with some portion of our actual experience. This, by the way, also happens to be the view of none other than Bohm, who arrived at it from his grasp, not of psychic phenomena, but of the history of physics.

Against the former, the very robust persistence of the reality of the psyche itself—of phenomena like telepathy, clairvoyance, trance personalities, precognitive dreams, and out-of-body experiences—offers eloquent testimony to the foolishness, if not sheer idiocy, of trying to reduce the meaning of "experience" to "physical experience *only,*" or "the senses" to "the five physical senses *only.*" We have nonphysical senses and nonphysical experiences, and that's that. Experience is far too rich and complex a field to simplify and impoverish it beyond recognition. Roberts was adamant about not denying the existence of the elephant in the living room.

In both of these recommendations, she echoes none other than William James, who got into trouble with his scientific and philosophical colleagues (not to mention mine) for saying remarkably similar things. It therefore strikes me as no accident that, at one point in her explorations of the interior universe, she found herself tuning into material she identified as the "worldview" of the deceased James.

In *The Afterdeath Journal of an American Philosopher: The World View of William James* (1978), Roberts did not claim to be in contact with James's disembodied spirit in the literal sense, but rather in a metaphorical sense—the "spirit" of his postmortem mind as it ruminated on those very "mystical" and philosophical matters that had occupied his attention while he was alive on earth:

> I am the William James that was, but I am no longer William James in the same way that the adult is not the child. Furthermore, I have learned much more about consciousness in general, and my own in particular. Perhaps more important, I recognize the limitations of definitions regarding identity and selfhood, for they are bound to be based upon impossibly confusing misconceptions and misunderstandings that appear as a result of earth experience itself.[33]

James's ruminations—his "World View" of the book title—were "recorded" and made available for inspection in a place Roberts called simply "The Library." This was her image for a particular altered state of consciousness, or nonphysical energy system, that many others down through the ages had also reported visiting—sometimes using similar, or even quite different, names like the Akashic records. (I know The Library exists because I've "visited" it myself on a number of occasions.)

Some critics—even some who are otherwise sympathetic, including Colin Wilson—have dismissed *The Afterdeath Journal* as exhibiting a quality of writing unworthy of the historical William James.[34] However, I believe it is a valuable document in its own right, one that offers valuable insights into Roberts's processes of thinking and their intellectual kinship with a prior American revolutionary who experienced his own "breakthrough" of the indigenous sensibility. Translations of nonphysical perceptions are tricky in any case, even for the most practiced psychic. But the fact that her sympathies led her to pick up on the spirit of James is telling, indeed.

Though Jane Roberts was no professional academic philosopher—and thank heaven for that—temperamentally, intellectually, and, dare I say, spiritually, she and James were two peas in a pod—two genuine American originals, giants of a kind and pioneers of a truly scientific form of consciousness exploration. What they shared above all was the ideal of science as an attitude and a method of inquiry: the patient investigation of human experience, uniting reason with intuition, leavened with equal measures of healthy curiosity and skepticism.

Impressions Not Commonly Felt

This brings us to the second half of psychic naturalism—the "naturalism" part. To say that psychic abilities are "natural" is not just an affront to those whose definition of nature does not include the nonphysical or those who see such categories only as evidence of pathology. It also disturbs those for whom such things are viewed as either supernatural gifts of God's divine grace or supernatural curses of the Devil's minions (or both) or as the fruits (either highly valued or eminently disposable) of much striving for spiritual perfection.

The former possibilities are those endorsed by the Western, biblical forms of religion. The latter represent the two ends of the spectrum of views embraced by Eastern yogis, for whom such things are mere distractions or powers worth pursuing that, in any case, result only from great effort expended under the tutelage of a guru with absolute authority. They are markers of spiritual progress, or perhaps temptations to the unwary, but not a natural endowment universally shared by all human beings as part of our standard-issue equipment when we enter what Robert Monroe called the Earth-Life System (ELS).

Of course, both these religious views support the outlook and value—not to mention the authority—of the religious systems in question. Powers and abilities that seem godlike to some can be viewed as divine gifts for the saints to employ or diabolical ploys to ensnare unwary sinners.

In either case, the centrality of God and the crux of the sin/atonement program is reinforced. The same is true with respect to the Eastern emphasis on spirituality as an attainment based on an extended apprenticeship and measurable, hierarchically arranged levels of achievement—much like merit badges for Boy Scouts. Who is ahead? Who is behind? Where are you on the path? These are the burning questions of guru-ism.

Once again, the primacy and authority of the system of judgment, and thereby the importance of remaining within its defined boundaries, are re-inforced. God or guru: they are functionally identical. Both point the way to the Great Ending, conceived as a final mass judgment and destruction of the wicked or as individual salvation and escape from the wicked.

But what if it turns out that you don't need either God or guru? That upsets the apple cart—both carts, you see. If the problem is not how to obtain (or to refuse) psychic or mystical or other non-ordinary experiences, but simply to get out of their way and let them happen—or, alternately, to simply remove the blocks that prevent us from realizing that they are already happening, unnoticed, right under our very noses—then the whole *raison d'être* of the re-ligious system collapses, and with it goes the bleak myth of the End. If nature basically gives us the tools, we don't need to buy them from others or wait to cash in our green stamps of spiritual redemption at the nirvana center. It's all right here, now. Just take a fresh look.

Sloughing off the dead cultural carapace of what we proudly call "civiliza-tion" reveals a soft and pliable living body of knowledge and self-knowledge that defies all the artifice—the blaring stereotypes and idiotic propaganda—that passes for true, i.e., natural, wisdom. This is, as Jane Roberts well un-derstood, a "gut knowing, a biological spirituality," and it is our rightful inheritance as human beings.

Once upon a time, this wisdom was part and parcel of an everyday exis-tence lived within the largesse of nature's rhythmical patterns. "I believe," declared Ohiyesa, "that such nearness to nature as I have described keeps the spirit sensitive to impressions not commonly felt [today], and in touch with the unseen powers."[35]

Amen to that.

We don't need to be hit by lightning to find that wisdom, although we may need to make ourselves available to the trauma of psychological thunderbolts.

But are these storms, either inner or outer, really just sheer accidents?

Perhaps, from a more expansive perspective, it may not have been mere happenstance that Tony Cicoria endured electrocution and temporary death. Any more than it was a freak accident that Jane Roberts found herself hurled through the tissue-paper-thin membrane that passes for the rigid boundary line of hard fact in physical-matter reality and plunged straight down the rabbit hole of a psychic Wonderland. For what some invite from the inside, through hard questions both consciously and unconsciously asked, others whose temperaments are of a decidedly more extroverted and self-consciously practical bent may have to perceive as external in order for them to accept the resulting explosion that effectively signals the coming end of their world.

Then again, there may be some extraordinary types who find themselves on the receiving end of both kinds of stimuli: inner and outer.

We'll meet such a one in the next chapter.

CHAPTER NINE

DOING THE BEST YOU CAN

It takes courage to do what you want. Other people have a
lot of plans for you. Nobody wants you to do what you want
to do. . . . Follow your bliss.

JOSEPH CAMPBELL, *A Joseph Campbell Companion:*
Reflections on the Art of Living (1991)

You do the best you can.

ROBERT MONROE, *Far Journeys* (1985)

Usually, lightning strikes but once. That's why Joseph Campbell liked to
cite the old proverb: "Dread the passage of Jesus, for He does not return."[1] At other times, however, we may be granted multiple opportunities
to heed the call to end our world, only—nothing happens. This raises some
important questions.

Puzzled and Preoccupied

For one thing, does the proverbial lightning strike—actual or metaphorical—that leads to insight and the establishment of a different overview,
thus effectively ending our old world, radically "rewire" our brains/nervous
systems, thereby somehow altering our consciousness? Or does the strike
merely wipe the hard disk clean of culturally installed software, so that the

hardware—if it so chooses—can revert to its "factory settings" and operate as nature intended?

Certainly it was not the lightning strike *per se* that transformed Tony Cicoria. Many people are struck by lightning every year, but not everyone who is struck by lightning has a near-death experience. The strike was therefore not, in scientific terms, the cause of the NDE. Furthermore, some evidence suggests that even some individuals who have NDEs may repress all conscious memory of the event for many years, perhaps even a lifetime. Others who do consciously recall their NDEs may nevertheless find the event and its implications so disturbing or challenging that they strive to ignore or minimize its effects. This is true for other unusual experiences as well.

Jane Roberts, for example, could well have chosen to dismiss her initial "Idea Construction" revelatory ecstasy as a bout of temporary depressive psychosis, or perhaps a wild creative fantasy triggered by family problems, psychological stress, and the unmet need for artistic inspiration. Then she could have resumed writing bleak poetry and retained her conventional ambitions for fame, fortune, and recognition by the lions of the literary establishment.

The strategies of evasion and denial are, alas, legion.

This is why my late friend, parapsychologist Rhea White, distinguished between what she called "Exceptional Experiences," or EEs, and "Exceptional *Human* Experiences," or EHEs.[2] The difference between EEs and EHEs is the difference between the event itself and the meaning we ascribe to it. The meaning gives the experience its specifically human dimension. We must choose to humanize our experience by making the effort to dialogue with it, reflect on it, and allow it to go to work on us by working on it—in short, by cultivating and nourishing the initial seed episode. Otherwise, it remains a mere unrealized potential, incapable of creating change.

In other words, ending our world is never an automatic, mechanical process; it is not something that just happens to us, even on the individual level, where it is understood symbolically rather than literally. It is rather something that we must choose to bring about. Cicoria could have decided to ignore that vague but insistent "pressure to do certain things" that he felt in the aftermath of his NDE. Dismissing the persistent urge to learn to play the piano, he could have elected to play eighteen holes of golf instead, and then headed over to the clubhouse for a beer or two with his buddies. Nothing was foreordained.

The many forms that evasion, repression, and denial take are an expression of what Campbell termed the mythological motif of "the refusal of the call." We can always just turn a blind eye or a deaf ear and pretend that nothing has really happened. But we pay a steep price for such rejection.

One of my favorite examples of this kind of refusal is told by Swami Radha in her book, *Realities of the Dreaming Mind*. Born Ursula Sylvia in Germany in 1911, Swami Radha was a disciple of the Hindu guru Swami Sivananda, and was one of the first women to bring yoga to the West in 1956. After her initiation, she returned to Canada, where she had emigrated after World War II, and set up her ashram.

Once, during a visit to one of the big cities, she met a psychiatrist who told her of an extraordinary dream he'd had. It seems that he dreamt of her ashram in the clearest, most precise detail. He described the buildings, including the guest lodge and the office, the grounds, and even the appearance of a young man with particularly large blue eyes. Swami Radha confirmed the accuracy of every detail and then invited the psychiatrist to the ashram so he could see for himself.

When the psychiatrist arrived at the ashram for his planned ten-day visit, he was astounded as he roamed the grounds. He recognized all of the landmarks from his dream experience—even the young man with the blue eyes.

Frightened out of his wits, the psychiatrist left after only a few hours.

"He had to accept his dream experience," observes Radha, "because he had verified it through his visit, but he did not want to accept it." Why not? "Fear! 'I have to change my perception of the world.' Fear! 'I have to change my perception of my life.' Fear! 'I have to change my idea of what my senses can do.' Fear! 'I have to take more responsibility for what I perceive.'"[3] Such fears can be paralyzing.

Another favorite example comes from the memoir by the late Rosalind A. McKnight, *Cosmic Journeys: My Out-of-Body Explorations with Robert A. Monroe*. McKnight was one of Monroe's first Explorers, the test subjects in his laboratory during the early days of his experimentation with the use of sound to induce altered states of consciousness, back in the early 1970s. McKnight quickly discovered that she had an ability to "lift out" of her body with ease, helped by four nonphysical "beings."

One day, McKnight could not make her regular appointment for a laboratory session. It so happened that a female psychologist from the Washington, D.C. area was visiting Monroe that day to ask questions about his new techniques. She was very skeptical, however, so Monroe invited her to lie down in one of the isolation booths and listen to the sounds through headphones. Not long after the session began, the psychologist pressed the intercom button to speak with Monroe, who was in the control room monitoring the proceedings.

"There is someone else in the booth with me," said the psychologist.

"Are you sure?" Monroe replied.

"Of course, I am sure. As a matter of fact, there are four of them," she answered.

"Are you sure there are four?" Monroe persisted.

The psychologist was insistent: "I can perceive them very clearly," she said. "There are two at my feet and two at my head."

Monroe then asked her what they were doing. "They are trying to lift me out of my body, if you can believe that," she replied.

Now a fifth being showed up and began arguing with the other four, telling them not to remove her from her body. Then they all disappeared. Monroe told the woman to relax and gave her time in the booth to drift into a refreshing nap. Then he realized with a start that she was occupying the same booth typically used by McKnight and at the very same time that McKnight had her weekly appointment. Evidently McKnight's "helpers" had been expecting her—and made a slight mistake.

When the psychologist emerged from the booth, she was bewildered, but remained deeply skeptical. Monroe explained about McKnight's activities and her canceled appointment. Then he played for her a recording of one of those previous sessions in which McKnight described the beings "lifting her out." The psychologist was stunned into silence and left "very puzzled and preoccupied."

Monroe never heard from her again.[4]

The Stranger

As the plastic mask of civilization rattles, loosens, and falls away, individuals gazing into the mirror may be frightened out of their wits by the stranger staring back. Before they know it, they've glued the culture mask back on more tightly than ever, covering nature once again with artifice, just like the suburban householders who cut down trees to make room for swimming pools, trampolines, swing sets, and sod so perfect in color and texture it resembles the manicured greens at a country club golf course.

The question is, then, what marks the subtle, but critical, difference between those who desperately cling to the mask, adamantly refusing the call to end their world, and those who accept the call and choose to remove it.

Monroe's case is particularly interesting, because he would seem to be among those least likely to choose to end their world. He was not, at the time, some poor, starving wannabe, existing at the margins, off somewhere in the hinterlands, angling for fame and fortune. Rather, he was a wealthy and successful businessman with offices in midtown Manhattan and an enviable manse in tony Croton-on-Hudson, a posh suburb located in one of New York's premier venues, Westchester County.

He was, in fact, an archetype of our patriarchal culture: highly competitive, ambitious, practical, nuts-and-bolts, and no-nonsense. He did not suffer fools gladly. As Monroe's biographers have noted, he was a true "man's man," delighting in such macho pursuits as driving fast cars (that he built himself) and piloting airplanes and light gliders, not to mention enjoying the company of a succession of beautiful women, most of whom he either proposed to or actually married.

Monroe, in short, "had it all" by every conventional measure. Yet despite his considerable investment in the cultural status quo of the mid-20th century (including an abiding faith in the scientific worldview), he became a mystic, psychic, and philosopher whose passage through our culture may yet prove to be one of the most creative disturbances witnessed by the 20th century—or any other. As Monroe himself might have opined, only time will tell.

The Tapestry Unravels

It is neither my intention nor my desire to give a comprehensive account of Robert Monroe's life in what follows. That, in any case, would be thoroughly redundant. For that task has already been ably performed by author Ronald Russell in his recent biography, *The Journey of Robert Monroe: From Out-of-*

Body Explorer to Consciousness Pioneer. Russell's book offers a candid, well-rounded picture of the man—warts and all—in addition to many excellent insights into his work.

Also of value is the late journalist Bayard Stockton's earlier biography of Monroe, *Catapult*, which was published in the late 1980s, while Monroe was still alive. In the memorable phrase of Henry James, Stockton's book is a "loose, baggy monster": a congenial, ambling, rambling conversation, peppered with anecdotes of Stockton's own experiences at the Monroe Institute's workshops, as well as commentary by Monroe's friends and associates. Despite all its flaws, however, *Catapult* is still highly useful—and a whole lot of fun to read.

The sketch I offer here is highly selective: compressed and impressionistic. My limited aim is simply to give you some idea of how supremely and securely ensconced Monroe was in his personal world—a world that remains a major thread in the tapestry of our mass consensus reality—when he realized that he had to end it.

At the time his world began to end, Monroe was a highly successful, hard-driving, middle-aged man. I doubt whether he ever would have thought of his experience as a "midlife crisis," not only because he was not then especially given to such inward psychological self-analysis, but also because he did not seem to be consciously aware of any looming problems. Sure, he had ulcers, but that was often the price paid for success among hard-driving, "Type-A" personalities, right? As for the periodic pangs of restlessness—well, they were to be expected, after all. How can you achieve new heights if you don't keep setting your sights higher and higher, and looking in new directions? Wondering what might lie over the next hill or around the next curve was simply the spur to conquer new worlds.

Ah, but what sort of worlds might these be?

War of the Worlds

Monroe, who always preferred the East Coast, never "went Hollywood." In 1958, he was at the very top of his game as a master of the entertainment universe, New York division. A man of many talents, he had been an innovative sound engineer (among the first, as Russell points out, to use magnetic recording tape[5]), as well as a writer, director, producer, music composer, and the prime creative force behind hundreds of radio programs. He was, for example, the producer of *The Shadow*, and the creator of such radio quiz-show staples as *Name That Tune*. [6]

Monroe subsequently repeated his success in television, though radio remained his favorite medium. He became the head of his own production company, while also serving as an executive for Mutual Broadcasting. Branching out to ownership, he eventually purchased two radio stations, both in southern states. He had a glamorous wife, two young daughters, and, of course, he enjoyed all of the material accoutrements of his media success, including being mentioned in newspaper gossip columns like Walter Winchell's.

What, in retrospect, may well have been a decisive turning point occurred in 1956. Stressed out from his overachieving lifestyle, Monroe resigned his position at Mutual Broadcasting. Because of a happenstance contact, he journeyed down to Ecuador to meet up with a prospective business partner named Ernesto "Chicho" Estrada, who turned out to be an exceedingly wealthy and powerful friend, as well as a would-be patron. Tremendous opportunities beckoned: oil concessions, crystal mines, banana liqueur manufacturing plants, you name it. Had he moved his family to South America, Monroe could have been more than simply rich; he could have lived like a veritable king. The opportunities presented had the alluring promise of fantastic wealth and power, minus the unbearable pressure cooker of the New York media circus he could no longer abide.

Monroe was sorely tempted. Yet he said no. He loved Ecuador and got along famously with Chicho. Nevertheless, he balked. He gave himself good, practical reasons—for instance, it would not be good for his daughters to grow up so far from home. But there were other, less tangible concerns. Indeed, as he admitted later, "he felt that something seemed to be pulling him back to the States."[7] What was this mysterious "something"? Was it the first stirrings of his deeper self, come to call?

When he returned to New York in late 1956, Monroe was no longer involved with the full-time production of radio programs. He had time on his hands to explore other avenues. What he chose to investigate, as Russell notes, were two up-and-coming ideas: sleep-learning and "a new process called Biorhythm, based on the idea that one's life is affected by rhythmic biological cycles, physical, emotional, and intellectual."[8] Although nothing much came of the latter project, much, as we shall see, was to come of the former.

The sleep-learning project was close to Monroe's interest in the creative use of sound. He chose—as he always did—to experiment on himself first. He produced audiotapes with exercises designed to improve recall of basic facts like multiplication tables and stock phrases in foreign languages like Spanish and French. He added the simulated sounds of ocean surf, which were designed to induce a state of relaxation and encourage sleep. And, as Monroe noted in *Journeys Out of the Body*, perhaps most important, he recorded a suggestion to remember and recall whatever was experienced during the exercise.

While his family was at church one Sunday morning, Monroe, all alone in his quiet country house, lay down in what he described as "a highly isolated environment" and listened to his self-made audiotape. When his family returned from church, they all had brunch. An hour or so later, he was, in his own words, "seized with a severe, iron-hard cramp which extended across my diaphragm or solar plexus area just under my rib cage. It was a solid band of unyielding ache."[9]

At first, he thought it might be food poisoning. But no one else fell ill, and they'd all eaten the same scrambled eggs and bacon. Nothing in the home medicine cabinet alleviated the intense cramp and pain, which lasted a full twelve hours, until he fell asleep from sheer exhaustion. He probably should have gone to a hospital, but he didn't. They did call around to several doctors they knew, but the physicians were either out of town or on the golf course. In any case, by morning, it was completely gone. There seemed to be no lingering aftereffects, except for some minor residual soreness of his muscles.

Monroe inevitably began to wonder whether something on his sleep-learning tape had triggered the strange physical pain, because it had occurred so soon after his initial trial run. He couldn't imagine what this "something" might be, but he wasn't about to take any unnecessary chances either. So he put all his self-experiments on hold until he could determine if there was, in fact, a connection.

In the meantime, he decided to take it easy. A few weeks later, on another Sunday morning while the family was off to church, he lay down on the living room couch to take a nap. Almost immediately, he was struck by "a beam or ray" of light that seemed to come out of the sky and strike him, causing his body to shake violently or "vibrate." He was, he said, "utterly powerless to move. It was as if I were being held in a vise."[10] Shocked and frightened, he fought the paralysis until he managed to move his limbs. The vibrations faded, and he felt fine.

The same pattern of violent vibrations and paralysis repeated itself over the next couple of months. It happened nine times, always when Monroe was lying down to go to sleep or take a brief nap. He was afraid he might be ill, but a thorough physical exam revealed no underlying problems. The doctor told him to lose weight and stop smoking—good basic advice, but in this case, an admission of ignorance.

On one occasion when the vibrations arrived, Monroe had the distinct sense that his body was being wrapped in a kind of flaming coil or oscillating electrical ring of sparks about two feet in diameter, which he said he could "see"—or perhaps more accurately, "perceive"—moving up and down the entire length of his body if he closed his eyes.

Thinking he might be hallucinating, Monroe nervously consulted his friend, a well-known psychologist, for advice. The psychologist simply laughed at the idea that he was mentally ill. He told him that he should study the phenomena—that it had some meaning, and that he had to figure out what it was for himself.

That meaning soon became apparent.

I Think I See the Light

If it were not for what soon followed and what developed from it, the two incidents with the "beam or ray" of light and the "ring of sparks" might have been written off as mere aberrations. Viewed historically, however, they fit a familiar pattern well known to the great mystics and medicine people of all times and places. Flames, sparks, fire, and light: these are but variations on a common theme, members of a single family of non-ordinary experiences known the world over.

Moses, of course, spoke to the Burning Bush and the bush talked back, while the ancient Greek philosopher Heraclitus experienced fire as the basic world principle: "There is an exchange of all things for fire and of fire for all things."[11] René Descartes had a waking vision or dream of sparks that led to his reformulation of philosophy in accordance with the principles of science.[12] Descartes' great intellectual enemy and critic, Blaise Pascal (1623–1662), had his own great mystical awakening, the essence of which he recorded in a single word— Fire.[13]

Many of those who have near-death experiences encounter, or in some cases merge with, a magnificent Being of Light or experience some form of meeting with unusual lights. A woman, for example, who suffered a miscarriage was being rushed to the hospital by her husband when they became involved in an automobile accident. She wound up losing the equivalent of four quarts of blood. As the operation began to remove her dead fetus, she drifted out of her body and floated up to the ceiling, then into the gray cloudy sky. "In the far distance on my right," she recalls, "was a soft-white globe of light that I felt drawn toward. When I got nearer the light it was all encompassing, but it wasn't white. It was molecular light made of fantastic colors. It was moving in ever-changing geometric patterns." She adds: "I realized that this light [which had a consciousness, both masculine and feminine] is what everything is made of."[14]

Dr. Richard Maurice Bucke was a 19th-century Canadian psychiatrist and contemporary of William James. In his classic study of mysticism, *Cosmic Consciousness* (1901), he described his own mystical encounter as suddenly being "wrapped around as it were by a flame-colored cloud" as he rode home in a hansom cab one evening after a meeting with some friends.[15] Indeed, Bucke's volume is a compendium of similar cases in which individuals both famous—like Moses and St. Paul—and not-so-famous (or anonymous) "see the light" and are transformed.

In *Shamans, Healers, and Medicine Men*, German anthropologist Holger Kalweit notes that, "the most dramatic form of shamanic initiation is initiation by the lightning bolt."[16] In tribal cultures all over the world, from the Asian Buryats, to the ancient Greeks, to the indigenous peoples of the Andes, the most powerful and venerated shamans are the lightning shamans— those "lucky few" who have survived being literally thunderstruck, blown away by a bolt from heaven. As a result, they acquire heaven's blessing-curse: mediumistic powers to talk with the dead, as well as the ability to diagnose and treat illnesses and foretell the future. These primitive, "archaic" peoples would not have been at all shocked or dismayed by the case of Tony Cicoria. They would have understood perfectly.

Then there is the intriguing case of the late science-fiction writer Philip K. Dick. In February of 1974, Dick experienced a prolonged series of highly unusual visionary episodes, all of which seemed to be initiated by his being struck in the face by a "pink light beam."[17] He felt that the pink light was a living intelligence providing him with information, some of which actually checked out.

For example, he was told that his young son, Christopher, suffered from a potentially fatal inguinal hernia—a diagnosis that was subsequently confirmed by medical authorities. Corrective surgery was performed in the nick of time, saving the boy's life. Dick spent the rest of his life puzzling over, writing about, and being inspired in his fiction by these bizarre episodes.

Dick's case in particular raises some pertinent questions: Did he and Monroe perceive being struck by "beams" of light because that is the way 20th-century, technologically besotted folks like us interpret what a 19th-century fellow like Bucke would describe as a "flame-colored cloud"? Are they, in essence, experiencing the same thing, only using different words to describe it? Or are they different—if perhaps, ultimately related—phenomena?

Some may complain here that I'm mixing up apples and oranges. What, after all, do these plainly inward, visionary experiences have in common with an actual, physical lightning strike? The circle of sparks that was visible to Monroe, for example, he admittedly "saw" only with his eyes *closed*. As far as the ray or beam of light goes, he acknowledged that it couldn't be "real" sunlight: "Only this was daylight and no beam was visible, if there truly was one. . . . I thought it *was* sunlight at first, although this was impossible on the north side of the house."[18] Moreover, aren't purely physical events like lightning strikes nothing more than meaningless, random accidents, unlike inward, psychological events that have some sort of meaningful relationship to the individual's personality and its history?

To all these questions I simply reply: take a long, hard look at the evidence; then make up your mind. Study the actual phenomena even as you ignore the shrill protests of your "common sense," which is—as my own philosophy professor used to quip—just the graveyard of dead philosophical theories. To paraphrase William James: Eat the food, not the menu.[19]

In Cicoria's case, an exterior physical cause had dramatic interior effects—spiritual, psychic, creative, and psychological. In Monroe's case, an interior psychic cause had pronounced physical effects: the severe cramp, pain, and soreness. What we're looking at, then, are just two sides of the same coin. As David Bohm says, reality is an unbroken whole.

With Flaming Spears

Actually, the closer one looks, the more difficult it becomes to say where the inner world leaves off and the outer one begins. The usual division we tend to make between "the physical" and "the mystical" (or "the psychological") gets harder and harder to maintain. Our friend, The Light, is a true metaphysical border-crosser.

In his second book, *Far Journeys,* Monroe recounts an out-of-body episode in which he was guided to relive and recall a forgotten incident from his childhood. He was a mere toddler at the time, having fun riding his tricycle and playing outside the front of his house, when suddenly a thunderstorm came up.

Lightning struck a nearby power pole and—carried undoubtedly through the wet grass and the metal bike—the current, or perhaps the concussion of the strike, zapped him, knocking him off his tricycle and facedown into the mud.

As his body lay stunned and unmoving, Monroe momentarily experienced himself as what he was before his human incarnation: a "curl" of intelligent light-consciousness, separate from his physical body. The realization only lasted briefly before his father rushed out and carried the shaken youngster into the house.

"I hope that doesn't mean that everyone has to get almost struck by lightning to begin to wake up," Monroe told his nonphysical guide. "It wouldn't be a very popular method."[20]

Not popular, to be sure, but perhaps not as unusual as we'd like to think.

Recall that, when nine-year-old Black Elk was taken to visit the Great Lodge in the sky in his ecstatic vision, the first "Grandfather" to address him was the Power of the West—Wiyopeyata—and that he was given the power to "make live" (the cup containing life-giving rains), and "the power to destroy" (the bow, symbolizing the lightning and thunder of the storms of the great plains). Black Elk, in other words, was a lightning shaman.

It was from the West that Black Elk derived his visionary and curative powers. It was the constant rumblings of the West Power that he heard and most feared, even in earlier childhood years. When he was but five years old, a thunderstorm presaged a waking encounter with a talking kingbird that presented him with a kind of Zen koan—"The clouds all over are one-sided," it announced. This was followed by a vision of two men zooming down from the clouds like lightning bolts, as he heard a sacred song and—in the booming storm—drumming: "Behold, a sacred voice is calling you," went the song, "All over the sky a sacred voice is calling."[21]

When it was time for Black Elk to have his Great Vision, these same two spirit men "with flaming spears"[22] reappeared to escort him to the great Sky Lodge. And afterward, when he remained too timid to share his vision (as he was meant to), it was the West Power that hounded him relentlessly: "When the frosts began I was glad, because there would not be any more thunder storms for a long while, and I was more and more afraid of them all the time, for always there would be the voices crying: 'Oo oohey! It is time! It is time!'"[23]

Isn't it about time for us to give up our simplistic ideas and rigid categories?

It Is Time

David Bohm would say that consciousness goes all the way "down" to the level of the subatomic particles, and correlatively that some sort of form—no matter how difficult or impossible to translate in terms of human language—goes all the way "up" to the highest levels of consciousness or spirit. If everything is part of one whole, this must be so. There is no absolutely "dumb, passive, and blind" matter, but neither is there any completely formless Void or Absolute Consciousness. Both extremes are ruled out.

The problem, you see, is that philosophy, religion, and mainstream science—which borrows liberally from both—have taught us to think, and even to perceive, in dualistic, dichotomous, either/or terms. From Aristotle, we inherited the logical law of the excluded middle, which states that a given proposition is either true, or not true—but not both. From religion, we have inherited a raft of either/or divisions: spirit versus nature, God versus the world, sin versus atonement, good versus evil, belief versus unbelief, and so forth. Science gives us mind versus matter. So we are led to ask: Is it internal or is it external? Is it by accident or by design? Is it an individual or a mass event? Is it essentially private and personal, or public and shared? Is it real or merely imaginary? Is it physical or visionary? And we believe in these questions.

"Such questions," writes Jane Roberts, "are legitimate." However, she adds, it is also wise to question our questions, along with the unexamined assumptions that often, if not characteristically, underpin them—the very task that Bohm acknowledges it is so difficult for "thought" to accomplish. But, she adds, try we must:

> It is very possible that our ideas of reality are severely limited. Even the type of questions that we ask are determined by what we believe to be possible and not possible. And our questions limit our investigations and determine their nature.[24]

Joseph Chilton Pearce—our erstwhile cosmic egg-cracker—would heartily agree: "For me no 'universal out-there truth' was given," he says of his passionate metaphysical quest to find the ultimate nature of reality. "Rather, I saw that the only 'truth' for us is the process of questioning what truth might be, and receiving answers in keeping with the nature of our questions."[25]

Quantum physics, of course, insists that, however paradoxical and illogical it seems intellectually, light is both a particle and a wave, and that by observing reality we are also creating it. Not rational, perhaps—but true, nevertheless.

And yet, we didn't have to wait until only recently to rummage around at the far margins of exotic scientific inquiry in order to see the limitations of our old dualisms.

Our everyday experience, if examined carefully, teaches us to do this, as in those odd coincidences Jung labeled "synchronicities," wherein a seemingly "mere" psychological event—for instance, thinking about someone I haven't heard from in many months—is juxtaposed by an occurrence in the physical world. For out of the blue, the very next day I receive an e-mail from this individual telling me that she suffered a computer crash and lost most of her electronic address book. Is this mind or matter? The answer, of course, is:

both. It's a crossover from each to the other.

The great shamans and the indigenous cultures have always known this. And modern shamanic initiates like Cicoria, Jane Roberts, and Robert Monroe, deprived of their cultural safety nets of assumptions, have merely rediscovered for themselves this great truth of nature's circle: Everything is distinct, but nothing is apart. When Cicoria stated that "Nothing is black and white to me anymore; everything is gray," he wasn't, I suspect, siding with the drop-melts-back-into-the-ocean-of-the-Absolute type of thinking prevalent in the Hindu-Buddhist traditions that denies the ultimate reality of distinctions and looks forward to the annihilation of everything individual, including the personality.

Polish philosopher Mishka Jambor, echoing this tradition, views a soul's incarnation as a "fall" or descent into individuality—a rather sad, unfortunate event—"a fall from divinity, and simultaneously a fall, or 'involution' . . . into worldliness" that "reflects that primordial split of undifferentiated consciousness, the Beyond."[26] Or, as Jambor's spiritual hero, Sri Aurobindo, would have it:

> Even the highest individual perfection, even the most blissful cosmic condition is no better than a supreme ignorance. All that is individual, all that is cosmic, has to be austerely renounced by the seeker of Absolute Truth.[27]

No. By "gray," Cicoria does not mean a featureless, nondescript void, but rather that which falls between the apparent extremes. There are, in short, no absolute dualisms, not even between the Beyond and the World—or, in the succinct terms that Monroe came to employ, "There" and "Here." Why else would the incursions of light be of value and importance to those in the dark?

Black Elk learned—as would Monroe and other modern shamanic initiates—that he had to share his visions in order to complete them, and that ending his own world was not sufficient. The private vision and the public event are not neatly divisible, after all. For the true world-ender, the nitty-gritty particulars of the world are to be embraced lovingly, not renounced austerely.

Black Elk did not speak of his Great Vision until he was seventeen. During that time, he was afflicted by the aforementioned fears. The West Power kept tormenting him. When, in desperation, his parents called in an old medicine man named Black Road for help, he listened to Black Elk's story of his visit to the Sky Lodge. Black Road then told him he must fulfill the will of the Six Grandfathers and perform his vision for the community. "Then the fear will leave you," said Black Road, "but if you do not do this, something very bad will happen to you."[28]

Following Black Road's advice, Black Elk enlisted the participation of the members of the village, who helped him perform his "Horse Dance" in imitation of the movements of the spirit horses he had seen in his vision. Then, as Black Road had predicted, the fear did leave him—and he found that he could cure others.

Black Elk found his calling, and answered his call, by conquering his fear and bringing the two worlds together, seeing that they were parts of one whole circle—one to which he, too, belonged. He created the hoop and joined it at the same time.

This Robert Monroe also learned to do after his encounter with the light.

A Sledgehammer Blow

Several months after Monroe's experience with the ring of sparks, he was still periodically assaulted with vibrations that disturbed his efforts to sleep as well as his peace of mind. Little by little, he got used to them until, he says, it "almost became boring"[29] lying in bed, feeling the odd sensations, and waiting for them to pass.

Then one night, something very odd indeed occurred. With his arm draped over the side of the bed, he found he could stretch his fingers out and touch not only the rug, but also the floor underneath the rug, and even penetrate the floor and go on through the surface of the ceiling below, lingering only to feel around a stray, triangular-shaped chip of wood, a bent nail, and some sawdust. Impossible! Was it a hallucination? He was half-tempted to cut a hole in the floor to see if the wood chip, nail, and sawdust were where he had felt them. But how could he have? A physical arm can't go through solid objects, can it? Monroe was not yet able to ask: But what about a nonphysical "appendage"—namely, consciousness?

"It was becoming fairly confusing,"[30] Monroe admitted. Here he had a solid background in engineering, science, and medicine. His mother was a physician, and he had originally majored in biology at college. Consequently—like many or most of us—he had come to rely on science and, as he said, to "expect some kind of answers or at least promising opinions from modern technology."[31]

Alas, none were forthcoming.

Finally came the breaking point. One night, while he was lying in bed trying to distract himself from the onset of the vibrations, he imagined how nice it would be to fly in his glider the following afternoon as he'd planned.

The next thing he knew, he found himself in a state of utter confusion. He seemed to be pressed up against the wall. Had he fallen out of bed? He didn't think so. Odder still, this "wall" had no windows, no furniture, and no doors. No, he slowly realized, it wasn't a wall at all. It was the ceiling—and he was bouncing against it! How could this be? Looking down on the bed below, he saw the sleeping figure of his wife. Well, if this were a dream, he reasoned, I wonder whom I would dream to be in bed with my wife? As he gave a closer look, he realized who the second sleeping form was: It was none other than himself. His body, that is. Fearing now that he was on the brink of death, he dove straight down and back into his body.

This was the beginning of Monroe's career as "the out-of-body man." It took him a long time to overcome his inner fears, as well as the outer dismissals his experiences earned him. He had never even heard of this concept before—leaving one's physical body. His physician informed him that was because he hadn't had a very good philosophy professor in college—an excellent diagnosis, if I do say so myself.

In any case, the books he now read on "astral travel" were of little help, as he did not find the obscure occult terminology and concepts helpful. He wasn't about to go to India and study in an ashram for thirty years. Most of the religious clergy he consulted thought this was something either vaguely demonic or outright diabolical. Even university professors interested in "extrasensory perception" took no interest in out-of-body travel, as they did not want to be tarred with the "occult" brush.

Most disappointing of all, however, was the deafening silence—or outright ridicule—of the scientific establishment. *Journeys Out of the Body* thus charts his own lonely course in meticulously gathering evidence that these excursions were not dreams, hallucinations, or some other pathological condition of body or mind. Bear in mind that this was in the 1950s, late in the buttoned-up, Eisenhower era—well before the psychic explosion of the 1960s and two decades before the New Age.

Then it finally hit Monroe—hard, right between the eyes—that it was all quite real, and that somehow his consciousness was not limited to his physical body and the perceptions of his five senses. The first structural cracks in his cosmic egg became undeniably apparent, even to the staid businessman of Westchester:

> That first evidential experience was indeed a sledgehammer blow. If I accepted the data as fact, it struck hard at nearly all of my life experience to that date, my training, my concepts, and my sense of values. Most of all, it shattered my faith in the totality and certainty of our culture's scientific knowledge. I was sure our scientists had all the answers. Or most of them.[32]

Do you hear the ominous, creaking sound of a decrepit world about to collapse and meet its well-deserved end?

CHAPTER TEN

BARRIER-BREAKER, WORLD-ENDER

The most difficult mental process of all is to consider objectively any concept which, if accepted as fact, will toss into
discard a lifetime of training and experience.

ROBERT MONROE, *Journeys Out of the Body* (1971)

Fear is the great barrier to human growth.

ROBERT MONROE, *Ultimate Journey* (1994)

According to the great German philosopher Friedrich Nietzsche, the
founders of religions and others who have had visions and other unusual experiences are typically dishonest with themselves. "They have never
made their experiences a matter of conscience for knowledge," he com-
plains. In other words, they don't ask themselves the tough questions: What
did I really experience? What was going on in my life and my environment
at the time? Was I thinking clearly? Was I skeptical enough? Did I look for
evidence, or avoid looking?

No, sighs Nietzsche, in mock exasperation. These so-called "visionaries"
pull their punches because they *want* to believe. They *need* to believe. And
so they do. Psychology trumps epistemology. You may recall in the *X-Files*,
the poster above FBI agent Fox Mulder's desk—a picture of UFO with the

caption: "I Want to Believe." This, you see, is the problem. Visionaries adore the irrational.

"But we," Nietzsche adds with a semi-conspiratorial wink to his readers, "we others who thirst after reason, are determined to scrutinize our experiences as severely as a scientific experiment—hour after hour, day after day." He concludes, with a bold flourish: "We ourselves wish to be our experiments and guinea pigs."[1]

Their Own Guinea Pigs

And this is precisely what Jane Roberts and Robert Monroe did. Neither really "wanted to believe"—nor did they, at least at first. Neither was consciously looking to end their respective worlds. Both subjected themselves to as much independent scientific testing as was available to validate their claims, or at least, their suspicions. And both ultimately had to rely on their own resources—and their own considerable acumen—to figure out just what was going on and what it might mean. They scrutinized themselves and their experiences relentlessly and with hard noses, before they came to embrace ideas that ran counter to old beliefs.

Neither Roberts nor Monroe avoided reason and its questions—though both saw the need for opening their own thinking process to accommodate and evaluate experiential data that their culture insisted on ignoring or dismissing out of hand. Roberts lamented the uncritical adulation that she received from "fans" all too eager to give away their power to her (or Seth). And Monroe came to the conclusion that the development of the good old, left-brained rational intellect was one of the prime reasons for entering human form in the "Earth-Life System" and must, therefore, never be denied. Neither was a gullible wishful thinker. Each became exactly what Nietzsche required of a scrupulously honest world-ender: their own guinea pigs, hour after hour, and day after day.

In this ongoing living experiment, however, Monroe enjoyed certain distinct and undeniable advantages, not the least of which was his relative wealth. This financial independence provided access to material and personnel resources not readily available to everyone encountering odd and challenging circumstances like the ones he faced. The important question is: What did he do with those resources? And what do his choices tell us, not simply about him, but about ourselves and about our freedom to end the Myth of the Great Ending?

Shifting Centers

By the early 1960s, Monroe's geographic center of gravity had shifted south to Virginia—first to Richmond and later to Charlottesville and its rural environs, where he and his family took up residence.

On the surface, this move made good, sound business sense. No longer the producer of radio and TV programs, he had shifted into the ownership of radio stations—one in Winston-Salem, the other in Durham, North Carolina—as well as a recording studio in Richmond. He now had many friends and contacts in the area. As a result, other lucrative, and some not-so-successful, ventures would subsequently beckon, including the ownership of the cable-television franchise in Charlottesville, which was one of the first in the nation. Well, so far, so good.

But on another, perhaps unconscious, level, there may have been more to the relocation than that. One suspects that the quieter, slower pace of southern life, far removed from the East Coast hustle-bustle of Gotham, was more suitable to an individual still struggling to separate the signal from the noise, so to speak, as he learned to listen to the inner promptings that were coming from his true self.

Like all shrewd and successful businesspeople, Monroe undoubtedly used his intuition and instincts without even thinking about it, or at least without thinking of them as "inner promptings from his true self." But this was different. These bizarre signals were coming from a more profound source of awareness, and their effect was not so much to support, but to radically upend, his previous practical interests and daily concerns. Monroe eventually divested himself of all his ties to the business world in order to concentrate his full attention on his out-of-body experiences, which continued. In retrospect, his move south thus looks like an evolutionary step of the extroverted mover-shaker and man-of-action toward the keen listener-observer whose focus is mainly inward, preparing the way for his strange talent and the exploration of the farther realms of consciousness.

In this exploration, Monroe was ultimately in good company, or at least had some vital assistance. Initially, however, he was very much alone, and—as his biographer Ronald Russell points out—it is not too difficult to read between the lines of his meticulously kept, coldly objective reportage in *Journeys Out of the Body* and detect hints of what must have been the loneliness and sheer terror that a previously solid, conventional, practical, emphatically nonphilosophical and nonmystical type felt grappling with the odd predicament of finding himself thrust out of his physical body. Was he also out of his mind? This is the question to which Monroe kept returning, time after time, until he was able to answer—at least to his own satisfaction—"No, I guess it's real after all." But it took years and the accumulation and analysis of much experiential data before he arrived at this conclusion.

Initially, in his out-of-body state, Monroe found himself unable to leave the environs of his bedroom to collect data. Once he overcame his fear that he was dying and his considerable sex drive, which he said tethered him to his physical body, he was able to go places and visit people he knew, and at least attempt to contact them. Sometimes they recalled his visits; sometimes they did not. On occasion, he was able to collect verifiable information about people and their activities that he did not previously know, but that subsequently checked out. Slowly, as Monroe himself often said, his fear was replaced by something far better and more useful: curiosity.

Other out-of-body adventures were not so earthbound. The deaths of his father and two close friends—lawyer and inventor Agnew Bahnson and Dick Gordon, the physician he had initially consulted about his "vibrations"—provided new opportunities to visit other realms. And to verify.

The Gordon episode in particular was telling. Once out of body, Monroe requested a meeting with the deceased Dr. Gordon. But the youthful figure with the prominent shock of hair he encountered in his OBE bore no resemblance to his seventy-year-old doctor friend. Monroe was puzzled. However, later, when he paid an embodied visit to Gordon's widow, she showed him a photograph of her husband in his earlier years. It was the man he recognized from his OBE.[2]

Monroe took many other types of out-of-body voyages, some to environments we might call "parallel worlds," in which he found himself in an earthlike environment, living an ordinary life with a family and a somewhat strained marriage. On another occasion, he visited a parklike setting, complete with "carefully tended flowers, trees, and grass, much like a large mall with paths crisscrossing the area. There were benches along the paths, and there were hundreds of men and women strolling by, or sitting on the benches." While some were calm and peaceful, others, he noted, were "apprehensive, and many had a dazed or shocked look of disorientation."[3] He intuitively knew that this was a meeting place for recently deceased souls. "The Park," as he would come to call it, was a nonphysical locale he remembered and returned to many years later.

While some of his visits to non-earthly environments, or what he called "Locale II," strained his ability to express them in human language terms, many others had as their common theme the experiencing—and perhaps purging—of buried fears. These fears, he now realized, had been ruling his life. Both their enormity and his inability to control them, he admitted, were embarrassing. What were they? Fear "of the unknown, of strange beings (nonphysical), of 'death,' of God, of rule-breaking, of discovery, and of pain, to name only a few."[4] Fear was the great barrier that had to be surmounted, over and over. It was as if he were a student being given a course in fear management, with the most terrifying tests and quizzes imaginable. This was a tough curriculum, not tailor-made for the faint of heart or weak of mind.

However, one nonphysical locale in particular proved to be the antithesis of the fear curriculum: an almost indescribable, harmonious state of being or "place" (the raised-eyebrow quotation marks are his own) he dubbed, simply, Home that he says he visited on three occasions. Here, in his own deeply affecting words—the words, mind you, of one not easily given to any sort of overt expression of emotion, especially of the tender sort—is how he managed to describe this mystical interlude:

> To me, it was a place or condition of pure peace, yet exquisite emotion. It was *as if* you were floating in warm soft clouds where there is no up or down, where nothing exists as a separate piece of matter. The warmth is not merely around you, it is of you and through you. Your perception is dazzled and overwhelmed by the Perfect Environment [italics mine].

Suddenly, however, and without any transition, Monroe quietly drops the "as if" qualifier to give a more densely physical description of this supreme bliss:

> The cloud in which you float is swept by rays of light in shapes and hues that are constantly changing, and each is good as you bathe in them as they pass over you. Ruby-red rays of light, or something beyond what we know as light, because no light ever felt this meaningful. All the colors of the spectrum come and go constantly, never harshly, and each brings a different soothing or restful happiness. It is as if you are within and a part of the clouds surrounding an eternally glowing sunset, and with every changing pattern of living color, you also change. You respond and drink into you the eternity of the blues, yellows, greens, and reds, and the complexities of the intermediaries. All are familiar to you. This is where you belong. This is Home.[5]

The poetical lyricism of this description is undeniable. But Monroe himself was not content with simply describing his experiences, no matter how detailed or accurate he tried to be. Like Jane Roberts, he was acutely, even painfully, aware of the difficulties, both in translating nonphysical data into physical terms, and in not tainting those translations with extraneous or misleading concepts and beliefs. Yet description was not enough, no matter how well done. He wanted—no, demanded—to understand his experiences. What was the larger significance of all this? Why was it happening to him? What was he supposed to do with it?

In *Journeys Out of the Body,* Monroe claimed that a major reason he wrote the book was to help others who had suffered through similar experiences and doubts by letting them know that they weren't alone—or psychotic, or "possessed"—and that their seemingly eccentric perceptions had a solid basis in fact, even if that factual basis was highly unpalatable to conventional science and religion. The OBE is real, not a mere dream or hallucination. But beyond that, what? What did it all mean? What was really going on underneath all of these wild perturbations?

He just knew he had to find out. And he had some help along the way.

"Where" Is "Here"

The publication of *Journeys Out of the Body* produced (or perhaps merely exacerbated) strains in Monroe's marriage. As a result, he and his wife, Mary, decided to divorce. In 1971, he remarried, this time to his good friend and business partner, Nancy Penn. The Monroes, along with their extended families, soon settled in on a 430-acre spread named Whistlefield, a half-hour's ride from Charlottesville, in Albemarle County—rural, but still tony. There they remained until 1977, when they sold the estate and moved to neighboring Nelson County—even more rural, and not tony at all. It was there, on the Roberts Mountain property in Faber, that Monroe built the research and educational center that became known as the Monroe Institute. But it all began in a few small outbuildings at Whistlefield.

Monroe had saved all the careful records of his OBE adventures, as well as miscellaneous laboratory equipment like a galvanic skin-response monitor and electrodes that he'd picked up along the way. But now he determined to do something more systematic and disciplined in the way of investigations.

Perhaps because of his earlier aborted experiments with the relaxation and sleep-learning tapes, as well as his previous background as a sound engineer and musical composer, he hit on the idea of somehow using sound to induce out-of-body experiences. After all, "if sound could send you to sleep," writes Monroe biographer Ronald Russell, "it followed that sound could alter your state of consciousness."[6] If he could replicate the OBE at will, he could study it, and perhaps even learn its secrets.

Thus began the long, laborious process of trial-and-error research that Monroe undertook—helped along by unpaid employees, including engineers and psychologists, as well as test subjects from his pool of staff, family, and other volunteers—to create and perfect the audio technology that was eventually dubbed "Hemi-Sync" (short for hemispheric synchronization), designed to put listeners into brain states propitious for the induction of altered states of consciousness, from deep sleep to creative inspiration and out-of-body travel.[7]

This audio technology operates through what are called "binaural beats"—basically, an electrical invitation sent to the brain that creates a third sound inside of itself, when two slightly different sounds or tones are introduced separately into each ear through a pair of stereo headphones, thereby producing a synchrony between the right and left cerebral hemispheres. It is such coherent, highly focused states of awareness that provide a launching pad for consciousness. Monroe acquired patents for certain elements of his audio technology, so there is no question of his originality, though the concept of binaural beats was not his own invention.[8]

How and why did Monroe initially divine a connection between altering consciousness and having OBEs? For this link is neither obvious nor immediately apparent. Let me explain.

In *Journeys Out of the Body*, Monroe gave the name of the "Second Body" to the admittedly quite elastic, plastic, evidently non-material form that "exited" his physical body, seemingly "bounced" against his bedroom ceiling, and "took off" through his bedroom walls or ceiling for visits to friends both living and dead, and beyond the earthly realm to places like "Home." This vivid language of motion and place reflected his attempt to convey his firsthand experience that he—that is, his real, nonphysical self—was indeed traveling. In other words, he was going somewhere where he had not already been, and would not be—or would not be in the process of perceiving—unless he first *went* there.

Now there is a tension here, as Monroe himself seemed to recognize at times. For example, he talks of "seeing" sparks with his closed eyes, and uses metaphors to describe his trips Home. This results from having to use physical terms to describe nonphysical processes and perceptions. Russell concurs: "Monroe's concept of the Second Body arises from his attempts to rationalize his experiences . . . to explain them, to make them fit, bizarre though many of them are, into a frame or pattern, something that the intellect can get hold of."[9]

Yet this problem is not altogether dissimilar to the difficulties we all face in translating our dreams—which, from the standpoint of our conscious awareness may seem bizarre and incomprehensible—into a form that our rational, waking self, or ego, can grasp and handle. The same is true of the simultaneous unfolding of events in near-death experiences, which defy our ordinary sequential concept of time, as well as powerful experiences of mystical oneness, which defy our normal, Newtonian thinking and the principle that two objects cannot occupy the same space at the same time. A true prospective world-ender, however, must face up to the limits of human language and find some creative way around them.

This Monroe did. Even as early as *Journeys Out of the Body*, he expressed some misgivings about talk of "going out" of the body. In one key passage, he speculates that the world or worlds of Locale II—or what he would subsequently refer to simply as "There"—were not really "somewhere else," or a "place" to which one "journeyed" in a quasi-physical "Second Body." Rather, these realms were unnoticed dimensions of one continuous reality, analogous to wave frequencies in the electromagnetic spectrum, of which we can become aware simply by shifting the focus of our attention. We don't have to *go* anywhere, or *get out* of something—the physical body; we just have to let the blinders drop, open our eyes, and see for ourselves:

> Except for rare or unusual conditions, our "natural" senses and our instruments which are extensions thereof are completely unable to perceive and report this potential. If we consider this premise, the "where" [of Locale II] is answered neatly. "Where" is "here."[10]

This may provide an answer as to how Monroe connected the OBE to changes of consciousness. It also throws the whole issue into a new perspective.

Hemi-Sync, whose benefits Monroe made available for all willing participants at the institute's numerous educational programs—*Gateway, Guidelines, Lifeline*, etc.—is essentially what I would call a blinder-removal tool, an antitechnology technology, or a cultural deprogramming device. Properly speaking, Hemi-Sync isn't a vehicle that takes you to some other place; it just helps you remove the narrow limits on your natural, wider perception. Then you can see what is—and that you are, in fact, already—There. Which is, of course, right Here.

Or, as Monroe put it much later, our consciousness is constantly flickering between Here and There, with little or no awareness on our part. The point is to become aware of what we are already doing and being, of the full range of operations of our consciousness. To be conscious is not the same thing as being aware. Much of the activity of our consciousness takes place below, or above, the threshold of awareness. The trick is to stop constricting that threshold.

Culture is the great boa constrictor that attacks and suffocates our awareness. By monopolizing our attention with technological baubles, it convinces us that there's no such thing as consciousness—or else it warns us not to expand our awareness, lest we fall into the clutches of the devil. Thus, it's not a doing, but rather, a "not-doing"—a carefully calibrated demolition of obstacles to our fuller perception—that frees us. To unlearn all that has been so assiduously learned—that is what ends our personal world.

"Do that which consists in taking no action, and order will prevail," advises the *Tao Te Ching*. This is the Taoist concept of *wu wei*: acting by not acting, or rather, by allowing the order of nature to unfold as it will, and trusting in it. Which is, of course, the very antithesis of the control fetishism of civilization, Eastern and Western.

Monroe came to see the limitations of this attitude in his own case. In fact, by the early 1970s, he admitted that he was becoming somewhat bored and frustrated with his own OBE activity. In his second book, *Far Journeys* (1985), he likens his previous experiences to aimless Sunday driving on the back roads—strictly "local traffic" stuff—versus zooming along on the interstate. What made the difference was a key decision: "The limiting factor was my conscious mind. . . . I was too much in control—this left-brain 'I.' What would happen if I turned this [OBE] process over to my total self (soul?), who was purportedly conversant with such activities."[11]

Once he did that and relinquished conscious control, he reports, "there began for me an entire new era in my out-of-body activities."[12] While there was some sensation of lifting out of his physical body, the shift in consciousness was now almost instantaneous—and profound. The mover and shaker was learning the wisdom of allowing the process to unfold on its own, in its own way.

The Philosophical Radical

The out-of-body experiences that Monroe enjoyed from 1972 to the early 1990s, and which he attempted to relate in his second book, *Far Journeys*, and in his third and final book, *Ultimate Journey* (1994)—published a year after the death from cancer of his beloved wife, Nancy, and only a year before his own death in 1995 at the age of 80—are far removed indeed from the "local-traffic" episodes recounted in *Journeys Out of the Body*.

This shift to the "interstate" presented further challenges in translation and communication, but ones he knew he had to face if he was to fulfill what he was coming to see as his true purpose. He felt he needed to convey certain information, but without falsifying data or confusing his audience. The question was: How?

The opening sections of *Far Journeys,* which deal with the creation of Hemi-Sync and the institute's early programs, read like Monroe's straightforward, reportorial style in *Journeys Out of the Body.* However, the second—much longer—part of the book, which presents his account of his own post-1972 experiences, reads like a seriocomic fable of what it means to forget and re-member one's true self. Chris Lenz, one of the early members of the Monroe Institute team of workshop leaders, once called it "an analogy of an analogy," and compared it to a creative work of science fiction. Of course, good fiction can convey truth, which is not the same as sheer fact. So Lenz quite rightly added: "Those for whom it was written got a rare and delightful twinge of recognition. *Far Journeys* was an attempt to lead people to There. He needed to take a certain number of people with him."[13]

This cryptic statement applies also, I believe, to all of Monroe's books, the development of Hemi-Sync, and the establishment of the institute and its educational programs—it is all of a piece, as he himself came to see toward the end, as both he and Nancy prepared to take their ultimate journeys. To fathom that purpose, and thus to appreciate just how far he had come from his conventional beginnings, his worldview, and his lifestyle, you really have to read the books for yourself. There is no substitute. But there are a few observations that can be made from the philosophical sidelines in the meantime, as an incentive to do so.

The first observation concerns what I think Monroe came, in the course of his actual investigative practice, to appreciate as the basic requirements of self-exploration. The first is the willingness to question absolutely everything, without exception. This is what I call "radical iconoclasm." The second, related, principle is what I call "radical empiricism." Allow me to explain each in turn.

An iconoclast is one who shatters the images we worship and cannot bring ourselves to question. "Radical" is usually taken to mean "extreme," which has a decidedly negative, somewhat sinister, connotation, calling to mind wild-eyed, bomb-throwing, fanatical types. But this is a distortion. Our English word "radical" comes from *radix*, the Latin word for "root." To get rid of a weed, you must pluck it out by its root, so it won't just grow back. Hence the original, proper sense of "radical" is thorough and complete, or getting down to the deepest root source.

For a radical iconoclast, then, every card is placed on the table: All of our previous dearly held beliefs, values, assumptions, and presuppositions must be examined. There are no holds barred, no stones unturned, and no sacred cows left to munch their cuds, peaceful and undisturbed in the verdant pasture. This is exactly what Monroe declares to be his methodological credo in *Ultimate Journey*:

> What we need to do, whether in- or out-of body, is to ignore or tear down the No Trespassing signs, the taboos, the notice that says Holy of Holies, the distortions of time and translation, the soft black holes of euphoria, the mysticisms, the myths, the fantasies of an eternal father or mother image, and then take a good look with our acquired and growing left brain. Nothing is sacred to the point where it should not be investigated or put under inquiry.[14]

Radical empiricism, on the other hand, draws on another meaning of "radical." The dictionary defines empiricism as the philosophical "theory that all knowledge originates in experience." Here Monroe was "radical," or absolutely thoroughgoing, in two distinct, but related senses.

In the first place, he insisted on not interpreting "experience" as narrowly as materialist philosophers and most mainstream scientists are wont to do, so that it only includes the inputs of our five physical senses. Monroe's field of experience thus includes impressions, perceptions, intuitions, and other data acquired in the exploration of nonphysical reality or other focus levels of consciousness.

Moreover, Monroe was absolutely thoroughgoing in his insistence that experience always trumps belief, no matter how firmly entrenched. Ever since St. Paul made the profession of certain beliefs—in the memorable phrase of philosopher Walter Kaufmann—"the gate to salvation,"[15] thus making the new religion of Christianity into a more saleable commodity, belief in general became a kind of fetish, not only for religion, but also for philosophy and science. "Standing up for one's beliefs" is seen as a mark of good character rather than as a kind of neurotic tic.

But such passionate love of conviction often interferes with the recognition and assimilation of experiences that don't fit any of our preconceived notions. Had Monroe listened to the religious and scientific authorities he had consulted after he had his initial out-of-body episodes, he would have concluded that he was possessed or deranged. There were also those "occultists" who knew all about "astral projection" and practitioners of yoga who had their own prejudicial views about the nature and value of the OBE as a kind of psychic "distraction" on the path to true enlightenment.

Yet Monroe rejected all of these firm opinions in order to let the experiences unfold as they did. For a long time, he had to endure living in the uncomfortable intellectual limbo of not having a framework in which to interpret them. But, by allowing the experiences themselves, rather than any ideas about them, to guide him, he opened up vast new territories of consciousness for exploration.

If and when we follow suit, what shall we find? Or perhaps we should ask, what did Monroe discover for himself, if for no one else (as he himself often put it)?

Certainly, as Monroe's biographer Ronald Russell points out, fairly early on in his out-of-body career, Monroe came to accept "some kind of immortality" for the individual.[16] This seemed to follow, not only from his felt sense of separation from the physical and his increasing comfort therewith, but also from his convincing afterlife encounters with friends and family.

Yet, as his journey of self-discovery took him farther afield from mere "local traffic," and further and further along the vast interstate of consciousness, Monroe's concept of "the individual" was stretched beyond his wildest imaginings. Indeed, what he came to view as the "self," from his own direct experience, resembles the model constructed by Jane Roberts based on her adventures in consciousness.

According to this mind-boggling picture, the source of our identity is a kind of multidimensional jellyfish with multitudinous tentacles of every conceivable permutation and combination—gender, personality trait, etc.—that stretch into every habitable corner of time and space, all times and all places on earth, and even beyond—into the far-flung nonphysical dimensions of reality, as well as the more local, postmortem surroundings of the Earth-Life System, like the place Monroe had previously visited, and now revisited, called "the Park." What Jane Roberts had called the "Source Self" Monroe dubbed his "I-There," which contains all previous and present life person-alities. There are multiple incarnations, reincarnations, and selves of every conceivable and inconceivable sort. Moreover, each "I-There" is bonded to vast numbers of other "I-Theres" in what he termed "clusters."

The Park, he came to understand, was not simply a meeting place for the recently deceased, but also a kind of convalescent and educational center. More properly, it was a state of consciousness given earthlike form to make new arrivals comfortable, where souls regrouped from their last earth life—a much-valued assignment precisely because it's so tough—and decided upon their next move. But this could only be possible if these souls were, first of all, aware that they had "passed over"—which, he discovered to his great surprise, many were not—and if they did not become "stuck" in what he dubbed the "Belief Systems Territories."

These are the heavens and hells created and sustained by organized reli-gions and their followers, as well as the enacted fantasies of total obliteration created by those hard-core materialists who dogmatically reject postmortem survival. "Belief" thus turns out to be the ultimate "gated community."

You get what you pay for—or at least what you expect.

Eventually, those souls trapped by their ignorance are offered rescue by other parts of their own I-There, or other guides and would-be helpers, in hopes of offering them an opportunity to free themselves from their self-imposed limitations. These unfortunates may be hovering around the earth-plane, attached to their old homes and families, refusing to accept their own death, or else traumatized by the suddenness or violence of it. Or they may be inhabitants of one of the Belief Systems Territories, unable to understand that their blissful after-death reward or awful punishment is strictly a collec-tive illusion of their own making.

To his own considerable surprise, Monroe found himself taking part in a number of such rescues, sometimes of what he intuitively realized were aspects of his own I-There, but in other cases, not. As when he assisted an elderly woman, moaning and gasping in a hospital bed, to realize that she had already expired:

> "Can't you see I'm hurting?" I asked her why. "I'm dying, that's why. I've been dying for years but nobody would believe me." I believe you, I told her "That's all you doctors say, but you don't mean it." I told her I wasn't a doctor, and that I did believe her. . . . There was no need to wish for death, I told her. It was all over. She was dead.[17]

Once she was convinced that she was, in fact, already dead, Monroe tried to get the old woman to accompany him to the Park, but found that he "lost" her somewhere in one of the Belief Systems Territories, to which she must have been attracted.

Soul Retrieval

Though he gave no evidence of being aware of it, what Monroe was re-discovering for himself through his own direct experience was none other than the ancient shamanic healing art called soul-retrieval.[18] After many such episodes, however, some of which didn't work out quite the way he'd intended, he began to question the point and purpose of offering such assistance. After all, he reasoned, he could spend every minute of every hour of every day doing this sort of thing, and not even begin to make a dent in retrieving the number of "lost" or stuck souls.

Eventually, however, he realized that these episodes were meant to be of educational value, to shock him into realizing that this was, in effect, what he had been doing all along, in all of his work: with the books, the audio technology, the institute programs—including a new program called *Lifeline*, specifically geared to teaching others to perform retrievals of parts of themselves, as well as other souls.

This was the missing truth—what he called "the Basic"—for which he had long searched, the true purpose of his deepest self, which went beyond any of his conscious intentions or even his constantly affirmed desire to offer "something of value" to humanity. "It was the Basic; the collection and unification of the 'parts,' not only the errant and missing ones in my own I-There but the parts of the entire I-There cluster to which I am bonded."[19] Monroe had no idea how many others this might be—thousands, perhaps hundreds of thousands. But trying to aid this completion, with each part bringing with it "a multitude of gifts of experience and love,"[20] he now saw had been his underlying aim.

And what would happen then? That answer, he admitted, is unknown. But it would involve a never-ending evolution of consciousness beyond the human and even the meta-human levels, to who knows what.

This was soul retrieval on a grand, even cosmic, scale. As Russell points out, however, the heart of *Ultimate Journey*—and Monroe's greatest adventure of self-discovery—comes when he makes a nearly indescribable and emotionally wrenching voyage to the very center of universal intelligence, the creative source of the physical world that he calls, simply, "the Emitter." There he receives an instantaneous holographic telepathic communication—what he called a "ROTE"—which he subsequently does his best to translate:

> There is no beginning, there is no end,
>   There is only change.
> There is no teacher, there is no student,
>   There is only remembering.
> There is no good, there is no evil,
>   There is only expression.
> There is no union, there is no sharing,
>   There is only one.
> There is no joy, there is no sadness,
>   There is only love.
> There is no greater, there is no lesser,
>   There is only balance.
> There is no stasis, there is no entropy,
>   There is only motion.
> There is no wakefulness, there is no sleep,
>   There is only being.
> There is no limit, there is no chance,
>   There is only a plan.[21]

This is a vision, according to Russell, that is at once "the most profound experience recorded in any of [Monroe's] books," and "especially remarkable in its originality," as it owes nothing to the teachings of organized religion or existing spiritual systems, "with nothing derived from any belief system or ancient text."[22] I heartily concur.

The onetime hard-boiled objective reporter has become an unabashed poet at last—perhaps even a mythmaker.

But this is no morbid, sad-sack Myth of the Great Ending. It is a joyous, profoundly awesome vision of the Grand Infinite, which neither begins nor ends—the true infinite: the never-ending hoop of life, to which we all equally belong, not by belief or special election, but by our indelible nature, which is the nature of all.

And so, a world ends. Will a new one begin?

CHAPTER ELEVEN

THE CIRCLE OF DREAMS AND THE ENDS OF MYTH

The myth is the public dream and the dream is the private
myth.

JOSEPH CAMPBELL WITH BILL MOYERS,
The Power of Myth (1988)

Dream, vision, god. The gods of heaven and hell are what
might be called the cosmic aspect of the dream. And the
dream is the personal aspect of the myth. Dream and myth
are of the same order.

JOSEPH CAMPBELL, *The Hero's Journey* (1990)

Dreams, said Carl Jung, are the voice of nature within us. Hermann Hesse predicted that when enough individuals begin to listen to nature's voice and pay heed to their own dreams—including their visions, intuitions, and instinctive promptings—the greatest revolution in all history will unfold. This is not an ending, but rather a beginning. The image Hesse used is that of a Great Goddess named Mother Earth, also known to us as Eve, giving birth to a galaxy of shooting stars—stars of individual destiny. When each of us chooses to embrace our true self and follow our own star, the real revolution will commence.[1]

Yet it must be said that Hesse was no cockeyed optimist. He made his prophetic pronouncement—dressed in the protective garb of fictional characters, of course—in the closing pages of *Demian*, written in the aftermath of the End of the World—the end, that is, of World War I, the bloody War to End All Wars, which also marked the end of the old European order. Hesse knew the old myth up close and personal, inside and out. And he knew the facts, too.

Axis Denial

Our imaginations can be corrupted as well as inspired. We must choose what kind of inner nourishment to seek: healthy food or junk food. Which is it?

The Myth of the Great Ending is junk food for the imagination. Actually, it is much worse than that: It is a deadly poison circulating in the body of human consciousness. It must be purged from our bloodstream, brought to the surface of our skin, and, finally, expelled. Then the open wound can be cauterized properly. The morbid yearning for the End of the World, in the customary sense of world-escape or world-destruction, hides a repressed, healthy longing for reconciliation with our inner and outer worlds, here and now—with nature, in short. That longing must be recognized, expressed, and acted upon. There simply is no alternative.

Many of us already realize this. For those who do, the ancient vision quest has become a mandatory part of the core curriculum of contemporary life rather than a mere optional elective. This quest can no longer be dismissed as a mere frill or, worse, denigrated as a fashionable New Age throwback to "the superstitions of ignorant primitives." Our very lives must take on the character and resonance of an old Indian ceremony. It's do or die.

But what if—even knowing all this—we still stubbornly avoid signing up for the required course? What if we still cling to our basest fears and can't let go?

I have left out something essential, you see. It's the personal factor; what William James identified as the true *axis mundi*. I must now try and make amends.

Cafeteria Crisis

Several years after my disheartening meeting with Dan that I described in chapter 8, it was my turn. The shoe was now squarely on the other foot.

A professor colleague in another department asked to meet with me. Dave, as I'll call him, had read my previous book and was anxious to discuss it. "I love the way you handle the dream material," Dave enthused. "I have trouble even remembering my dreams."

Dave is a clinical psychologist who gave up his private practice to teach. He positively radiates good will and an almost contagious sense of calm. His merry eyes twinkle and he has a beard. If he were a hundred pounds heavier, and significantly grayer of beard, he might be mistaken for Old St. Nick on his off-season, marking time before the holidays by doing a volunteer stint at a local community college.

Dave and I met for lunch in the drab faculty dining room, where we brought our sandwiches and salads. We'd always been friendly with each other in a casual, offhand way, exchanging greetings and chatting in the halls. But this was the first time we'd actually sat down together for any kind of sustained conversation. In truth, we hardly knew each other, despite the fact that we obviously liked one another, based on—well, based on pretty much nothing, if you want to know the truth. At least, it was nothing in a verifiable, scientific sense. Back in the '60s, we would have said, "It was just a vibe, man"—that is, an intuitive sense. Nothing you could put your finger on, after all; just some inchoate inner promptings.

I told Dave enthusiastically that I was always pleased—if a bit surprised— to meet a fellow academic who took not only dreams, but also psychic experiences, seriously. I asked him how he got interested in this kind of "woo-woo" stuff.

Dave explained that he'd been going through a particularly rough period, both personally and professionally. He'd been overworked and exhausted from his practice, counseling traumatized survivors of the Long Island Railroad shooting, a bloodbath that occurred some years back when a madman with a pistol calmly strode down the aisle of a commuter train shooting innocent victims like fish in a barrel. A number of people were killed or maimed for life. And there were some other family issues weighing heavily on his mind as well.

One afternoon, Dave was walking past a storefront that advertised psychic readings. He was never "into" such things, but spontaneously—on the sheer spur of the moment, more or less as a lark—he walked in and asked for a reading. Now he had never been in this particular neighborhood before, so no one knew him. And he was very careful not to tell the psychic anything about himself, either verbally or with his body language or other behavioral cues. He just wanted a reading, he said.

What the psychic told Dave floored him—specifics about the names and ages of his children, and many other details that this individual just could not possibly have known through ordinary means, unless a private detective had been hired to follow Dave around. But, of course, Dave himself hadn't known that he was going to do this, so how did the psychic know? Must be psychic!

But it wasn't only the facts that impressed Dave so much. It was also the quality of the psychic's advice. So, ever since, once a year Dave treats himself to a reading with his favorite psychic to get his annual update. No scoffer, he.

Now, however, it was my turn.

Dave repeated his earlier kind comments about my book and my handling of dream material. Then, his eyes narrowing somewhat, he said gently, "With all of your sense of connection to nature, and your own dreams, why is it, do you think, that you seem so out of sorts lately?"

I was stunned. I think my mouth hung open, if just a bit. I hadn't quite realized anyone else had noticed my mood—or would care to comment. I didn't know what to say, so I sat there speechless. I felt like a kid with his hand caught in the cookie jar. No, worse yet, I felt like a garden-variety hypocrite.

"I mean," Dave added apologetically. "I see you in the hallway, getting upset about little things. You know, trivial stuff. But I would think someone with your wider perspective would have a solid handle on all that."

It was true. And I knew that Dave wasn't saying what he was saying just to put me on the hot seat or to do a therapist's number on me: "Yes, and how do *you* feel about that?" He was genuinely concerned. But he was also demanding an answer. And so was I.

Appearing to mull it over, as if performing an internal file search, I made an effort to find my lost mental footing. Regaining my composure, I mumbled something about feeling at wit's end over teaching. The students had changed over the years. Add to that the annoying distractions of cell phones, computers, and all the new technology, all of which makes it difficult to gain and hold students' attention—unless, of course, you're entertaining them. We're now in the edutainment business.

"We're pressured to use tools that do more harm than good," I said grumpily. "Plus, during the semester, I don't really have the time or energy to do much of that inner dream-work, or commune with nature, and I guess that puts me out of sorts."

Dave nodded sympathetically, appearing to accept my response as genuine. On one level, I suppose, it was. However, on another, deeper level—the gut variety—I sensed it was, at best, a half-truth. There *had* been a dream— or rather more than that. I'd been doing my level best to ignore it, even though that was impossible. How could I ignore the clamorous sound of my own world ending?

Two, Plus One

The first two things troubling me were definitely dreams.

In the first, I'm in the house, alone with the dog. I become increasingly anxious that there is a ghostly presence that means to do us harm. I move carefully through the house, checking each room, but find nothing. Finally, I come to the room I use as my study. The fear is overwhelming, as if I have been grabbed at the throat. I feel as if I'm choking to death. I'm paralyzed. After making what seems like a Herculean effort, I manage to scream—and, waking from my nightmare in a cold sweat, actually find myself yelling out loud with my physical vocal chords.

Cynthia groans and rolls over in bed beside me.

After what seems like a long time, I fall back asleep, and my second dream begins. Now I find myself teaching a philosophy class in a darkened, dingy room, where even the blackboards are falling apart, all peeling and cracked. As I walk over to the board to write something down, I begin to feel dizzy. I'm losing my balance. But instead of falling, I find myself stumbling around the walls of the classroom, which I now realize is circular. I can't regain my balance, but I can't stop walking around the room, either. Faster and faster I go! It's as if I'm one of those astronauts in training, spinning in a giant centrifuge. The dizziness increases exponentially, and I feel as if I'm either going to pass out or "take off." It's the "wicked spins" times ten.

I awaken, breathless and shaken. What the hell is going on?

Tossing and turning, I can't get back to sleep for what seems like hours, although I know that if I look at my watch to find out how much time has passed, that will only make things worse. I'll feel under more pressure. Tomorrow—or rather today, certainly by now—is Sunday, so at least I won't have to get up early and go to work. But the more I lie there in bed, the higher my anxiety level rises. What if this? What if that? How can I fix this? What if I can't handle that? I can feel the fear meter edging farther and farther into the red zone. The tension is becoming unbearable. I try to talk myself out of my worries, or ignore them. But the more I do this, the worse it seems to get.

Suddenly, out of nowhere, I get an idea: Instead of trying to erase or combat my fears, I'm going to just accept them. No, more than that: love them. What would it be like to feel total love and acceptance, I wonder, even of my fears? I do my best to imagine the feeling. I send out "love rays" everywhere, in all directions, inside and out. As I do this, I realize something: If I can imagine this feeling so vividly, it must be real, both within and without me. As I think this thought, I sense the fear and tension just melting away. What remains is a warm, satisfying glow, a peaceful, flowing feeling. With this, I drift into sleep, and into the third—and final—experience.

I'm in the car, off to do my grocery shopping, driving down a familiar local street in the direction of the supermarket. In the background, I can hear a voice, very faintly, off in the distance, talking about visiting "the museum." I assume this is a radio playing somewhere, although it doesn't seem to be coming from inside my car.

Meanwhile, I notice that I'm wearing a very peculiar kind of hat. I take it off my head to examine it. The hat has all these funny little flaps on it, like the neat, crisp folds of a paper airplane. And I really can't tell the front from the back. This seems very odd, and I don't know what to make of it.

Just then, I turn the corner. As I do, I am totally flabbergasted: Where suburban houses and ugly strip malls should be, there is a shoreline. The ocean waves are lapping on the beach. But we're inland, a good forty miles from the shore, I think to myself. This is all wrong. How can it be?

In a moment, I recognize the incongruity, and it's as if a light switch is suddenly turned on. It dawns on me, with great excitement: *This is a dream!* Now I exclaim out loud, as if shouting from the rooftops: *"This is a dream!"*

Instantly, I lift out of the car, shooting like a rocket right through the roof and into the sky, just like Superman. I'm doing barrel rolls and streaking through the air at an incredible, dizzying speed. Everything is absolutely gorgeous and crystal clear. The sun has just come up, and the warm sunlight is pouring through puffy white clouds. The blue of the sky is the bluest blue I've ever seen. I just can't believe how awfully beautiful it all is as I look down below to where the ocean meets the shore.

My "body" now begins to pulsate, to vibrate, and the vibration keeps increasing at an incredible rate. The feeling is so pleasurable it's ecstatic—way beyond anything I've ever experienced before. I know now that I'm not in my physical body anymore. The vibrant energy of pure joy is cascading through every cell in my "body," shaking me to my very core. The sense of freedom is unbelievable! I'm streaking higher and higher, through the clouds and on into the atmosphere.

"It's *all* a dream!" I shout out.

Liquid ecstasy continues to pour through me to the very center of my being. I'm not sure I can handle much more of it. The exhilaration is indescribable—so intensely pleasurable that it is painful. Meanwhile, my speed keeps increasing. I'm shooting through the atmosphere and on into space. I close my "eyes" and lose all orientation. I can't tell up from down, or where I am. I just feel the speed . . . the pulsations . . . the ecstasy . . . the joy . . . the freedom . . . the pain-pleasure—all in one.

Then, suddenly, without warning, it all stops, as if a valve had shut.

I awaken, in bed, incredulous.

I lie there for some time, just trying to fathom what happened, basking in the afterglow of something so wonderful, so profoundly moving. Tears stream down my face. I just can't believe I've been given this incredible gift.

I look over at my watch on the nightstand: 6:30 AM. I realize that I have to get up and take the dog outside. As I put on my sweat suit for protection against the cold January air, I feel like Scrooge on Christmas morning, after the visits by the three ghosts. I could almost do a jig, as he did, I'm so happy. I'm walking on air.

I slip into my clogs. The dog follows me from the bedroom to the back door. I put the collar around his neck and snap on the leash. Opening the door, I let him walk out in front of me, and don't even bother to look as he slides down the two rather steep and narrow concrete steps. The afterglow of my experience is still too much with me. I haven't fully "come back" yet. So I fail to notice the thin, nearly invisible layer of ice that coated the steps and driveway during the night.

It all happens in a split second.

Grinning like an idiot, I step out the door, putting down my right foot. But before I can even figure out what is happening, I'm flying, feet first, into the air—I never even feel my foot touch the step—and bam! I'm flat on my backside.

The dog stops in his tracks, turns around, and just looks at me as if I'm some kind of clown. I'm stunned. My body is throbbing. At first, I just lie there, not moving, wondering if I've broken something. My rear end hurts like hell, and so does my back. I realize I'm lucky that I didn't hit my head and crack open my skull.

So much for grand ecstasies and out-of-body voyages to the great beyond, I groan inwardly. I've flopped back down to earth—in a damn hurry. It's the "Chop wood, carry water" express.

Later, I told a couple of people I knew would be understanding about the episode, then pretty much filed it away on a back shelf in my memory warehouse. Don't get me wrong: I sensed it was important— even very important— but I didn't really know what to do with it. Or perhaps I didn't want to know.

I'd had numerous experiences in non-ordinary states of consciousness before—I've even written about them—but nothing quite like this. It started with the nightmares, progressed through a lucid dream—the kind of dream in which you're aware that you're dreaming—and culminated in what I was certain was an out-of-body experience flavored with mystical bliss. It was all a bit too much.

In the aftermath of my discussion with Dave, however, I intuitively knew that I had to revisit that January night and take a fresh look at what had happened and why.

An Inconvenient Truth

Joseph Campbell quips somewhere that, if you really want to insult an artist, ask them what their work means. And if they really want to insult you back, they'll tell you.

Well, I won't insult you or try your patience by slogging through the many details of the conclusions I reached about that night, or try to convince you that my interpretations are the right, or only possible, ones. That would be pointless and tiresome. You can draw your own conclusions. I'll just mention a few points of interest.

It seemed fairly clear to me in retrospect that the first, "haunting" nightmare as well as the second, "spinning classroom" bad dream grew out of my negative feelings about my work. In the first dream, I'm in the house alone with my "dog," which represents instinct, or the guide and protector of souls. I'm afraid that the dog will come to harm—which, of course, it has. I'm in my study, where I write and do all my left-brain, intellectual work, when I encounter the fearsome phantom. At first, I'm paralyzed, unable to scream out—that is, to express myself and my emotions.

The second dream addresses my unhappiness with academic teaching—the symbolism of the dark, decaying atmosphere is pretty obvious. But it is also, I now realize, much more than that. The spinning, the stumbling around the classroom, is not just the negative merry-go-round effect. When the room morphs into the centrifuge, evoking the image of an astronaut in training, the positive aspect of the circle emerges. There is great energy stored and available there—in my frustrations, fears, and disappointments—with sufficient power to enable me to "take off." This, I think, was an effective prologue to what happened later, in the actual out-of-body flight.

Author and teacher Patricia Leva points out that children have instinctive ways of trying to alter the "normal" state of their awareness—spinning like wild dervishes until they almost pass out being chief among them. She reports that she remembers doing this herself when she was a very young girl.[2] And, of course, there are the actual whirling dervishes, the Muslim Sufi mystics who reach ecstatic states of consciousness through the practice of certain dizzying forms of dance.

What happened while I was awake, after the two "nightmares," was equally important and facilitated a further transmutation of that "negative" energy into the rocket fuel that propelled my third adventure. When I stopped trying to cap that energy—in other words, to talk myself out of it, suppress or avoid it—and embraced it lovingly, that's when everything shifted.

The loving affirmation of all that is—what Joseph Campbell calls the "joy-terror" of existence—is, of course, the true meaning, in his view, of "the end of the world." I'd read about this in his books, of course, but I didn't really grasp it until I experienced it for myself.

In my final experience on that night, I literally and figuratively turned the corner and took off, like a rocket, into the sky. That was ecstasy in both senses: the thrill of literally being out-of-body and the rapture of freedom beyond compare. The only ghost was the disembodied voice on the distant radio talking about the "museum," which is a place that houses things from the past. But that specter was left behind early on. Recognizing the incongruity of the presence of the ocean—the great sea of consciousness—allowed my intellectual left-brain ego to make the dream lucid. What followed was no dream, lucid or otherwise. Though, of course, I can't prove that.

In a way, however, I didn't have to—the experience itself reminded me of this. When I exclaimed excitedly, "It's *all* a dream!" I was making a statement that throws the whole problem into a new perspective. For myself, this can't mean that what we think of as "reality" is a mere illusion (as it may be to some), or even that physical reality is just an illusion (as it does seem to some), for the simple reason that I never denigrated or pooh-poohed dreams. "Oh, that was just a dream," someone might say to calm a child's anxieties. Or, worse yet, "You're dreaming," which some people say to others when they think their ideas or aspirations are "unrealistic." To me, however, dreams were always as, if not more, real and important than waking life. "Dream" was thus never a synonym for a put-down—at least, not in my book.

To say, then, that "it's all a dream," is to say that it's all equally real, powerful, vibrant, meaningful, and worthy of our attention. I could just as easily have said, "Nature is," or, "The circle is unbroken." In other words, my declaration was just a verbal form of the grand affirmation of love I made, on the feeling level, while I was lying in bed awake, tossing and turning, and grappling with my multiplying fears.

Heyoka Power

Finally, it struck me that my "accidental" pratfall was no real accident after all. The second, physical flight down the icy steps mimicked the first, nonphysical flight to the stars in a kind of mocking turnabout reminiscent of the Indian *heyokas*: the sacred clowns who do things backward. The key is to maintain a balance of energies, or, rather, a balance between alternate expressions of what is, ultimately, one and the same Energy—it's the circle (hoop) of nature, once again.

This is precisely how Black Elk explained the significance of the heyokas to John Neihardt. The old medicine man's comments are worth citing here at length:

> Only those who have had visions of the thunder beings of the west can act as heyokas. They have sacred power and they share some of this with all the people, but they do it through funny actions. When a vision comes from the thunder beings of the west, it comes with terror like a thunder storm; but when the storm of vision has passed, the world is greener and happier; for wherever the truth of vision comes upon the world, it is like a rain. The world, you see, is happier after the terror of the storm.
>
> But in the heyoka ceremony, everything is backwards, and it is planned that the people shall be made to feel jolly and happy first, so that it may be easier for the power to come to them. You have noticed that the truth comes into this world with two faces. One is sad with suffering, and the other laughs; but it is the same face, laughing or weeping.[3]

Falling down flat on my behind like some vaudeville comic was thus a none-too-gentle reminder to come down out of the clouds, not be too self-important, and bring my visionary experience back down to earth, where it must be put to good use.

Which is what we all must do.

Jung says somewhere that anyone can dream the most fantastic and important dreams. The key is to find the courage and will to express them, to anchor them in waking reality. We can do this by writing them down, painting pictures of their images, making sculptures, or doing something to bring the dream message and its energy into this world. Otherwise it's a waste and a kind of psychic self-inflation to think, "Well, I have these grand dreams and visions, so aren't I grand."

Of course, there will be all kinds of inner resistances to doing this work. You'll think to yourself, "Oh, this is just a waste of time and effort; that experience wasn't so important after all," or, "I'm not really worthy of this." But these inner obstacles must be overcome. They are demonic tricks of the small self—the culture-bound, "civilized" ego—to keep your deeper, natural, truer self at bay.

In Joseph Campbell's terms, the genuine hero is one who returns from the journey capable of offering boons to others, in hopes of inspiring his or her own degree and level of heroism. Those who are able to end their own world, then, must take it upon themselves to help others end theirs.

No Blame

Once a visionary insight has been formulated and expressed, openly and publicly, there is no going back. You either shoulder the responsibility for making it real or you shirk it. There is only one way in which there is a middle ground. As René Descartes observed, if you are tearing down your house in order to rebuild it from the foundation up, it makes sense to find temporary shelter—a lean-to or trailer will do in a pinch—while the brand-new structure is being constructed. This new thought structure is the equivalent of what Robert Monroe called a "different overview." A provisional worldview is like a sweater borrowed from a friend. It keeps you cozy and warm in the short term, but you don't intend to keep it.

The final lesson, of course, is: There is no final lesson, no different overview that is not, in the end, merely provisional. Better to have a movable tepee you can take with you than a grand castle made of stone that you cannot. But this is a difficult—for some, impossible—truth to grasp.

Thus, to borrow a familiar phrase from the *I Ching*, there is "no blame" if you end your old world gradually, in stages, while creating a whole new world to inhabit. Sometimes the destruction of the old mental habitation may be so sudden and catastrophic that there will be no opportunity for piecemeal solutions. This is what author and consciousness-explorer Bruce Moen aptly refers to as a "belief systems crash."[4] In other instances, however, it may be feasible to ease the transition in a somewhat more gentle fashion.

This logically leads to the next point: Just as ice cream comes in many flavors, so revolutions come in many different colors. There is Soviet Red and, of course, The Blues. They also sport different textures—like Czech Velvet and Hard Rock—and different sounds—like the transition from silent movies to yappy talkies. In other words, not everyone who seeks to follow the promptings of their true inner self, heed the call of nature, and listen to their heart, will necessarily experience a full-blown mystical ecstasy or a visionary insight into the ultimate nature of reality. There are many different ways to end your world. Some are more subtle than dramatic, but these are no less significant on that account.

It just so happened, for example, that, as I was working on this very book chapter, the latest issue of my college alumni magazine arrived in the mail. The article advertised on the front cover of the periodical read: "Act Two: Five Alums Who Ditched Their Careers and Followed Their Hearts."[5]

This fascinating piece featured a successful patent attorney who chucked his law practice in order to follow his lifelong passion: balloon sculpture; a financial services guru who opened up a café that features organic and fair-trade food, housed in a building designed with renewable resources, energy-efficient products, and recycled materials; a forty-five-year-old woman who gave up a lucrative career in the music industry in order to make ceramics; and an M.B.A. who spent twenty-five years developing and marketing medical devices, but decided, at the age of sixty, to become a minister instead.

Each of these intrepid individuals is no less a heroic "world-ender" than Jane Roberts, Robert Monroe, or Tony Cicoria. By following their dreams and allowing the natural faces of their true inner selves to shatter their carefully contrived, artfully constructed, culturally sanctioned masks, they are removing the underpinnings—one pin at a time, of course—of a dysfunctional system that thrives on fear, guilt, deception, manipulation, exploitation, boredom, negativity, thoughtlessness, literalism, dogmatism, and the overall constriction of consciousness.

Any chink made in the armor is a major victory, heralding the day when the light will shine through all of the disparaging mythic memorabilia that keeps us mentally preoccupied and satisfied captives in what Plato called the darkness of the cave of ignorance. On the day when we can all laugh at the Myth of the Great Ending, we will finally see it revealed for what it truly is: a seriocomic road sign pointing inward to our own deepest being, and outward to its own inevitable and felicitous dissolution.

TRUST THE PROCESS

And so, Cathy, that's what I would have said to you, that day in the stairwell, in answer to your question about the End of the World. It's a myth. And that means it's true and powerful, but also false and weak. It depends on how you look at it. The world may end, but only if you make it happen

You can choose to end your world, but the world won't be ended for you. Christ will not be returning triumphant and militant to make a new heaven and earth; human consciousness won't magically be transformed; alien spacecraft won't be landing on the White House lawn. Some individuals may be disappointed by this, while others may breathe a genuine sigh of relief. Still others, arms folded self-righteously, may smugly say, "I told you so."

But they are all missing the main point: the Myth of the Great Ending is not really about the future; it is a distorted echo of the distant past, and the catastrophic end of our once harmonious relationship to nature. But it also serves as a coded reminder of the true magic that is still available in the present moment when we choose to align ourselves with nature and with our own true, deepest nature. As for the future—well, you must make it for yourself. It's up to you. Of course, you can always give away your authority, or passively wait on the sidelines for a Day of Judgment or Terminal Doom. But that, too, is your choice.

I apologize for going on at such length, Cathy, and for repeating myself from time to time. I always reassure myself—just so I feel better, mind you—that repetition never hurts the learning process. I'm sorry for telling you far more about history and old, outdated philosophical theories than you probably ever wanted to hear. Of course, I am a college professor, after all—*mea culpa*.

But, when you boil it all down, it comes to this: Do whatever it is that you—the *real* you—truly want to do. Don't be afraid of the future. And whatever you do, don't take the Myth of the Great Ending at face value. In fact, you'd be better off ignoring it altogether. Go out and buy yourself a notebook. Then write down your nightly dreams. In my view, that would be time and money well spent.

Now, I grant you that all this may seem like simple advice—maybe too simple. However, I remind you that, in order to discover who and what you really are, and what it is that you actually desire, you must ask yourself some hard and uncomfortable questions. They may be especially uncomfortable for people whom you are used to trying to please and impress—friends, family, teachers, bosses, lovers, and just about everybody else who forms a judgment of you.

Don't be afraid of this, either. For who you really are and what you really want are the very things that nature has given you as her finest gifts. There's great beauty in that, and truth. And some ugliness and lies, too—just to round things out. That's just how nature is. It's how she works. Everything tries to be round. Go with it.

Never, ever worry about leaving home—because you're never far from Home. All points along the circle of life—all times and all places—are equidistant from the center. And as Black Elk said, "anywhere is the center of the world."

Years ago, when I was in a difficult place myself, a friend offered me some well-meaning advice: "Trust the process," she said gently.

At first, I was miffed. I thought my friend was just trying to soothe me with some banal catchphrase she'd learned to say in such situations. It took me a good long while—years, in fact—to realize just how wrong I was. For what she told me then was profound, and perhaps the wisest thing that anyone can ever say.

Trust the process.

ACKNOWLEDGMENTS

In the words of the old Sioux holy man, Black Elk, "no good thing can be done by any man alone."[1] The task of creating a book—one both joyous and onerous—provides a striking and powerful illustration of this great truth.

First, I want to thank my publisher, Jan Johnson, for taking on the project and having great faith in it. I am also grateful to my editor, Gary Leon Hill, for his enthusiastic support and suggestions for the manuscript. One of the delights of the journey is to encounter kindred spirits along the way. Gary is certainly such a one.

Thanks also to Susie Pitzen, Lisa Trudeau, and everyone at Red Wheel Weiser/Hampton Roads who had a hand in helping to shape and produce the book.

My good friend Sue Ray of Moment Point Press first encouraged me (five years ago) to write on the Myth of the Great Ending. She read and commented on earlier drafts, and helped me to find my voice. Her assistance was indispensable. Thank you, Sue.

Kudos to my resourceful web master, Palyne Gaenir (an intrepid explorer of consciousness in her own right), whose generosity and patience are deeply appreciated.

My wife, Cynthia, helped me to find the time to write. Meanwhile, our golden retriever, Wakanda, wisely made sure that I enjoyed timely breaks for much needed strolls in the park. Without their help, this project would never have been completed.

The Dedication acknowledges a debt both personal and collective, aspects of which are addressed in the pages of this book, particularly in the later chapters. What is owed to these three intrepid explorers of the inner space of human consciousness—in other words, the abyssal depths of the soul—is immense indeed.

Robert Monroe and Jane Roberts—along with her husband, Rob Butts, the cocreator of the Seth material—were individuals of enormous personal integrity who ventured into the far reaches of the human psyche. Armed only with insatiable curiosity, sharp intellects, and a blanket disdain for all forms of dogma and mystification, religious or scientific, they sought to answer their own burning personal questions and expand the range of human possibilities.

They were thus true heroes, in Joseph Campbell's specific sense of the term. "A hero ventures forth from the world of common day into a region of supernatural wonder," he wrote in *The Hero with a Thousand Faces*. "Fabulous forces are there encountered and a decisive victory is won: the hero comes back from this mysterious adventure with the power to bestow boons on his fellow man."[2]

Heeding the call of a greater destiny, Monroe and Roberts abandoned the comfortable, but false, security of their smaller selves to undertake perilous voyages beyond the pale of consensus reality. Having endured numerous trials and received illuminating revelations, they returned from their metaphysical adventures with not only a new form of awareness and altered sense of self, but also with great gifts of information, knowledge, and wisdom to bestow. The body of work they left behind will someday be recognized for what it most certainly is: the most important record of human endeavor in and reflections on the nature of consciousness yet produced.

While I did not have the good fortune to meet Monroe or know him personally, I have derived great benefit from his three books, the audio technology he developed for exploring consciousness and inducing expanded states of awareness—"Hemi-Sync"—and the educational programs offered at the institution he founded in Faber, Virginia. I have written elsewhere about my experiences at these programs and their impact on my thought and life.[3]

That impact includes meeting many friends whose support and conversation I have been privileged to enjoy. I am especially grateful to both Kearns Kelly and Gina Galate. I also want to thank fellow Hampton Roads author (and Institute alum) Bruce Moen, who has provided inspiration, encouragement, and advice, both through his excellent books and through personal communication over the years.

In 2006, I had the honor of being invited to give the keynote address to the Monroe Institute's Professional Division seminar.[4] This gave me the opportunity to meet with many of the physicians, therapists, psychologists, teachers, and other professionals from all over the world who employ Monroe's Hemi-Sync audio technology in their respective practices and fields. To all of them, and to my many friends at and around the Institute, I am especially grateful. Shirley Bliley, Dr. Darlene ("Dar") Miller, Frank DeMarco, Nancy ("Scooter") McMoneagle, Karen Malik, Lee Stone, Carol Sabick, and Franceen King all deserve special mention and appreciation, as does the late Laurie Monroe, Robert's daughter and his eventual successor as head of the institute.

As for Jane Roberts and Rob Butts, I never met them in person. I discovered the Seth material in the late 1970s during a period in which I was grappling with my own inner experiences. I dropped them a line from time to time over the years, right up until some months before Rob's death. To say that I appreciated their support is putting it mildly. Many years ago, Jane encouraged me to write and use my creative abilities. Coming, as it did, from an established author whose work I greatly valued and respected, that advice was pure gold.

For insights into Jane Roberts's life and work, I am indebted to Sue Watkins's moving personal memoir of her friend and mentor, *Speaking of Jane Roberts*. Mary Dillman, who has devoted much time—along with her boundless energy and enthusiasm—to the enormous task of organizing and cataloguing the Jane Roberts archive at Yale University's Sterling Library, provided crucial research assistance.

Ronald ("Russ") Russell's comprehensive recent biography, *The Journey of Robert Monroe*, was instrumental in helping me to discern the heroic dimensions of Monroe's life career. And since I count both Russ Russell and Sue Watkins among my true friends and fellows in the life of spirit, I hereby offer each of them a full disclaimer of responsibility. Any mistakes or misstatements are all mine.

I am also indebted to an earlier biography of Monroe, *Catapult*, by the late journalist Bayard Stockton. In addition, over the past nine years, I've met a number of Monroe's friends or associates. Our personal conversations sometimes naturally touched upon topics related to the man or his work. I learned much from these discussions. Unfortunately, it is not always easy to disentangle what I recollect from these personal encounters from what I've read in written sources. Once again, I apologize to all concerned for any inadvertent confusions, errors, omissions, or distortions of fact. My interpretations, of course, are my own.

Speaking of heroes and myths, the name of the late, great mythologist Joseph Campbell figures prominently in these pages. And therein lies a tale.

In the mid-1980s, I was at Oxford University on an overseas fellowship doing research for my dissertation. My writing process, however, was severely stuck. If I hadn't accidentally stumbled across the four volumes of Campbell's *Masks of God* series while browsing through the aisles of the cavernous Blackwell's bookstore one rainy afternoon, I might well never have finished the work on my Ph.D.

At the time, blinkered by the narrow confines of academic specialization, I had no idea who Campbell was. I was taught that "real" philosophers didn't read "mere" mythologists—especially ones influenced by Carl Jung. I was ignorant of *The Hero with a Thousand Faces*. But Campbell's unique perspective on religion enabled me to rethink my own, and thereby to resume my research and writing with renewed confidence. Eventually I completed my dissertation.

Several years later—after Campbell's death and the posthumous celebrity brought about by the *Power of Myth* public television interviews with Bill Moyers—I learned more about his life and work. It struck me as no small irony that, following the completion of his own overseas research fellowship, he returned from his mind-expanding trip to Europe only to abandon work on his own doctoral thesis, which he suddenly found too narrow and confining—too academic, in other words. Yet it was his own subsequent series of investigations, arising out of the ashes of that bold rejection, that helped me to complete the very task he had happily abandoned.

There was another irony yet to be discovered. A conversation with a family friend of Campbell's revealed an interesting coincidence. It turned out that, if I had followed an acquaintance's well-meaning advice and attended some lectures being given at the Jung Institute (located just outside of Chicago, where I was a graduate student at the time) in the early 1980s, I might well have met Joseph Campbell in the flesh, several years before I serendipitously encountered his words in print. And who knows what effect that meeting might have had on my quest?

More than a decade ago, I wrote a lengthy essay on Campbell that was later published in the *Journal of the American Academy of Religion*.[5] I viewed that article as a mere down-payment on the large debt I owe to him. My running conversation with Campbell and his ideas about the Myth of the Great

Ending that are woven throughout the pages of this book I regard as but a further installment on that considerable debt.

Several years back, another friend and mentor, Hal Zina Bennett, introduced me to the wisdom of an old Cherokee prayer to the Great Spirit. It goes like this:

> Help me always to speak the truth quietly,
>
> To listen with an open mind when others speak,
>
> And to remember the peace that may be found in silence.

By chance, I came across a framed copy of that Indian prayer. It sits on a shelf directly above the computer desk in my study where I do most of my writing. It serves to remind me of simple, but rock-solid, verities. Thank you, Hal.

One of these truths is that endings are an integral element of the order of things: the constant ebb and flow of life. Often, they are more prosaic than mythical. With this book, I have come to the end of a long and winding trail of thought. So I happily pass the talking-stick to others, who will have their own say. I've said my piece as best I can. Now I look forward to the peace that may be found in silence.

This does not mean quitting the world or ignoring our present challenges. There was no world-disdain among the Indians. They had an intimate and loving conversation with nature—with "all their relations." But they recognized that, in every conversation, there must be pauses to listen. "Silence meant to the Lakota," said Chief Luther Standing Bear, "what it meant to Disraeli when he said, 'Silence is the mother of truth.'"[6] Those who always speak and never listen know no truth.

Coming full circle, I return to Hermann Hesse, who wrote: "We can understand one another, but each of us is able to interpret himself to himself alone."[7]

The paradoxical truth is that both Hesse and Black Elk are right: We are One; all of us, together, after all. Yet, at the same time, we are also many, apart; each of us a unique individual, walking down our own, solitary paths, in our own, special way.

May it ever be so!

Chapter One

(1.) See Edgar Allen Beem, "Apocalypse Then," *Down East* (October 2007), *www.downeast.com.*

(2.) St. Augustine, *Retr.* i. 13, quoted in E. E. Evans-Pritchard, *Theories of Primitive Religion* (Oxford: Clarendon Press, 1965), 3.

(3.) R. G. Collingwood, *Speculum Mentis* (Oxford: Clarendon Press, 1924), 144.

(4.) Terence McKenna, *The Archaic Revival* (San Francisco: HarperSanFrancisco, 1991), 20.

(5.) Quoted in Mark Stevenson, "2012 Isn't the End of the World, Mayans Insist," *Associated Press* (October 11, 2009), *http://abcnews.go.com.*

(6.) Charles Dickens, *A Christmas Carol* (New York: Pocket, 1963), 196.

(7.) St. Augustine, *Confessions*, trans. R. S. Pine-Coffin (Baltimore, MD: Penguin, 1961), 56.

(8.) C. G. Jung, *The Undiscovered Self*, trans. R. F. C. Hull (New York: Signet, 2006), 3. In his comments here about prophecy and apocalyptic visions, Jung's tone is emphatically scholarly and objective. However, his true relationship to such prognostications—and the fundamental questions regarding the possible linkage between the private precognitive visions of individuals and future public mass events—was of a deeply personal and intimate nature. In his posthumously published reminiscences, *Memories, Dreams, Reflections* (ed. Aniela Jaffe, trans. R. and C. Winston, rev. ed. [New York: Vintage, 1965], 175–76), Jung describes a series of disturbing visions of catastrophe he had in the autumn of 1913—including a horrifying vision of flowing rivers of blood covering the Swiss countryside—that, in retrospect, he interpreted as predictive of the coming conflagration of World War I. Also, in an interview included in a film on Jung's work and life, *Matter of Heart* (videocassette, directed by Mark Whitney [New York: Kino Video,

1985]), Jung's protégé, the late Marie-Louise Von Franz revealed that, on his deathbed in 1961, Jung experienced a vision of a coming global catastrophe that suggested to him that human beings—who would be responsible for this catastrophe—might have only another fifty years left on the clock. But in the closing pages of *The Undiscovered Self*—published only three years prior to his death—Jung expressed his firm belief that humanity would undergo a positive spiritual transformation over the next several hundred years. This far more optimistic view of the future accords with what he told psychiatrist Max Zeller in 1949 about the coming into being of a new, post-Christian religion, a historical process that would take about 600 years to complete. When Zeller asked Jung how he knew this, Jung replied that this message was contained in the dreams of his patients, as well as in his own dreams. See Meredith Sabini and Margaret Laurel Allen, "Christ Comes Down from the Cross: The Evolution of an Archetype," *Chrysalis* 9:1 (Spring 1994), 21–32.

(9.) Russell Shorto, "How Christian Were the Founders?" *The New York Times Magazine* (February 14, 2010), www.nytimes.com.

(10.) "Religious Right Activist Calls for Execution of Homosexuals," *Church and State* 63:2 (February 2010), 21.

(11.) David Bohm, *Wholeness and the Implicate Order* (London: Routledge and Kegan Paul, 1980), 1.

(12.) Bohm, *Wholeness and the Implicate Order*, 1.

(13.) Uki Goni, "Tests on Skull Fragment Cast Doubt on Hitler Suicide Story," *The Sunday Observer* (September 27, 2009), www.guardian.co.uk.

(14.) Joseph Campbell, *The Hero's Journey: Joseph Campbell on his Life and Work*, ed. P. Cousineau (San Francisco: Harper & Row, 1990), 134–36. This was one of the guiding themes of all of Campbell's work in mythology. Perhaps the most mature and passionate statement of it may be found in *The Inner Reaches of Outer Space: Myth as Metaphor and as Religion* (New York: Alfred Van Der Marck, 1985).

(15.) This (and all subsequent quotations from the Bible cited in the text) is taken from *The New Oxford Annotated Bible with the Apocrypha, Revised Standard Version*, ed. H. G. May and B. M. Metzger (New York: Oxford University Press, 1973).

(16.) R. G. Collingwood, *The New Leviathan* (New York: Thomas Y. Crowell, 1942), 73.

Chapter Two

(1.) See Joseph Campbell, *The Masks of God: Primitive Mythology* (New York: Penguin, 1969), 342; and Michael Grosso, *Soulmaking: Uncommon Paths to Self-Understanding* (Charlottesville, VA: Hampton Roads, 1997), 35.

(2.) *Annie Hall*, videocassette, directed by Woody Allen (Culver City, CA: MGM/UA Home Video, 1977).

(3.) Bertrand Russell, "A Free Man's Worship," in *The Basic Writings of Bertrand Russell*, ed. R. E. Egner and L. E. Denonn (New York: Simon & Schuster, 1961), 61.

(4.) Quoted in Frank Waters, *Pumpkin Seed Point: Being Within the Hopi* (Athens, OH: Ohio University Press, 1969), 69.

(5.) John Neihardt, *Black Elk Speaks: Being the Life Story of a Holy Man of the Oglala Sioux* (New York: Washington Square Press, 1972), 10.

(6.) In Kent Nerburn, ed., *The Wisdom of the Native Americans* (Novato, CA: New World Library, 1999), 48.

(7.) Nerburn, *Wisdom of the Native Americans*, intro., xi. Nerburn's other books on Native culture include: *Neither Wolf Nor Dog: On Forgotten Roads with an Indian Elder* (Novato, CA: New World Library, 1994), *Chief Joseph and the Flight of the Nez Perce: The Untold Story of an American Tragedy* (San Francisco: HarperSanFrancisco, 2005), and *The Wolf at Twilight: An Indian Elder's Journey through a Land of Ghosts and Shadows* (Novato, CA: New World Library, 2009). All are indispensable guides to an outsider's understanding of the First People's ways.

(8.) Nerburn, *Wisdom of the Native Americans*, intro., xiii. Ohiyesa's book was originally published in 1911. The version used here is the one found in Nerburn's collection. Another edition of the book was published by the University of Nebraska Press, but I prefer the language in Nerburn's version, which is slightly different.

(9.) Ohiyesa (Charles Alexander Eastman), *The Soul of an Indian and other writings*, in Nerburn, *Wisdom of the Native Americans*, 121–122.

(10.) Richard Erdoes and Alfonso Ortiz, eds., *American Indian Myths and Legends* (New York: Pantheon, 1984), 467.

(11.) Jeffrey McDonald, "Does Maya Calendar Predict 2012 Apocalypse?" *USA Today* (March 27, 2007) *www.usatoday.com*.

(12.) Neihardt, *Black Elk Speaks*, 164–165.

(13.) Neihardt, *Black Elk Speaks*, 165.

(14.) Julien Offray de la Mettrie, *Man: a Machine*, trans. G. C. Bussey and M. Carret (LaSalle, IL: Open Court, 1912), 92.

(15.) Stanislav Grof, with Hal Zina Bennett, *The Holotropic Mind: The Three Levels of Consciousness and How They Shape Our Lives* (San Francisco: HarperSanFrancisco 1992), 4. I am indebted, throughout this section, to Grof's sketch of the materialistic standpoint.

(16.) Herbert Butterfield, in the preface to *The Whig Interpretation of History* (London, 1931), quoted in David Hackett Fischer, *Historians' Fallacies: Toward a Logic of Historical Thought* (New York: Harper and Row, 1970), 139.

(17.) *Groundhog Day*, videocassette, directed by Harold Ramis (Culver City, CA: Columbia/Tristar, 1994).

(18.) C. G. Jung, *Modern Man in Search of a Soul*, trans. W. S. Dell and C. F. Baynes (New York: Harcourt Brace Jovanovich, 1933), 103.

Chapter Three

(1.) W. B. Yeats, *Selected Poems and Three Plays of William Butler Yeats*, 3rd ed., ed. M. L. Rosenthal (New York: Collier Macmillan, 1962), 89.

(2.) For an earlier version of the arguments found in this chapter, see my essay, "Parapsychology Without Religion: 'Breaking the Circle' or Circling the Wagons?" *The Journal of the American Society for Psychical Research* 93:3 (July 1999), 259–279.

(3.) Ken Wilber, "Physics, Mysticism, and the New Holographic Paradigm: A Critical Appraisal," chapter in Wilber, ed., *The Holographic Paradigm and Other Paradoxes: Exploring the Leading Edge of Science* (Boston: Shambhala, 1985), 162.

(4.) Joseph Campbell, *The Masks of God: Oriental Mythology* (New York: Penguin, 1976), 36.

(5.) Joseph Campbell, *The Masks of God: Creative Mythology* (New York: Penguin, 1976), 420–421.

(6.) Carl B. Becker, *Breaking the Circle: Death and the Afterlife in Buddhism* (Carbondale, IL: Southern Illinois University Press, 1993), 2.

(7.) Campbell, *The Masks of God: Creative Mythology*, 421.

(8.) Joseph Campbell, *The Masks of God: Occidental Mythology* (New York:

Penguin, 1970), 121. See also Campbell, *The Masks of God: Creative Mythology*, 420.

(9.) Mircea Eliade, *Shamanism: Archaic Techniques of Ecstasy*, trans. W. R. Trask (Princeton: Princeton University Press, 1972), 466ff.

(10.) G. W. F. Hegel, *The Philosophy of Right*, trans. T. M. Knox (Oxford: Oxford University Press, 1975), 13.

(11.) J. W. von Goethe, *Faust*, trans. Bayard Taylor, I. iv. 509-14, quoted in T. M. Knox's translator's notes to Hegel's *Philosophy of Right*, 304.

(12.) Hegel, *Philosophy of Right*, 13.

(13.) Campbell, *The Masks of God: Occidental Mythology*, 192.

(14.) "Zoroaster~Zarathustra," *http://personalpages.tds.net*.

(15.) In chapter 23 (par. 1459a 17-21) of the *Poetics*, Aristotle writes: "As for the poetry which merely narrates, or imitates by means of versified language (without action), it is evident that it has several points in common with tragedy. . . . The construction of its stories should clearly be like that in a drama; they should be based on a single action, one that is a complete whole in itself, with a beginning, middle, and end, so as to enable the work to produce its own proper pleasure with all the organic unity of a living creature" Richard McKeon, ed., *The Basic Works of Aristotle* (New York: Random House, 1941), 1480.

(16.) John Herman Randall Jr., *Aristotle* (New York: Columbia University Press, 1960), 290.

(17.) Sir David Ross, *Aristotle*, 5th ed. (London: Methuen & Co., 1977), 281.

(18.) Campbell, *The Masks of God: Occidental Mythology*, 260.

(19.) Daniel Quinn, *Ishmael* (New York: Bantam, 1992), 119.

(20.) A brilliant, visionary thinker, Quinn went on to develop his highly original and provocative view of human history and his spirited defense of animism in subsequent works, fiction and nonfiction alike, including: *Beyond Civilization: Humanity's Next Great Adventure* (New York: Three Rivers Press, 1999); *My Ishmael* (New York: Bantam, 1997); and *The Story of B* (New York: Bantam, 1996). In his autobiographical work, *Providence: The Story of a Fifty-Year Vision Quest* (New York: Bantam, 1995), he notes that, among the scholars of our civilizations, animism with its manifold array of spirit powers, tolerance of different forms of worship, and lack of defined creeds "is judged not to count as a religion at all, is judged to be merely a pre-religion, a crude evolutionary stage that people had to pass through in order to arrive at the enlightened and advanced religions [of civilization] that evoke such murderous fervor among [their adherents]" (154). Compare this biting witticism with the words of Chief Joseph of the Nez Perce, who long ago declared: "We do not want churches because they will teach us to quarrel about God, as the Catholics and Protestants do. We do not want to learn that." See Nerburn, *The Wisdom of the Native Americans*, 35.

(21.) Betty Bethards, *The Dream Book: Symbols for Self-Understanding* (Petaluma, CA: New Century, 2006), 43–44.

(22.) John Neihardt, *Black Elk Speaks: Being the Life Story of a Holy Man of the Oglala Sioux* (New York: Washington Square Press, 1972), 205.

(23.) Brad Steiger, *Revelation: The Divine Fire* (New Brunswick, NJ: Inner Light, 1988), 125.

Chapter Four

(1.) On the natural depravity and powerlessness of human will (along with the corruption of human desire and reason), see, for example, Luther's "Preface to St. Paul's Epistle to the Romans" (1522), and also his earlier essay, "The Freedom of a Christian" (1520), in which he flatly declares: "Although the commandments teach things that are good, the things taught are not done as soon as they are taught, for the commandments show us what we ought to do but do not give us the power to do it. They are intended to teach man to know himself, that through them he may recognize his inability to do good and may despair of his own ability" See Martin Luther, *Selections From His Writings*, ed. J. Dillenberger (Garden City, NY: Anchor Doubleday, 1961), 57. In other words, the Ten Commandments are strictly a pedagogical device, a teaching tool designed to make us realize how utterly evil and worthless we are, and will remain, in the absence of divine grace. But how does Luther know this? When he opines that, "They are intended to teach man to know himself," the intentions of which he is speaking here are, of course, none other than God's. How can Luther read God's mind? Is this not an audacious claim for one with a corrupt reason, desire, and will, completely spoiled by Original Sin? Would we trust the operations of a computer we knew to be infected with a virus? Luther's answer is that the Holy Spirit himself guides the mind of the saved to a true understanding of scripture. But how can we be sure that it is the Holy Spirit guiding our interpretation and not the Devil whispering in our ear? That calls for a judgment—a human intellectual judgment. If we are thoroughly corrupt, all judgment is rendered corrupt and untrustworthy—Luther's, too. The total depravity of nature means that we can never know anything, including that nature is depraved. It is thus a self-refuting—not to mention, a deeply insidious—claim.

(2.) René Descartes, Discourse, II: 19, in *Discourse on Method and Meditations on First Philosophy*, 2nd ed., trans. D. A. Cress (Indianapolis, IN: Hackett, 1980), 10.

(3.) I say "supposedly" because there is disagreement over the interpretation of Bacon's language in his *Meditations* (1597). For a defense of Bacon against the charge that he sought to do violence against Mother Nature by "torturing" the secrets out of her, see, e.g., Peter Pesic, "Wrestling with Proteus: Francis Bacon and the 'Torture' of Nature," *Isis*, 90:1 (March 1999), 81–94. Regardless of the outcome of this debate, there is no doubt that the ideal of the experimental method as an objective, value-free inquiry designed not simply to gain theoretical understanding, but to enhance human power, and Bacon's concomitant coupling of truth with utility, or scientific knowledge with technological manipulation, is grandly, if not grandiosely, optimistic. From a religious (that is, biblical) standpoint, this could be read—quite apart from any belief in the impotency of human agency owing to the taint of Original Sin—as an attempt to fulfill the commandment to subjugate nature that God issued to Adam and Eve in Genesis 1, prior to the disastrous "Fall" that Christians believe was recorded in Genesis 2: "Be fruitful and multiply and fill the earth and subdue it; and have dominion over the fish of the sea and over the birds of the air and over every living thing that moves upon the earth" (Gen. 1:28). But whether the scientific project is read as an arrogant repudiation of human sinfulness and the necessity of salvation (as many conservative Christians believe to this day), or as a faithful, humble adherence to prelapsarian divine injunctions, it makes little difference. The aim of technology, as an extension of the agriculturalist project begun 10,000 years ago, is to subdue, manage, and control nature without regard to "emotional attachments" or other "subjective" factors that can't be quantified or measured. The clinical attitude may not, in itself, express violence, but it does violence to relationships that are non-instrumental in character, and to sensibilities that find in nature the vital expressions of consciousness, intelligence, knowledge, and even personality. "You ask me to plow the ground. Shall I take a knife and tear my mother's bosom?" said Wovoka. "You ask me to dig for stones! Shall I dig under her skin for her bones? . . . You ask me to cut grass and make hay and sell it, and be rich like white men, but how dare I cut my mother's hair?" (In Kent Nerburn, ed., *The Wisdom of the Native Americans* (Novato, CA: New World Library, 1999), 6).

(4.) Ronald Russell, *The Journey of Robert Monroe: From Out-of-Body Explorer to Consciousness Pioneer* (Charlottesville, VA: Hampton Roads, 2007), 339.

(5.) Michael Specter, "A Life of Its Own: Where Will Synthetic Biology Lead Us?" *The New Yorker* (September 28, 2009), 56.

(6.) Specter, "A Life of Its Own," 56.

(7.) Specter, "A Life of Its Own," 58.

(8.) *Dr. No*, videocassette, directed by Terence Young (Culver City, CA: MGM/UA, 1963).

(9.) See Jerome Groopman, "Eyes Wide Open: Can Science Make Regular Sleep Unnecessary?" *The New Yorker* (December 3, 2001), 52–57.

(10.) See chapter 9 of the present work.

(11.) Jane Roberts, *Psychic Politics: An Aspect Psychology Book* (Englewood Cliffs, NJ: Prentice-Hall, 1979), 266.

(12.) Jack Weatherford, *Indian Givers: How the Indians of the Americas Transformed the World* (New York: Fawcett Columbine, 1988), 120.

(13.) Weatherford, *Indian Givers*, 121.

(14.) Hermann Hesse, *Demian: The Story of Emil Sinclair's Youth*. Trans. M. Roloff and M. Lebeck. (New York: Bantam, 1970), 87.

(15.) Hesse, *Demian*, 88.

(16.) Edward Hoffman, *Visions of Innocence: Spiritual and Inspirational Experiences of Childhood* (Boston: Shambhala, 1992), 55.

(17.) Marie-Louise von Franz, *On Dreams and Death: A Jungian Interpretation*, trans. E. X. Kennedy and V. Brooks (Boston: Shambhala, 1987), intro., viii.

(18.) Ingo Swann, *Your Nostradamus Factor: Accessing Your Innate Ability to See Into the Future* (New York: Fireside/Simon and Schuster, 1993), 26.

(19.) Peter Fenwick and Elizabeth Fenwick, *The Hidden Door: Understanding and Controlling Dreams* (New York: Berkley, 1999), 168–169.

(20.) Swann, *Your Nostradamus Factor,* 25.

(21.) Bohm, *Wholeness and the Implicate Order,* 211.

(22.) Fred Alan Wolf, *Mind Into Matter: A New Alchemy of Science and Spirit* (Portsmouth, NH: Moment Point Press, 2001).

Chapter Five

(1.) John Neihardt, *Black Elk Speaks: Being the Life Story of a Holy Man of the Oglala Sioux* (New York: Washington Square Press, 1972), 166.

(2.) J. Allen Boone, *Kinship with All Life* (San Francisco: HarperSanFrancisco, 1976), 62.

(3.) David Bohm, *Thought as a System* (New York: Routledge, 1992), 18–19.

(4.) Bohm, *Thought as a System,* 23.

(5.) *Joseph Campbell and the Power of Myth with Bill Moyers, Part 6 of 6: The Masks of Eternity,* first broadcast June 27, 1988 by PBS, prod. Catherine Tatge, transcript (New York: Journal Graphics, 1988), 4.

(6.) C. G. Jung, "Foreword to the *I Ching,*" chapter in *Psychology and the East: From the Collected Works of C.G. Jung,* Vols. 10, 11, 13 and 18, Bollingen Series XX, trans. R. F. C. Hull (Princeton: Princeton University Press, 1978), 196. Of special note is that Hull, the English translator of Jung's collected works, acknowledges in a footnote his indebtedness to Cary F. Baynes, the original translator of the Foreword that Jung wrote (in 1949) especially for the English version of Richard Wilhelm's translation of the *I Ching,* which was originally published in 1950. Apart from expressing his gratitude, Hull says that he followed Baynes's translation scrupulously, with the exception of "a few minor changes." Yet Hull's alteration is far from superficial and goes to the very heart of the matter under discussion. In Hull's translation, the key statement of Jung's reads: "This is the classical etymology. The derivation of *religio* from *religare,* 'reconnect,' 'link back,' originated with the Church Fathers" (Bollingen Series XX, 196). But compare this with the earlier rendering by Baynes: "This is the classical etymology. The derivation of *religio* from *religare,* 'bind to,' originated with the Church Fathers" (C. G. Jung, Foreword to the *I Ching or Book of Changes,* trans. R. Wilhelm and C. F. Baynes [London: Routledge & Kegan Paul, 1985), xviii]. "Bind to" is clearly stronger than "reconnect" or "link back" in its emphasis on the contrast between yielding to, or harmonizing with, nature on the one hand, versus being bound or obliged to obey divine laws that are regarded as contrary to a nature that is fallen, on the other. The former is much closer to Jung's intended meaning, as well as to the poet Robert Graves's strikingly similar etymological derivation (see below).

(7.) Robert Graves, *The White Goddess: A Historical Grammar of Poetic Myth*, 2nd ed. (New York: Farrar, Straus and Giroux, 1948), 477–478.

(8.) In Kent Nerburn, ed., *The Wisdom of the Native Americans* (Novato, CA: New World Library, 1999), 15.

(9.) See Vine Deloria, Jr., *The World We Used to Live In: Remembering the Powers of the Medicine Men* (Golden, CO: Fulcrum, 2006).

(10.) In his essay, "Tribal Religious Realities" (*Spirit and Reason: The Vine Deloria, Jr. Reader*, ed. B. Deloria, K. Foehner, and S. Scinta [Golden, CO: Fulcrum, 1999]), Deloria writes: "The great bond of experience [the Indians had] with nature, no matter how vaguely defined, incorporates the emotional and intuitive dimension of our lives much better than do the precise creeds, doctrines, and dogmas of the great world religions" (360).

(11.) Chang Chung-yuan, *Creativity and Taoism: A Study of Chinese Philosophy, Art, and Poetry* (New York: Harper & Row, 1963), 12.

(12.) Chuang Tzu, *Inner Chapters*, in Jacob Needleman and David Appelbaum, eds., *Real Philosophy: An Anthology of the Universal Search for Meaning* (New York: Penguin/Arkana, 1990), 180.

(13.) Quoted in Chang, *Creativity and Taoism*, 5.

(14.) In Nerburn, *The Wisdom of the Native Americans*, 5.

(15.) Paul Starr, *The Social Transformation of American Medicine* (New York: Basic Books, 1982). Starr notes that William James's resistance to the move toward the professionalization of medicine was linked to his critique of the mechanistic model of human beings; and this was expressed in his public opposition to the newly proposed practice of licensing physicians. Appearing before the Massachusetts legislature in 1898, James argued that, "licensing would interfere with the freedom of research in medicine. James had personally tried an assortment of healers and was pursuing his own research into psychic cures. At a time when Christian Science was a great subject of controversy, he defended the right of 'mind curers' to test out their new modes of therapy" (Starr, 105). Of course, the licensing measure passed in spite of such opposition, and the professionalization of medicine along allopathic lines proceeded apace. Though James's prediction about the stifling of research into alternative modes of treatment would hold true for the most part over the next century, by the 1980s, the sudden explosion of interest in mind-body medicine, including the burgeoning field of psycho-neuroimmunology, which studies the relationship between cognitive and emotional states on the one hand and the body's immune and nervous systems on the other, began to alter the medical landscape—at least somewhat. But James got there first, ahead of them all.

(16.) William James, *The Varieties of Religious Experience: A Study in Human Nature* (New York: Modern Library, 1936), preface, xv. For his forceful critique of the narrow and illegitimate reductionism inherent in what he dubbed "medical materialism," see the chapter on "Religion and Neurology," 3–26.

(17.) Many of James's essays on "psychical research," as the field of parapsychology used to be known, may be found collected in G. Murphy and R. Ballou, eds., *William James on Psychical Research* (New York: Viking, 1969).

(18.) James, *The Varieties of Religious Experience*, 488.

(19.) James, *The Varieties of Religious Experience*, 488.

(20.) James, *The Varieties of Religious Experience*, 490.

(21.) Bohm, *Wholeness and the Implicate Order*, 211.

(22.) David Bohm and F. David Peat, *Science, Order and Creativity* (New York: Bantam, 1987), 148–149.

(23.) In "The Physicist and the Mystic—Is A Dialogue Between Them Possible? A Conversation with David Bohm Conducted by René Weber, Edited by Emily Sellon," chapter in Ken Wilber, ed., *The Holographic Paradigm and Other Paradoxes: Exploring the Leading Edge of Science* (Boston: Shambhala, 1985), 192.

(24.) Bohm, *Wholeness and the Implicate Order*, 205.

(25.) Bohm and Weber, in Ken Wilber's *The Holographic Paradigm and Other Paradoxes*, 193.

(26.) Bohm, *Wholeness and the Implicate Order*, 211.

(27.) Itzhak Bentov, *Stalking the Wild Pendulum: On the Mechanics of Consciousness* (New York: Bantam, 1979), 75.

(28.) Bohm, *Wholeness and the Implicate Order*, 211.

(29.) Wolf, *Mind Into Matter*, 105.

(30.) Robert A. Monroe, *Ultimate Journey* (New York: Doubleday, 1994), 59.

(31.) Susan M. Watkins, *Conversations with Seth: The Story of Jane Roberts's ESP Class*, rev. ed. (Portsmouth, NH: Moment Point Press, 1999), 116. Watkins's book was originally published in two volumes by Prentice Hall in 1980 and 1981.

(32.) Susan M. Watkins, *Speaking of Jane Roberts: Remembering the Author of the Seth Material* (Portsmouth, NH: Moment Point Press, 2001), 3.

(33.) Wolf, *Mind Into Matter*, 116.

(34.) Wolf, *Mind Into Matter*, 116.

(35.) Bohm, *Wholeness and the Implicate Order*, 206.

(36.) Bentov, *Stalking the Wild Pendulum*, 93.

(37.) Bohm, *Wholeness and the Implicate Order*, 206.

(38.) Bohm, *Wholeness and the Implicate Order*, 206.

(39.) Joseph Chilton Pearce, *The Crack in the Cosmic Egg: Challenging Constructs of Mind and Reality* (New York: Bantam, 1973), intro., xiv. Pearce, by the way, would go on to become a friend, advisor, and neighbor to Bob Monroe, whose own first book, *Journeys Out of the Body*, was published in 1971—the same year that Pearce's book originally appeared in print.

(40.) Wolf, *Mind Into Matter*, 106.

Chapter Six

(1.) Joseph Campbell, *The Masks of God: Occidental Mythology* (New York: Penguin, 1970), 269.

(2.) By Wilson's own account, his first use of the term "robot" in this context occurred in an address, "Existential Psychology: A Novelist's Approach," subsequently published as an essay in *Challenges of Humanistic Psychology*, ed. J. F. T. Bugental (New York: McGraw Hill, 1967). He elaborated on this idea in New Pathways in Psychology: *Maslow and the Post-Freudian Revolution* (New York: Taplinger, 1972), *passim*.

(3.) In *Ultimate Journey*, Monroe defines "Different Overview" as "The gathering of knowledge minus the glitter of beliefs and animal commands" (New York: Doubleday, 1994), 272.

(4.) Jane Roberts, *The Seth Material* (Englewood Cliffs, NJ: Prentice-Hall, 1970), 256.

(5.) St. Augustine, *Confessions,* 164. On the nature of Original Sin (considered from the standpoint of the theology, history, and politics of the doctrine—including the gender politics), see Elaine Pagels, *Adam, Eve, and the Serpent* (New York: Random House, 1988). I am greatly indebted to her account.

(6.) Thomas Hobbes, *Leviathan: Parts I & II,* ed. H. W. Schneider (Indianapolis, IN: Bobbs-Merrill, 1958), 23.

(7.) C. G. Jung, *The Undiscovered Self.* Trans. R. F. C. Hull (New York: Signet, 2006), 11.

(8.) Jane Roberts, *The Coming of Seth* (New York: Bantam, 1976), intro., xi.

(9.) This is my gloss of the famous passage on personal identity found in Book I, section vi of Hume's *Treatise of Human Nature,* ed. L. A. Selby-Bigge (Oxford: Clarendon Press, 1975), 251ff. "Some philosophers" is a tacit reference to Descartes and his view of the soul.

(10.) Joel Kramer and Diana Alstad, *The Guru Papers: Masks of Authoritarian Power* (Berkeley, CA: Frog, 1993), 322.

(11.) Kramer and Alstad, *The Guru Papers,* 322.

(12.) Kramer and Alstad, *The Guru Papers,* 216.

(13.) J. M. Maher and D. Briggs, eds., *An Open Life: Joseph Campbell in Conversation with Michael Toms* (Burdett, NY: Larson, 1988), 72–75, 89–90.

(14.) Kramer and Alstad, *The Guru Papers,* 83.

(15.) Richard Rorty, *Consequences of Pragmatism: Essays: 1972–1980* (Minneapolis: University of Minnesota Press, 1982), introduction, xl.

(16.) The author is Margo Jefferson, *On Michael Jackson* (New York: Vintage, 2007), as quoted by Courtland Miloy, "A Man Who Loathed His Reflection," *Portland Press Herald* (July 1, 2009), A9.

(17.) Thomas S. Kuhn, *The Structure of Scientific Revolutions* (Chicago: University of Chicago Press, 1962).

(18.) R. G. Collingwood, *Religion and Philosophy* (London: Macmillan, 1916), 103.

(19.) R. G. Collingwood, *An Autobiography* (Oxford: Oxford University Press, 1970), 29–43.

(20.) See Louis O. Mink, *Mind, History, and Dialectic: The Philosophy of R. G. Collingwood* (Bloomington, IN: Indiana University Press, 1969), 8ff.

(21.) Monroe, *Ultimate Journey,* 1.

(22.) Joseph Campbell with Bill Moyers, *The Power of Myth*, ed. B. S. Flowers (New York: Doubleday, 1988), 5.

(23.) As quoted by Albert Camus in his essay, "The Absurd Man" in *The Myth of Sisyphus and Other Essays*, trans. J. O'Brien (New York: Knopf, 1955), 61.

(24.) The line, of course, is from Wordsworth's great poem, "Ode: Intimations of Immortality from Recollections of Early Childhood," in *William Wordsworth: Selected Poems*, ed. W. Davies (London: J. M. Dent & Sons, 1975), 107.

(25.) Edward Hoffman, *Visions of Innocence: Spiritual and Inspirational Experiences of Childhood* (Boston: Shambhala, 1992), 39.

(26.) Hoffman, *Visions of Innocence*, 39. According to those forms of mysticism that champion a total annihilation or erasure of the ego and a relinquishment of all individuality as we melt in a featureless All, there is an experience of the One without a second (ego). But this is a self-refuting claim. If there was such an experience, there would be no memory of it and no way to bring it "back," for there would have been no subject to record it as their own. The experience would be more than "ineffable" (i.e., indescribable); it would be a total blank. For even experiences that are ultimately beyond all description are given some sort of accounting by the subject, no matter how they might struggle with the language and insist that the episode exhausts all attempts at expression. In such experiences, the ego does not vanish; rather it becomes more porous and flexible as it opens to its wider connections with the web of life, in which there is diversity as well as unity. As a near-death experiencer cited by Dr. Jeffrey Long in his ground-breaking study of NDEs put it, "We live in a 'plural unity' or 'oneness.' In other words, our reality is 'unity in plurality and plurality in unity'" [Jeffrey Long with Paul Perry, *Evidence of the Afterlife: The Science of Near-Death Experiences* (New York: HarperOne, 2010), 158]. This was part of the wisdom that this woman received while she was "in the light," and according to Dr. Long, it is an idea commonly expressed by returning NDErs. Note that it also accords with David Bohm's view of the holomovement. (See chapter 9 for further discussion of these issues.)

(27.) Philip K. Dick, "How to Build a Universe That Doesn't Fall Apart Two Days Later," in *The Shifting Realities of Philip K. Dick: Selected Literary and Philosophical Writings*, ed. L. Sutin (New York: Pantheon, 1995), 261. This essay (originally an address) was originally published as the introduction to a short story collection of Dick's, *I Hope I Shall Arrive Soon* (New York: St. Martins, 1987).

Chapter Seven

(1.) C. G. Jung, "The Stages of Life," in *Modern Man in Search of a Soul*, trans. W. S. Dell and C. F. Baynes (New York: Harcourt Brace Jovanovich, 1933), 104.

(2.) Robert Bly, "Five Stages in Exiling, Hunting, and Retrieving the Shadow," in *A Little Book on the Human Shadow*, ed. W. Booth (New York: Harper & Row, 1988), 31.

(3.) Moody and Ring are the research pioneers of the near-death experience (NDE); without them there would not be a field. Each authored four important books on the subject. Moody wrote *Life After Life: The Investigation of a Phenomenon—Survival of Bodily Death* (Harrisburg, PA: Stackpole, 1976); *Reflections on Life After Life* (New York: Mockingbird, 1977); *The Light Beyond* (New York: Bantam, 1988); and his most philosophical book, *The Last Laugh: A New Philosophy of Near-Death Experiences, Apparitions, and the Paranormal* (Charlottesville, VA: Hampton Roads, ·1999). Psychologist and university professor Kenneth Ring augmented Moody's anecdotal approach with surveys, formal interviews, and statistical analyses. His four books are: *Life at Death: A Scientific Investigation of the Near-Death Experience* (New York: Quill, 1982); *Heading Toward Omega: In Search of the Meaning of the Near-Death Experience* (New York: Quill, 1985); *The Omega Project: Near-Death Experiences, UFO Encounters, and Mind at Large* (New York: William Morrow, 1992); and (with E. V. Valarino) *Lessons from the Light: What We Can Learn from the Near-Death Experience* (New York: Plenum, 1988), which has been republished by Moment Point Press (2006). There are literally hundreds of books on the NDE phenomenon. While this book was in press, several important volumes on the near-death experience appeared in print: *The Handbook of Near-Death Experiences: Thirty Years of Investigation*, ed. J. Holden, B. Greyson, and D. James (Westport, CT: Praeger Publishers, 2009); J. Long with P. Perry, *Evidence of the Afterlife: The Science of Near-Death Experiences* (New York: Harper-One, 2010); and P. van Lommel, *Consciousness Beyond Life: The Science of the*

Near-Death Experience (New York: HarperOne, 2010). Also of importance is Raymond Moody's latest study of shared-death experiences (SDEs), in which healthy individuals at the deathbed vigils of close relatives or friends join the newly deceased as they cross over to the other side. These experiences share many elements with the NDE, including its beneficent aftereffects. See R. Moody with P. Perry, *Glimpses of Eternity: Sharing a Loved One's Passage from This Life to the Next* (New York: Guideposts, 2010). The best way to view the field is to subscribe to the excellent professional (peer-reviewed) journal of the International Association of Near-Death Studies (IANDS), *The Journal of Near-Death Studies*, and the IANDS newsletter, *Vital Signs*.

(4.) "Interview: Dr. Tony Cicoria," *Vital Signs* 27: 4 (2008), 1.

(5.) Oliver Sacks, *Musicophilia: Tales of Music and the Brain* (New York: Knopf, 2007).

(6.) Interview, *Vital Signs*, 1.

(7.) Interview, *Vital Signs*, 5.

(8.) John Neihardt, *Black Elk Speaks: Being the Life Story of a Holy Man of the Oglala Sioux* (New York: Washington Square Press, 1972), 22.

Chapter Eight

(1.) Jane Roberts, *The Coming of Seth* (New York: Bantam, 1976), intro., xiv.

(2.) Jane Roberts, *Seth, Dreams, and Projections of Consciousness* (Walpole, NH: Stillpoint, 1987), 57.

(3.) Jane Roberts, *The Seth Material* (Englewood Cliffs, NJ: Prentice-Hall, 1970), 10.

(4.) Roberts, *The Seth Material*, 10.

(5.) Roberts, *Seth, Dreams, and Projections of Consciousness*, 42–43.

(6.) Roberts, *The Seth Material*, 10.

(7.) Roberts, *Seth, Dreams, and Projections of Consciousness*, 63.

(8.) Roberts, *Seth, Dreams, and Projections of Consciousness*, 60.

(9.) Jane Roberts, *Seth Speaks: The Eternal Validity of the Soul* (Englewood Cliffs, NJ: Prentice-Hall, 1972), intro., ix.

(10.) Originally published as *How to Develop Your ESP Power* by Frederick Fell in 1966, and subsequently reissued in mass-market paperback form as *The Coming of Seth*.

(11.) Roberts, *The Seth Material*, 17.

(12.) Roberts, *The Seth Material*, 19.

(13.) This quote is taken from chapter 2 "Seth Speaks to Me," in *The Road to Elmira*, a work in progress by Rich Kendall posted on his website at: *www.sethnet.org.*

(14.) Kathryn Ridall, *Channeling: How to Reach Out to Your Spirit Guides* (New York: Bantam, 1988), 1.

(15.) Plato, *Crito*, 46b in *Plato: Five Dialogues*, trans. G. M. A. Grube (Indianapolis, IN: Hackett, 1981), 48.

(16.) Bertrand Russell, *A History of Western Philosophy* (New York: Simon and Schuster, 1945), 90.

(17.) Roberts, *The Coming of Seth*, intro., xiii.

(18.) Eileen Garrett (1893–1970) was an Irish medium and eventual émigré to America. An exceedingly intellectually curious and open-minded psychic, she went on to found the Parapsychology Foundation in New York City, and thereby to engage with leading scientists and thinkers of the day, including the Jungian psychologist Ira Progroff, who authored a book on Garrett, *The Image of an Oracle* (1964). Garrett was originally trained in the traditions of Spiritualism, with its spooky séances, magical apports, and cloudy ectoplasmic materializations (though Garrett herself was not a physical medium and did not claim to be able to produce such phenomena). But she abandoned the Spiritualist movement because she felt it was too gullible and uncritical in its approach to psychic experience. Although her two main "spirit controls," Uvani and Abdul Latif—the facilitating personalities that acted as mediators between Garrett and other spirits or entities—insisted that they were disembodied spirits of the dead and thus existed fully independently of the medium's unconscious mind, Garrett herself remained agnostic about such claims and tended to view her controls as some kind of psychic amalgam. "I saw the configuration of the controls molded, as it were," she wrote in her autobiography, "in the images of those who believed in them. " See Eileen J. Garrett, *Many Voices: The Autobiography of a Medium* (New York: Dell, 1969), 225.

(19.) Jane Roberts, *The God of Jane: A Psychic Manifesto* (Englewood Cliffs, NJ: Prentice-Hall, 1981), 19.

(20.) Jane Roberts, *The Early Class Sessions, Book I, Sessions 9/12/67 to 11/25/69:*

A Seth Book (Manhasset, NY: New Awareness Network, 2008), 27.

(21.) John Neihardt, *Black Elk Speaks: Being the Life Story of a Holy Man of the Oglala Sioux* (New York: Washington Square Press, 1972), 36.

(22.) Anne A. Simpkinson, "On Past-Life Therapy: An Interview with Roger Woolger," *Common Boundary* 5:6 (November/December 1987), 26.

(23.) Roger J. Woolger, *Other Lives, Other Selves: A Jungian Psychotherapist Discovers Past Lives* (New York: Bantam, 1988), 60.

(24.) Simpkinson, "On Past-Life Therapy," 26.

(25.) Roberts, *The Seth Material*, 204.

(26.) Jane Roberts, *The "Unknown" Reality, Volume 2: A Seth Book* (Englewood Cliffs, NJ: Prentice-Hall, 1979), 463.

(27.) Vine Deloria, "If You Think About It, You Will See That It Is True," in *Spirit and Reason, The Vine Deloria, Jr. Reader*, ed. B. Deloria, K. Foehner, and S. Scinta. (Golden, CO: Fulcrum, 1999), 44.

(28.) In Kent Nerburn, ed., *The Wisdom of the Native Americans* (Novato, CA: New World Library, 1999), 118.

(29.) Nerburn, *The Wisdom of the Native Americans*, 119–121.

(30.) Roberts, *The God of Jane*, 256.

(31.) See the late philosopher of science Paul Feyerabend's account of this rather embarrassing episode in the recent history of science (or is it "Scientism"?) in his book, *Science in a Free Society* (London: NLB, 1978), 91–96.

(32.) Paul Kurtz and E. H. Wilson, *The Humanist Manifestos I and II* (Buffalo, NY: Prometheus, 1973), 16–17.

(33.) Jane Roberts, *The Afterdeath Journal of an American Philosopher: The World View of William James* (Englewood Cliffs, NJ: Prentice-Hall, 1978), 111.

(34.) See Colin Wilson with Damon Wilson, *The Encyclopedia of Unsolved Mysteries* (New York: Contemporary, 1988), 176.

(35.) In Nerburn, *The Wisdom of the Native Americans*, 121.

Chapter Nine

(1.) Campbell, *The Hero with a Thousand Faces*, 2nd ed. (Princeton: Princeton University Press, 1968), 59.

(2.) Rhea A. White (1931–2007) worked in the field of parapsychology for over forty years, beginning in the 1950s as a research associate to psychology professor J. B. (Joseph Banks) Rhine, who founded modern experimental parapsychology out of what had previously been called "psychical research" at his Duke University Parapsychology Laboratory. A professional librarian, White subsequently became the longtime editor of *The Journal of the American Society for Psychical Research* (as well as a contributor to the journal), and in the early 1990s went on to found the groundbreaking journal *Exceptional Human Experience*, in which she developed her own, more subjective, experiential-based approach to the study, not only of specifically psychic phenomena, but of the entire panoply of mystical, anomalous, spiritual, or what she termed (and meticulously catalogued as) "exceptional experiences." For one of her most cogent published statements of the deeply personal factors that motivated her lifelong study of these kinds of experiences, as well as the philosophical and methodological ramifications of her new approach, see her eloquent essay, "The Amplification and Integration of Near-Death and Other Exceptional Human Experiences by the Larger Cultural Context: An Autobiographical Case," *Journal of Near-Death Studies* 16: 181–204.

(3.) Swami Sivananda Radha, *Realities of the Dreaming Mind* (Boston: Shambhala, 1996), 138.

(4.) Rosalind A. McKnight, *Cosmic Journeys: My Out-of-Body Explorations with Robert A. Monroe* (Charlottesville, VA: Hampton Roads, 1999), 52–53. Her account is clearly based in part on what Monroe wrote about this incident in his own book, *Far Journeys* (New York: Doubleday, 1985), 47–48.

(5.) Ronald Russell, *The Journey of Robert Monroe: From Out-of-Body Explorer to Consciousness Pioneer* (Charlottesville, VA: Hampton Roads, 2007), 32.

(6.) I learned this interesting little tidbit from reading Dr. Charles T. Tart's Foreword to Ronald Russell's biography. Tart, who would go on to become one of the foremost authorities in the fields of parapsychology and transpersonal psychology, was a young psychology professor at the University of Virginia at Charlottesville in the early 1970s when he began what would become a long collaboration and friendship with Robert Monroe, which included performing one of the only published laboratory studies on Monroe's out-of-body abilities. It was Tart who was instrumental in getting Monroe's first book, *Journeys Out of the Body*, published (unbeknownst to Monroe, he had sent a copy of the manuscript to his own editor at Doubleday), and he provided the Foreword to that book. They would remain friends and colleagues up until Monroe's death in 1995. Tart couldn't attend Monroe's memorial service, but instead sent a eulogy that was read at the service. This unpublished reminiscence, "In Memory of My Friend Robert Monroe," is available on Tart's website: *www.paradigm-sys.com*.

(7.) Russell, *The Journey of Robert Monroe*, 37.

(8.) Russell, *The Journey of Robert Monroe*, 38.

(9.) Robert Monroe, *Journeys Out of the Body* (New York: Doubleday, 1971), 21.

(10.) Monroe, *Journeys Out of the Body*, 22.

(11.) Heraclitus, *The Cosmic Fragments* (Logion 28), in Jacob Needleman and David Appelbaum, eds., *Real Philosophy: An Anthology of the Universal Search for Meaning*. New York: Penguin/Arkana, 1990), 173.

(12.) See Willis Harman and Howard Rheingold, *Higher Creativity: Liberating the Unconscious for Breakthrough Insights* (New York: Tarcher/Perigee, 1984), 75. This account of Descartes' dreams is based on the one he himself provided to his biographer, Adrien Baillet, who published his work, *The Life of M. Descartes*, in 1691, or forty-one years after Descartes' death. Nevertheless, most scholars believe that Baillet's account is faithful to Descartes' experience, even though Descartes had lost his original journal notes and was speaking from memory.

(13.) Blaise Pascal, *Pensées*, trans. A. J. Krailsheimer (New York: Penguin, 1966), 309.

(14.) From an NDE account published in the online newsletter of IANDS: *The Monthly NDE* (September 2009), and available on their website, *iands.org*.

(15.) Richard Maurice Bucke, *Cosmic Consciousness: A Study in the Evolution of the Human Mind* (New York: Dutton, 1969), 9–10.

(16.) Holger Kalweit, *Shamans, Healers, and Medicine Men*, trans. M. H. Kohn (Boston: Shambhala, 1992), 46.

(17.) For a discussion of the pink light beam episode, see chapter 10 of Lawrence Sutin's biography, *Divine Invasions: A Life of Philip K. Dick* (New York: Citadel Twilight, 1989), 208–233. Dick incorporated some of these experiences into three of his novels: *Valis* (1980), *The Transmigration of Timothy Archer* (1982), and *Radio Free Albemuth* (1985). But his primary mode of expression was an 8,000-page handwritten journal, titled *Exegesis*, which he worked on for eight years, from 1974 up until his untimely death from a series of strokes in 1982.

(18.) Monroe, *Journeys Out of the Body*, 22.

(19.) On the prejudice against subjective experience and in favor of abstract theoretical ideas, he writes: "A bill of fare with one real raisin on it instead of the word 'raisin,' with one real egg instead of the word 'egg,' might be an inadequate meal, but it would at least be a commencement of reality" (William James, *The Varieties of Religious Experience* [New York: Modern Library, 1936], 490).

(20.) Monroe, *Far Journeys*, 109.

(21.) Neihardt, *Black Elk Speaks*, 16.

(22.) Neihardt, *Black Elk Speaks*, 19.

(23.) Neihardt, *Black Elk Speaks*, 134.

(24.) Jane Roberts, *The Coming of Seth* (New York: Bantam, 1976), 106.

(25.) Joseph Chilton Pearce, *The Crack in the Cosmic Egg: Challenging Constructs of Mind and Reality* (New York: Bantam, 1973), 23.

(26.) Mishka Jambor, "The Mystery of Frightening Transcendent Experiences: A Rejoinder to Nancy Evans Bush and Christopher Bache," *Journal of Near-Death Studies*, (1998) 16:2, 169.

(27.) Quoted in Jambor, *Journal of Near-Death Studies*, 174.

(28.) Neihardt, *Black Elk Speaks*, 135.

(29.) Monroe, *Journeys Out of the Body*, 25.

(30.) Monroe, *Journeys Out of the Body*, 27.

(31.) Monroe, *Journeys Out of the Body*, 27.

(32.) Monroe, *Journeys Out of the Body*, 31.

Chapter Ten

(1.) Friedrich Nietzsche, *The Gay Science*, trans. W. Kaufmann (New York: Vintage, 1974), 253.

(2.) Monroe, *Journeys Out of the Body* (New York: Doubleday, 1971), 108.

(3.) Monroe, *Journeys Out of the Body*, 80–81.

(4.) Monroe, *Journeys Out of the Body*, 77.

(5.) Monroe, *Journeys Out of the Body*, 123–124.

(6.) Ronald Russell, *The Journey of Robert Monroe: From Out-of-Body Explorer to Consciousness Pioneer* (Charlottesville, VA: Hampton Roads, 2007), 85.

(7.) Russell, *The Journey of Robert Monroe*, 79–86. See also Thomas Campbell,

My Big TOE: A Trilogy Unifying Philosophy, Physics, and Metaphysics, Book I: Awakening (Ypsilanti, MI: Lightning Strike Books: *www.LightningStrikeBooks.com*), 59–96. A NASA physicist and engineer, Campbell was one of the original researchers responsible for the early development and testing of Hemi-Sync at Monroe's Whistlefield lab in the 1970s.

(8.) For starters, see the two volumes of research papers edited by Ronald Russell, *Using the Whole Brain: Integrating the Right and Left Brain with Hemi-Sync Sound Patterns* (Norfolk, VA: Hampton Roads, 1993), and its successor/replacement, *Focusing the Whole Brain: Transforming Your Life with Hemispheric Synchronization* (Charlottesville, VA: Hampton Roads, 2004), plus the Appendix to Russell's biography of Monroe, "The Hemi-Sync Process," a 1999 paper authored by F. Holmes ("Skip") Atwater, the former research director and current president of the Monroe Institute. See also Atwater's book, *Captain of My Ship, Master of My Soul: Living with Guidance* (Charlottesville, VA: Hampton Roads, 2001), along with a more recent paper of his, "Binaural Beats and the Regulation of Arousal Levels, *TMI Journal* (Winter/Spring 2009), which is available on the TMI website: *www.monroeinstitute.org*. Russell observes in a footnote that, "It is likely Monroe's interest in the possibility of using sound to drive brainwaves derived from a conversation with Charles Tart [sometime in the 1970s], who had told him about the research by Andrew Neher, described in studies issued in 1961 and 1962, investigating how EEG responses could be driven by periodic acoustic stimuli, such as drumming. Neher used electrodes attached to the scalp to assess the effects. This study was replicated at Stanford in 2006 (Russell, *The Journey of Robert Monroe*, 113n.). Certainly there were many cooks in the kitchen, but Monroe was the indispensable head chef—the creative and organizational "magnet" (as Tom Campbell, in the course of a personal conversation, recently described him to me) who drew the various talents together and made the whole thing work. But if Monroe had not already been experimenting with the power of sound (and music) to alter consciousness, all the other research into binaural beats and kindred phenomena might not have registered.

(9.) Russell, *The Journey of Robert Monroe*, 10. "Russ" Russell—who has himself gone through numerous programs at the Monroe Institute, and thus has firsthand familiarity with altered states of consciousness in what Monroe dubbed the "focus levels"—recently reiterated this very point to me in an e-mail: "I think that much of what Bob wrote [in *Journeys Out of the Body*] was an attempt to rationalize experiences which are not rational and cannot satisfactorily be dealt with in this way. In later life he might say 'That's what it felt like then . . .' [*Journeys*] was a brave effort to do this, regardless of the possibility that he might open himself to ridicule" (personal correspondence with the author).

(10.) Monroe, *Journeys Out of the Body*, 76. For a more detailed account of the concept of "phasing" as Monroe would subsequently develop and employ it, see, for example, Frederick Aardma, Ph.D., "Focus 10: Mind Awake/Body Asleep," *www.monroeinstitute.org*. Monroe's own subsequent elaborations may be found in *Far Journeys* (New York: Doubleday, 1985), 3–7; 77–79, and also in *Ultimate Journey* (New York: Doubleday, 1994), 100–102.

(11.) Monroe, *Far Journeys*, 6.

(12.) Monroe, *Far Journeys*, 6.

(13.) Bayard Stockton, *Catapult: The Biography of Robert A. Monroe* (Norfolk, VA: Donning, 1989), 151.

(14.) Monroe, *Ultimate Journey*, 109.

(15.) Walter Kaufmann, *Critique of Religion and Philosophy* (Princeton: Princeton University Press, 1978), 294. Making belief, rather than rigorous practice (as in Judaism or Buddhism) central made it far easier to become a Christian, thereby facilitating the spread of the religion beyond its initial (Jewish) adherents. The very word, however, is suggestive of commodification. In his book Science, Order, and Creativity, David Bohm points out that the English word belief "is based on the Teutonic Aryan word lief, which means 'love,' so that what is believed is 'beloved.' The danger in belief should therefore be clear, for when the 'love' for a set of assumptions and their implications is strong, it may lead to playing false in order to defend them. The end result is inevitably destructive" (264).

(16.) Russell, *The Journey of Robert Monroe*, 71.

(17.) Monroe, *Ultimate Journey*, 129.

(18.) See, for example, Michael Harner, *The Way of the Shaman* (New York: Harper & Row, 1980) and Sandra Ingerman, *Soul Retrieval: Mending the Fragmented Self* (San Francisco: HarperSanFrancisco, 1991), two key works in the shamanic revival, for a discussion of the soul-retrieval process from an anthropological and neo-shamanic perspective. As I said, I can find no evidence that Monroe was aware of these parallel developments, or was in any way influenced by them—or vice versa, for that matter. Which points, yet again, to the fascinating and oft-reported phenomenon of simultaneous discovery that biologist Rupert Sheldrake has discussed in terms of "morphogenetic fields."

(19.) Monroe, *Ultimate Journey*, 226–227.

(20.) Monroe, *Ultimate Journey*, 227.

(21.) Monroe, *Ultimate Journey*, 217.

(22.) Russell, *The Journey of Robert Monroe*, 244.

Chapter Eleven

(1.) Hermann Hesse, *Demian: The Story of Emil Sinclair's Youth*. Trans. M. Roloff and M. Lebeck (New York: Bantam, 1970), 139.

(2.) Patricia Leva, *Traveling the Interstate of Consciousness: A Driver's Instruction Manual: Using Hemi-Sync to Access States of Non-Ordinary Reality* (Longmont, CO: Q Central Publishing, 1997), 3–4.

(3.) John Neihardt, *Black Elk Speaks: Being the Life Story of a Holy Man of the Oglala Sioux* (New York: Washington Square Press, 1972), 159.

(4.) Bruce Moen, *Afterlife Knowledge Guidebook: A Manual for the Art of Retrieval and Afterlife Exploration* (Charlottesville, VA: Hampton Roads, 2005), 50–59.

(5.) Cynthia K. Buccini, Katie Koch, and Natalie Jacobson McCracken, "Act 2," *Bostonia* (Winter 2008/2009), No. 4, 26–31.

Acknowledgments

(1.) John Neihardt, *Black Elk Speaks: Being the Life Story of a Holy Man of the Oglala Sioux* (New York: Washington Square Press, 1972), 2.

(2.) Joseph Campbell, *The Hero with a Thousand Faces*, 2nd ed. (Princeton: Princeton University Press, 1968), 30.

(3.) I discussed my experiences at the Monroe Institute's Gateway Voyage and Lifeline programs in three published articles: "My Gateway Voyage: An Experiential Account," *EHE News* 7:2 (September 2000), 17–26; "Through the Doorways of Change: A Philosopher's Inner Voyage Continues," *Excep-*

tional Human Experience 17:2 (2002), 180–89; and "Explaining Infinity to a Monkey: Challenges and Rewards of NVC [Non-Verbal Communication]," *TMI Focus* 24:1 (Winter 2002) 1, 4–8. I also included them in chapters 6 and 7 of my first book, *The Way Back to Paradise: Restoring the Balance Between Magic and Reason* (Charlottesville, VA: Hampton Roads, 2005), 139–188.

(4.) A highly condensed version of my keynote address appeared in the Institute's newsletter as, "Reasonable Magic and Magical Reason: The Philosophy of Robert Monroe," *TMI Focus* 28: 1&2 (Winter/Spring 2006), 1, 5–6, 8–9, 11. My friend Frank DeMarco subsequently published the complete original text on his weblog: *http://hologrambooks.com*

(5.) See my essay, "Was Joseph Campbell a Postmodernist?" *Journal of the American Academy of Religion* 114:2 (Summer 1996), 395–417.

(6.) In Kent Nerburn, ed., *The Wisdom of the Native Americans* (Novato, CA: New World Library, 1999), 10.

(7.) Hermann Hesse, *Demian: The Story of Emil Sinclair's Youth*, trans. M. Roloff and M. Lebeck (New York: Bantam, 1970), 4.

WORKS CITED

Aardma, Frederick. "Focus 10: Mind Awake/Body Asleep." *www.monroeinstitute.org* (2009).

Annie Hall. Directed by Woody Allen. Culver City, CA: MGM/UA Home Video. Videocassette, 1977.

Atwater, F. Holmes. "Binaural Beats and the Regulation of Arousal Levels." *TMI Journal* (Winter/Spring 2009). *www.monroeinstitute.org*.

———. *Captain of My Ship, Master of My Soul: Living with Guidance*. Charlottesville, VA: Hampton Roads, 2001.

St. Augustine. *Confessions*. Trans. R. S. Pine-Coffin. Baltimore, MD: Penguin, 1961. (Original work published in 397.)

Becker, Carl B. *Breaking the Circle: Death and the Afterlife in Buddhism*. Carbondale, IL: Southern Illinois University Press, 1993.

Beem, Edgar Allen. "Apocalypse Then." *Down East* (October 2007), *www.downeast.com*.

Bentov, Itzhak. *Stalking the Wild Pendulum: On the Mechanics of Consciousness*. New York: Bantam, 1979.

Bentov, Itzhak, with Mirtala Bentov. *A Cosmic Book: On the Mechanics of Creation*. Rochester, VT: Destiny, 1988.

Bethards, Betty. *The Dream Book: Symbols for Self-Understanding*. Petaluma, CA: New Century, 2006.

Bly, Robert. *A Little Book on the Human Shadow*. Ed. W. Booth. New York: Harper & Row, 1988.

Bohm, David. *Thought as a System*. New York: Routledge and Kegan Paul, 1994.

————. *Wholeness and the Implicate Order*. New York: Routledge and Kegan Paul, 1980.

Bohm, David, and F. David Peat. *Science, Order and Creativity*. New York: Bantam, 1987.

Boone, J. Allen. *Kinship with All Life*. San Francisco: HarperSanFrancisco, 1976. (Original work published in 1954.)

Buccini, Cynthia K., et. al. "Act 2." *Bostonia*. Winter 2008–2009. No. 4; 26–31.

Bucke, Richard Maurice. *Cosmic Consciousness: A Study in the Evolution of the Human Mind*. New York: Dutton, 1969. (Original work published in 1901.)

Bugental, J. F. T., ed. *Challenges of Humanistic Psychology*. New York: McGraw Hill, 1967.

Campbell, Joseph. *The Hero's Journey: Joseph Campbell on his Life and Work*. Ed. P. Cousineau. San Francisco: Harper & Row, 1990.

————. *The Hero with a Thousand Faces*. 2nd ed. Princeton: Princeton University Press, 1968. (Original work published in 1949.)

———. *The Inner Reaches of Outer Space: Myth as Metaphor and as Religion.* New York: Alfred Van Der Marck, 1985.

———. *A Joseph Campbell Companion: Reflections on the Art of Living.* Ed. D.K. Osbon. New York: HarperCollins, 1991.

———. *The Masks of God: Creative Mythology.* New York: Penguin, 1976.

———. *The Masks of God: Occidental Mythology.* New York: Penguin, 1970.

———. *The Masks of God: Oriental Mythology.* New York: Penguin, 1976.

———. *The Masks of God: Primitive Mythology.* New York: Penguin, 1969.

Campbell, Joseph, with Bill Moyers. *The Power of Myth.* Ed. B. S. Flowers. New York: Doubleday, 1988.

Campbell, Joseph, with Michael Toms. *An Open Life: Joseph Campbell in Conversation with Michael Toms.* Ed. J. M. Maher and D. Briggs. New York: Larson, 1988.

Campbell, Thomas. *My Big TOE: A Trilogy Unifying Philosophy, Physics, and Metaphysics. Book I: Awakening.* Ypsilanti, MI: Lightning Strike Books: *www.LightningStrikeBooks.com*, 2003.

Camus, Albert. *The Myth of Sisyphus and Other Essays.* Trans. J. O'Brien. New York: Knopf, 1955.

Chung-yuan, Chang. *Creativity and Taoism: A Study of Chinese Philosophy, Art, and Poetry.* New York: Harper & Row, 1963.

Collingwood, R. G. *An Autobiography.* Oxford: Oxford University Press, 1970. (Original work published in 1939.)

———. *The New Leviathan.* New York: Thomas Y. Crowell, 1942.

————. *Religion and Philosophy*. London: Macmillan, 1916.

————. *Speculum Mentis*. Oxford: Clarendon Press, 1924.

Deloria, Jr., Vine. *Spirit and Reason: The Vine Deloria, Jr. Reader*. Ed. B. Deloria, K. Foehner, and S. Scinta. Golden, CO: Fulcrum, 1999.

————. *The World We Used to Live In: Remembering the Powers of the Medicine Men*. Golden, CO: Fulcrum, 2006.

Descartes, René. *Discourse on Method and Meditations on First Philosophy*. 2nd ed. Trans. D. A. Cress. Indianapolis, IN: Hackett, 1980. (Original works published in 1637 and 1641.)

Dick, Philip K. *I Hope I Shall Arrive Soon*. New York: St. Martins, 1987.

————. *The Shifting Realities of Philip K. Dick: Selected Literary and Philosophical Writings*. Ed. L. Sutin. New York: Pantheon, 1995.

Dickens, Charles. *A Christmas Carol*. New York: Pocket, 1963. (Original work published in 1843.)

Dr. No. Directed by Terence Young. Culver City, CA: MGM/UA. Videocassette, 1963.

"Doomsday Machine." Episode no. 35 of *Start Trek* television series. Directed by Marc Daniels. Hollywood, CA: Paramount Home Video. Videocassette, 1978. (First broadcast October 20, 1967.)

Eliade, Mircea. *Shamanism: Archaic Techniques of Ecstasy*. Trans. W. R. Trask. Princeton: Princeton University Press, 1964.

Erdoes, Richard, and Alfonso Ortiz, eds. *American Indian Myths and Legends*. New York: Pantheon, 1984.

Evans-Pritchard, E. E. *Theories of Primitive Religion*. Oxford: Clarendon Press, 1965.

Felser, Joseph M. "Explaining Infinity to a Monkey: Challenges and Rewards of NVC." *TMI Focus* 24:1 (Winter 2002) 1, 4–8.

———. "My Gateway Voyage: An Experiential Account." *EHE News* 7:2 (September 2000), 17–26.

———. "Parapsychology Without Religion: 'Breaking the Circle' or Circling the Wagons?" *The Journal of the American Society for Psychical Research* 1999, 93: 259–279.

———. "Reasonable Magic and Magical Reason: The Philosophy of Robert Monroe." *TMI Focus* 28: 1&2 (Winter/Spring 2006), 1, 5–6, 8–9, 11.

———. "Through the Doorways of Change: A Philosopher's Inner Voyage Continues." *Exceptional Human Experience* 2002, 17:2, 180–189.

———. "Was Joseph Campbell a Postmodernist?" *Journal of the American Academy of Religion* 1996, 114: 395–417.

———. *The Way Back to Paradise: Restoring the Balance Between Magic and Reason*. Charlottesville, VA: Hampton Roads, 2005.

Fenwick, Peter, and Elizabeth Fenwick. *The Hidden Door: Understanding and Controlling Dreams*. New York: Berkley, 1999.

Feyerabend, Paul. *Science in a Free Society*. London: NLB, 1978.

Fischer, David Hackett. *Historians' Fallacies: Toward a Logic of Historical Thought*. New York: Harper and Row, 1970.

Garrett, Eileen J. *Many Voices: The Autobiography of a Medium*. New York: Dell, 1969.

Goni, Uki. "Tests on Skull Fragment Cast Doubt on Hitler Suicide Story." *The Sunday Observer* (September 27, 2009). *www.guardian.co.uk*.

Graves, Robert. *The White Goddess: A Historical Grammar of Poetic Myth*. 2nd ed. New York: Farrar, Strauss and Giroux, 1966. (Original work published in 1948.)

Grof, Stanislav with Hal Zina Bennett. *The Holotropic Mind: The Three Levels of Consciousness and How They Shape Our Lives*. San Francisco: HarperSanFrancisco, 1992.

Groopman, Jerome. "Eyes Wide Open: Can Science Make Regular Sleep Unnecessary?" *The New Yorker* (December 3, 2001), 52–57.

Grosso, Michael. *Soulmaking: Uncommon Paths to Self-Understanding*. Charlottesville, VA: Hampton Roads, 1997.

Groundhog Day. Directed by Harold Ramis. Culver City, CA: Columbia/Tristar. Videocassette, 1994.

Harman, Willis, and Howard Rheingold. *Higher Creativity: Liberating the Unconscious for Breakthrough Insights*. New York: Tarcher/Perigee, 1984.

Harner, Michael. *The Way of the Shaman*. New York: Harper & Row, 1980.

Hegel, G. W. F. *The Philosophy of Right*. Trans. T. M. Knox. Oxford: Oxford University Press, 1975. (Original work published in 1821.)

Hesse, Hermann. *Demian: The Story of Emil Sinclair's Youth*. Trans. M. Roloff and M. Lebeck. New York: Bantam, 1970. (Original work published in 1925.)

Hobbes, Thomas. *Leviathan: Parts I & II*. Ed. H. W. Schneider. Indianapolis, IN: Bobbs-Merrill, 1958. (Original work published in 1651.)

Hoffman, Edward. *Visions of Innocence: Spiritual and Inspirational Experiences of Childhood.* Boston: Shambhala, 1992.

Holden, Janice Miner, Bruce Greyson, and Debbie James, eds. *The Handbook of Near-Death Experiences: Thirty Years of Investigation.* Westport, CT: Praeger, 2009.

Hume, David. *Treatise of Human Nature.* Ed. L. A. Selby-Bigge. Oxford: Clarendon Press, 1975. (Original work published in 1888.)

Ingerman, Sandra. *Soul Retrieval: Mending the Fragmented Self.* San Francisco: HarperSanFrancisco, 1991.

Jambor, Mishka. "The Mystery of Frightening Transcendent Experiences: A Rejoinder to Nancy Evans Bush and Christopher Bache." *Journal of Near-Death Studies* (1998) 16: 163–176.

James, William. *The Varieties of Religious Experience.* New York: Modern Library, 1936. (Original work published in 1902.)

———. *William James on Psychical Research.* Ed. G. Murphy and R. Ballou. New York: Viking, 1969.

Jung, C. G. Foreword to the *I Ching or Book of Changes.* Trans. R. Wilhelm and C. F. Baynes. London: Routledge & Kegan Paul, 1985.

———. *Memories, Dreams, Reflections.* Rev. ed. Ed. A. Jaffé. Trans. R. Winston and C. Winston. New York: Vintage, 1965.

———. *Modern Man in Search of a Soul.* Trans. W. S. Dell and C. F. Baynes. New York: Harcourt Brace Jovanovich, 1933.

———. *Psychology and the East: From the Collected Works of C. G. Jung, Vols. 10, 11, 13 and 18.* Trans. R. F. C. Hull. Princeton: Princeton University Press, 1978.

————. *The Undiscovered Self.* Trans. R. F. C. Hull. New York: Signet, 2006. (Original work published in 1957.)

Kalweit, Holger. *Shamans, Healers, and Medicine Men.* Trans. M. H. Kohn. Boston: Shambhala, 1992.

Kaufmann, Walter. *Critique of Religion and Philosophy.* Princeton: Princeton University Press, 1978.

Kramer, Joel, and Diana Alstad. *The Guru Papers: Masks of Authoritarian Power.* Berkeley, CA: Frog, 1993.

Kuhn, Thomas S. *The Structure of Scientific Revolutions.* Chicago: University of Chicago Press, 1962.

Kurtz, Paul, and E. H. Wilson. *The Humanist Manifestos I and II.* Buffalo, NY: Prometheus, 1973.

Leva, Patricia. *Traveling the Interstate of Consciousness: A Driver's Instruction Manual: Using Hemi-Sync© to Access States of Non-Ordinary Reality.* Longmont, CO: Q Central, 1997.

Long, Jeffrey, with Paul Perry. *Evidence of the Afterlife: The Science of Near-Death Experiences.* New York: HarperOne, 2010.

Luther, Martin. *Selections From His Writings.* Ed. J. Dillenberger. Garden City, NY: Anchor Doubleday, 1961.

Maher, J. M., and D. Briggs, eds. *An Open Life: Joseph Campbell in Conversation with Michael Toms.* Burdett, NY: Larson, 1988.

Mann, A. T. *The Elements of the Tarot.* Rockport, MA: Element, 1993.

Matter of Heart. Directed by Mark Whitney. New York: Kino Video. Videocassette, 1985.

May, H. G., and B. M. Metzger. *The New Oxford Annotated Bible with the Apocrypha, Revised Standard Version*. New York: Oxford University Press, 1973.

McDonald, Jeffrey. "Does Maya Calendar Predict 2012 Apocalypse?" *USA Today* (March 27, 2007). *www.usatoday.com*.

McKenna, Terence. *The Archaic Revival*. San Francisco: HarperSanFrancisco, 1991.

McKeon, Richard, ed. *The Basic Works of Aristotle*. New York: Random House, 1941.

McKnight, Rosalind A. *Cosmic Journeys: My Out-of-Body Explorations with Robert A. Monroe*. Charlottesville, VA: Hampton Roads, 1999.

Mettrie, Julien Offray de la. *Man: a Machine*. Trans. G. C. Bussey and M. Carret. LaSalle, IL: Open Court, 1912. (Original work published in 1748.)

Meyer, Marvin W., trans. *The Secret Teachings of Jesus: Four Gnostic Gospels*. New York: Vintage, 1986.

Miloy, Courtland. "A Man Who Loathed His Reflection." *Portland Press Herald* (July 1, 2009).

Mink, Louis O. *Mind, History, and Dialectic: The Philosophy of R. G. Collingwood*. Bloomington, IN: Indiana University Press, 1969.

Moen, Bruce. *Afterlife Knowledge Guidebook: A Manual for the Art of Retrieval and Afterlife Exploration*. Charlottesville, VA: Hampton Roads, 2005.

Monroe, Robert A. *Far Journeys*. New York: Doubleday, 1985.

———. *Journeys Out of the Body*. New York: Doubleday, 1971.

————. *Ultimate Journey*. New York: Doubleday, 1994.

Moody, Raymond. *The Last Laugh: A New Philosophy of Near-Death Experiences, Apparitions, and the Paranormal*. Charlottesville, VA: Hampton Roads, 1999.

————. *Life After Life: The Investigation of a Phenomenon—Survival of Bodily Death*. Harrisburg, PA: Stackpole, 1976.

————. *The Light Beyond*. New York: Bantam, 1988.

————. *Reflections on Life After Life*. New York: Mockingbird, 1977.

Murphy, G., and R. Ballou, eds. *William James on Psychical Research*. New York: Viking, 1969.

Needleman, Jacob, and David Appelbaum, eds. *Real Philosophy: An Anthology of the Universal Search for Meaning*. New York: Penguin/Arkana, 1990.

Neihardt, John. *Black Elk Speaks: Being the Life Story of a Holy Man of the Oglala Sioux*. New York: Washington Square Press, 1972. (Original work published in 1932.)

Nerburn, Kent, ed. *Chief Joseph and the Flight of the Nez Perce: The Untold Story of an American Tragedy*. San Francisco: HarperSanFrancisco, 2005.

————. *Neither Wolf Nor Dog: On Forgotten Roads with an Indian Elder*. Novato, CA: New World Library, 1994.

————. *The Wisdom of the Native Americans*. Novato, CA: New World Library, 1999.

————. *The Wolf at Twilight: An Indian Elder's Journey through a Land of Ghosts and Shadows*. Novato, CA: New World Library, 2009.

Nietzsche, Friedrich. *The Gay Science.* Trans. W. Kaufmann. New York: Vintage, 1974. (Original work published in 1887.)

Pagels, Elaine. *Adam, Eve, and the Serpent.* New York: Random House, 1988.

Pascal, Blaise. *Pensées.* Trans. A. J. Krailsheimer. New York: Penguin, 1966. (Original work published in 1662.)

Pearce, Joseph Chilton. *The Crack in the Cosmic Egg: Challenging Constructs of Mind and Reality.* New York: Bantam, 1973. (Original work published in 1971.)

Pesic, Peter. "Wrestling with Proteus: Francis Bacon and the 'Torture' of Nature." *Isis,* 90:1 (March 1999), 81–94.

Plato. *Plato: Five Dialogues.* Trans. G. M. A. Grube. Indianapolis, IN: Hackett, 1981.

Pollack, Rachel. *Seventy-Eight Degrees of Wisdom: A Book of Tarot.* London: Thorsons, 1997.

Progroff, Ira. *The Image of an Oracle: A Report on Research into the Mediumship of Eileen J. Garrett.* New York: Helix Press, 1964.

Quinn, Daniel. *Beyond Civilization: Humanity's Next Great Adventure* New York: Three Rivers Press, 1999.

———. *Ishmael.* New York: Bantam, 1992.

———. *My Ishmael.* New York: Bantam, 1997.

———. *Providence: The Story of a Fifty-Year Vision Quest.* New York: Bantam, 1995.

———. *The Story of B.* New York: Bantam, 1996.

Randall, Jr., John Herman. *Aristotle*. New York: Columbia University Press, 1960.

Radha, Swami Sivananda. *Realities of the Dreaming Mind*. Boston: Shambhala, 1996.

Ridall, Kathryn. *Channeling: How to Reach Out to Your Spirit Guides*. New York: Bantam, 1988.

Ring, Kenneth. *Heading Toward Omega: In Search of the Meaning of the Near-Death Experience*. New York: Quill, 1985.

———. *Life at Death: A Scientific Investigation of the Near-Death Experience*. New York: Quill, 1982.

———. *The Omega Project: Near-Death Experiences, UFO Encounters, and Mind at Large*. New York: William Morrow, 1992.

Ring, Kenneth, with E. V. Valarino. *Lessons from the Light: What We Can Learn from the Near-Death Experience*. New York: Plenum, 1988.

Roberts, Jane. *Adventures in Consciousness*. Englewood Cliffs, NJ: Prentice-Hall, 1975.

———. *The Afterdeath Journal of an American Philosopher: The World View of William James*. Englewood Cliffs, NJ: Prentice-Hall, 1978.

———. *The Coming of Seth*. New York: Bantam, 1976. (Original work published in 1966.)

———. *The Early Class Sessions, Book I, Sessions 9/12/67 to 11/25/69: A Seth Book*. Manhasset, NY: New Awareness Network, 2008.

———. *The God of Jane: A Psychic Manifesto*. Englewood Cliffs, NJ: Prentice-Hall, 1981.

————. *The Individual and the Nature of Mass Events.* Englewood Cliffs, NJ: Prentice-Hall, 1981.

————. *Psychic Politics: An Aspect Psychology Book* Englewood Cliffs, NJ: Prentice-Hall, 1979.

————. *Seth, Dreams, and Projections of Consciousness.* Walpole, NH: Stillpoint, 1987.

————. *The Seth Material.* Englewood Cliffs, NJ: Prentice-Hall, 1970.

————. *Seth Speaks: The Eternal Validity of the Soul.* Englewood Cliffs, NJ: Prentice-Hall, 1972.

————. *The "Unknown" Reality, Volume 2: A Seth Book.* Englewood Cliffs, NJ: Prentice-Hall, 1979.

Rorty, Richard. *Consequences of Pragmatism: Essays: 1972–1980.* Minneapolis, MN: University of Minnesota Press, 1982.

Ross, Sir David. *Aristotle.* 5th ed. London: Methuen & Co, 1977.

Russell, Bertrand. *The Basic Writings of Bertrand Russell: 1903–1959.* Ed. R. E. Egner and L. E. Denonn. New York: Simon and Schuster, 1961.

————. *A History of Western Philosophy.* New York: Simon and Schuster, 1945.

Russell, Ronald. *The Journey of Robert Monroe: From Out-of-Body Explorer to Consciousness Pioneer.* Charlottesville, VA: Hampton Roads, 2007.

————. *The Vast Enquiring Soul: Explorations Into the Further Reaches of Consciousness.* Charlottesville, VA: Hampton Roads, 2000.

Russell, Ronald, ed. *Focusing the Whole Brain: Transforming Your Life with Hemispheric Synchronization.* Charlottesville, VA: Hampton Roads, 2004.

———. *Using the Whole Brain: Integrating the Right and Left Brain with Hemi-Sync Sound Patterns*. Norfolk, VA: Hampton Roads, 1993.

Sabini, Meredith, and Margaret Laurel Allen. "Christ comes down from the cross: the evolution of an archetype." *Chrysalis* 9:1 (Spring 1994), 21–32.

Sacks, Oliver. *Musicophilia: Tales of Music and the Brain*. New York: Knopf, 2007.

Shakespeare, William. *The Annotated Shakespeare, 3 Vols*. Ed. A. L. Rowse. New York: Orbis, 1978.

Shorto, Russell. "How Christian Were the Founders?" *The New York Times Magazine* (February 14, 2010). *www.nytimes.com*.

Simpkinson, Anne A. "On Past-Life Therapy: An Interview with Roger Woolger." *Common Boundary* 5:6 (November/December 1987), 7–9; 24–26.

Specter, Michael. "A Life of Its Own: Where Will Synthetic Biology Lead Us?" *The New Yorker* (September 28, 2009).

Starr, Paul. *The Social Transformation of American Medicine*. New York: Basic, 1982.

Steiger, Brad. *Revelation: The Divine Fire*. New Brunswick, NJ: Inner Light, 1988.

Stevenson, Mark. "2012 Isn't the End of the World, Mayans Insist." *The Associated Press* (October 11, 2009). *abcnews.go.com*.

Stockton, Bayard. *Catapult: The Biography of Robert A. Monroe*. Norfolk, VA: Donning, 1989.

Sutin, Lawrence. *Divine Invasions: A Life of Philip K. Dick.* New York: Citadel Twilight, 1989.

Swann, Ingo. *Your Nostradamus Factor: Accessing Your Innate Ability to See Into the Future.* New York: Simon and Schuster, 1993.

Tart, Charles T. Foreword to Ronald Russell, *The Journey of Robert Monroe: From Out-of-Body Explorer to Consciousness Pioneer.* Charlottesville, VA: Hampton Roads, 2007.

————. "In Memory of my friend Robert Monroe." Unpublished article, 1995. *www.paradigm-sys.com.*

Unsigned article (2008). Interview: Dr. Tony Cicoria. *Vital Signs* 27: 4, 3–5; 13; 16.

Unsigned article. "Religious right activist calls for execution of homosexuals." *Church and State* (2010) 63: 2, 21.

Unsigned article. *Zoroaster~Zarathustra.* (2009) *http://personalpages.tds.net.*

Von Franz, Marie-Louise. *On Dreams and Death: A Jungian Interpretation.* Trans. E. X. Kennedy and V. Brooks. Boston: Shambhala, 1987.

van Lommel, Pim. *Consciousness Beyond Life: The Science of the Near-Death Experience.* New York: HarperOne, 2010.

Waite, Arthur Edward. *The Pictorial Key to the Tarot.* Blauvelt, NY: Steiner, 1975.

Waters, Frank. *Pumpkin Seed Point: Being Within the Hopi.* Athens, OH: Ohio University Press, 1969.

Watkins, Susan M. *Conversations with Seth: The Story of Jane Roberts's ESP Class.* Rev. ed. Portsmouth, NH: Moment Point, 1999.

————. *Speaking of Jane Roberts: Remembering the Author of the Seth Material*. Portsmouth, NH: Moment Point, 2001. Weatherford, Jack. *Indian Givers: How the Indians of the Americas Transformed the World*. New York: Fawcett, 1988.

White, Rhea A. "The Amplification and Integration of Near-Death and Other Exceptional Human Experiences by the Larger Cultural Context: An Autobiographical Case." *Journal of Near-Death Studies* (1998) 16: 181–204.

Wilber, Ken, ed. *The Holographic Paradigm and Other Paradoxes: Exploring the Leading Edge of Science*. Boston: Shambhala, 1985.

Wilson, Colin. *New Pathways in Psychology: Maslow and the Post-Freudian Revolution*. New York: Taplinger, 1972.

Wilson, Colin, with Damon Wilson. *The Encyclopedia of Unsolved Mysteries*. New York: Contemporary, 1988.

Wolf, Fred Alan. *Mind Into Matter: A New Alchemy of Science and Spirit*. Portsmouth, NH: Moment Point Press, 2001.

Woolger, Roger. *Other Lives, Other Selves: A Jungian Psychotherapist Discovers Past Lives*. New York: Bantam, 1988.

Wordsworth, William. *William Wordsworth: Selected Poems*, ed. W. Davies. London: J. M. Dent & Sons, 1975.

Yeats, W. B. *Selected Poems and Three Plays of William Butler Yeats*, 3rd ed. Ed. M. L. Rosenthal. New York: Collier MacMillan, 1962.

INDEX

A

Adam and Eve, 11, 31, 106
Adventures in Consciousness (Roberts), 143
Afterdeath Journal of an American Philosopher, The (Roberts), 154–155
afterlife, 24, 27
Agricultural Revolution, 51, 61–62
Ahura Mazda, 47
Alexander the Great, 48
alive, experience of being, 118–119
Allen, Woody, 25
Alstad, Diana, 111–112
anatta (anatman), 111
anger, 20
animism, 31
Annie Hall (film), 25
anxiety, 13
apocalyptic beliefs, 5–13, 104, 112–113
Applewhite, Marshall Herff, 12, 28
Aquinas, Thomas, Saint, 61
Archaic Revival, The (McKenna), 7
Aristotle, 48–50, 55–56, 171
Asahara, Shoko, 12
atoms, 58
Augustine, Saint, 10–11, 82, 107

Augustine of Hippo, Saint, 7
Aum Shinrikyo cult, 12
Aurobindo, Sri, 173
axis mundi, 196

B

Bacon, Francis, 59
Bahnson, Agnew, 180
Barker, John, 68
Basic, the, 191–192
Becker, Carl, 40
belief systems crash, 207
Belief Systems Territories, 190–191
Bentov, Itzhak, 55, 91, 96–97
Bethards, Betty, 51
Bible, 5, 14, 19, 57, 105–107
Big Bang, 128, 129
Big Elk, 26
biology, synthetic, 60
birth and rebirth, 43, 48, 49
Black Elk
    circle of life theories of, 28–29, 76
    on death, 26
    Ghost Dance out-of-body experience, 52
    heyokas, significance of, 205
    value of vision sharing, 173–174

visions of, 128–129, 145–146,
170–171
Black Road, 174
Blavatsky, Mrs. H. P., 146
bleed-throughs, 148
bliss, 127, 159
Bly, Robert, 122
boggle threshold, 104
Bohm, David
on consciousness, 171
fragmentation theories, 15
insight experiences, 135
linear *vs.* psychological time, 91,
103
on memory, 96, 97
open-minded experiences, 153
quantum theory and
consciousness, 87–89, 92
relativity of time, 72–73
science and religion competition,
152
system definition by, 79
on thought, 75, 80
Boone, J. Allen, 78, 102
Brasseur de Bourbourg, Charles
Etienne, 6–7
Braun, Eva, 16
Breaking the Circle (Becker), 40
Brule Sioux, 28
Bucke, Richard Maurice, 168
Buddhism, 40, 43, 111–112, 147
Butterfield, Herbert, 31
Butts, Rob (husband of Roberts),
134, 138, 150

C

calendars, Mayan Long Count, 6–7
calls. *See* consciousness, non-
ordinary states of
Campbell, Joseph
art interpretation, 203
Christianity influences, 47
on dreams and myths, 195
on end of world, 67, 101, 102, 204,
206
formula for life, 127, 159
Great Reversal theory, 39–40, 41,
42
guru models and, 112
myth theories, 17, 18
natures of universe and man, 50
prehuman consciousness
evidence, 24
proverb on Jesus return, 159
self and experience, 118
wound themes, 77
Catapult (Stockton), 164
Catholic Church, 72
cause and effect, 30, 96
Cavell, Stanley, 114
celebrity, cult of, 115
Chang Chung-yuan, 83
channeling, 138–142. *See also* Seth
chariots, 42
children, 67, 118, 170, 203
Christianity
as anger religion, 20
Cartesian views of, 58
creation myths, 105–107
culture wars and, 14
end of world traditions, 6–7, 9

Luther's view of, 57–58
nature views, 19, 81–82, 84
pagan absorption and system
adaptation, 46–47, 80
practices condemned by, 72
religion, word origin and
interpretation, 82
as system, 80
time perception of, 29, 30–31
Christmas Carol, A (Dickens), 8
chutzpah, 37
Cicero, 82
Cicoria, Tony, 123, 124, 125–127,
160, 173
circle
collective mentality and, 66
Eastern traditions of life as, 43
gaps and breakage in, 38–45,
76–77
Native American view of nature
as, 28–29, 76
reality as, 145–146
of suffering, 39–40
time and, 28–29, 33–34
Zoroastrian symbols of, 47–48
clairvoyance, 137, 150
clusters, 190
collective mentality, 65–67, 69
Collingwood, R. G., 7, 20, 115–116
conformism, 130
consciousness. *See also* consciousness,
non-ordinary states of; out-of-
body experiences
Christian view of, 106–107
collective, 65–67
constriction of, 185–186

inner and outer relationships of,
65
materialistic view of, 59–60
modern order of reality and, 38
oscillating universe hypothesis
and, 96–97, 98
quantum theory and, 86, 88
self-transformation altering, 101–
104, 115, 196, 206–210
consciousness, non-ordinary states
of. *See also* out-of-body
experiences
acceptance *vs.* denial of, 159–164
children and, 67, 118, 170, 203
exceptional *vs.* exceptional
human experiences, 160
lack of scientific study on, 177–178
manifestations of, 164–169
near-death experiences, 123–127,
160, 184
control, 61, 65
Cosmic Consciousness (Bucke), 168
Cosmic Journeys (McKnight), 161–162
counterparts, 149–150
creation myths, 105–107
creation of self, 144–145
cults, 12–13
cycle concept, 28–29, 43, 48, 49. *See
also* circle
Cyrus the Great, King of Persia, 47

D
daimons, 141
Dakotas, 26–27
Dan (professor), 131–132, 197–199
Dante Alighieri, 121

Darwin, Charles, 14, 60, 108
dead, visits with, 180–181, 191
death
  denial of, 24–25
  Eastern traditions, 43, 48
  Greek view of, 49
  linear thinking response to,
    121–123
  Native American attitude toward,
    26–28
  near-death experiences, 123–127,
    160, 184
  prehistoric rituals, 24
  reincarnation cycle, 43, 48, 146–
    148, 150
  Taoist view of, 83
Deloria, Vine, Jr., 150
Demian (Hesse), 66, 104, 196
Democritus, 58
Descartes, René, 30, 57, 58, 168, 206
despair, 25
Dick, Philip K., 119, 169
Dickens, Charles, 8
dinosaur extinction, 16
disaster predictions, 68, 69–70
distress of society, 13–16
Divine Comedy, The (Dante Alighieri),
  121
"Doomsday Machine, The" (*Star Trek*
  episode), 18–19
Dr. No (film), 61
Dream Book, The (Bethards), 51
dreams
  acceptance *vs.* denial of, 161
  as altered consciousness, 168

author's experiences with, 199–
  204
Campbell on, 195
expression and response, 205–
  206
Hesse on, 195
Jung on, 195
limitations of self-knowledge and,
  109
as precognition, 67–73

E

Earth-Life System (ELS), 155, 178,
  190
Eastern traditions, 43, 48. *See also*
  specific religions
Eastman, Charles Alexander
  (Ohiyesa), 26–27, 150, 156
ecstasy (*ecstasis*), 124, 135, 201, 204
egg, cosmic, 99
ego, 64–65
egoism, 112
Einstein, Albert, 87
Eliade, Mircea, 43
ELS (Earth-Life System), 155, 178,
  190
Emitter, the, 192
empiricism, radical, 187
end of world
  desire for, 13–16
  literal interpretations of, 5–13,
    104, 112–113
  Native American stories of, 27, 28
  as self-transformation, 101–104,
    115, 196, 206–210
  shamanic perception of, 101

term usage, 16–17
Enlightenment, 30, 31, 58–59
entities, nonphysical, 93, 161–162.
    See also Seth
Erdoes, Richard, 27
Eve, Adam and, 11, 31, 106
Exceptional Experiences (EEs), 160
Exceptional Human Experiences
    (EHEs), 160
experience, human
    fear and, 118
    knowledge acquisition through,
        102–103
    as life goal, 118–119
    mechanistic materialism views
        of, 30
    midlife crisis as lack of, 122
    Native American perception of,
        150
    physical/sense *vs.* nonphysical,
        85–87, 151–152, 153–155
explicate (projected) order, 88, 96,
    97–98

F
Faravahar (Farohar), 47–48
Far Journeys (Monroe), 93, 170,
    186–187
Faust (play), 44
fear
    as barrier, 118, 161, 174, 180, 181,
        200
    of end of world, 8
    of living, 210
Fenwick, Peter and Elizabeth, 68
fire, 27, 28, 167, 168

flood, 27, 28
fragmentation, 15
Franz, Marie-Louise von, 67
freedom, 43–44, 114–115
Freud, Sigmund, 109, 146

G
Galileo, 152
Genesis, 105–107
Ghost Dance, 51–52
global warming, 15, 104
Gnostic Christianity, 84
God of Jane, The (Roberts), 143
Good *vs.* Evil, 45–46, 47, 57, 83, 107
Gordon, Dick, 180
Graves, Robert, 82
Great Book of Nature, 82
Great Goddess, 195
Great Mystery, 28
Great Reversal, 39–44
Grof, Stanislav, 30
Grosso, Michael, 24
Groundhog Day (film), 34
guru models, 111–113, 155–156
Guru Papers, The (Kramer and
    Alstad), 111–112

H
habits, 97, 98, 102
Heaven, 61
Heaven's Gate, 12
Hegel, G. W. F., 44
Hell, 57, 61, 106
Hemi-Sync (hemispheric
    synchronization), 183–184, 185
Heraclitus, 111, 142, 167–168

Hesse, Hermann, 66, 104, 126, 195–196
heyokas, 205
Hinduism, 43, 112
Hitchcock, Alfred, 114
Hitler, Adolf, 16
Hobbes, Thomas, 108
Hoffman, Edward, 67
holomovement, 89
Home (non-earthly environment), 181–182
Hopis, 27
horses, 43–44
Humanist Manifesto II (Kurtz), 153
Hume, David, 110–112, 113
Hurricane Katrina, 128, 129
hyperaggression, 76

I

I Ching (Jung), 82, 206
iconoclasm, radical, 187–188
"Idea Construction" revelation (Roberts), 136–137, 144
"I Have a Dream" (King), 19–20
illness foretelling, 168–169
imagination, 9–11, 19, 99, 196
implicate (enfolded) order, 88, 97–98
Indian Givers (Weatherford), 65–66
Inquisition, 72
in-seeing, 75, 78, 84, 102
insight. *See also* consciousness, nonordinary states of
    lightning bolt initiations, 168–169
    Native American view of, 75, 78, 84

from near-death experiences, 123–127
as out-of-body revelations, 134–135
as shift of perception, 77–78, 102
Inspec (entity), 93–94
intuition, 127, 151, 188
Ishmael (Quinn), 50
Islam, 80
I-There, 190
Ixion, 40

J

Jackson, Michael, 114
Jainism, 43
Jambor, Mishka, 173
James, William, 84–87, 88, 90, 154–155, 196
Jesus Christ, Second Coming of, 5, 9
John the Baptist, 19
Jones, Jim (Jonestown), 12
Jouret, Luc, 12
Journey of Robert Monroe, The (Russell, Ronald), 163–164
Journeys Out of the Body (Monroe), 93, 166, 176, 180, 182–183, 184
Judaism, 47
Jung, Carl
    distress and apocalyptic beliefs, 13
    dreams, 195, 205–206
    emotional maturity and life's problems, 34, 35
    midlife crisis, 122
    myths, 18
    nature and destructive forces, 19

religion, word origins, 82
science and consciousness, 109
self-knowledge, 121
synchronicities, 172–173

K

Kalweit, Holger, 168
karma, 147–148
Katrina, Hurricane, 128, 129
Kaufmann, Walter, 188–189
Keasling, Jay, 60
Kendall, Rich, 139–140
King, Martin Luther, Jr., 19–20
King Lear (play), 37, 39, 40
knowledge
    Christian creation myths and,
        105–106
    experience and, 102–103, 109
    Native American views of, 82
    near-death experiences
        implanting, 125–127
    out-of-body experiences
        implanting, 136
    self-, 107, 108–110, 113–118, 130
Korzybski, Alfred, 87–88
Kramer, Joel, 111, 112
Kurtz, Paul, 153

L

Lenz, Chris, 187
Leva, Patricia, 203
Libet, Benjamin, 95
"lie in the soul," 19
life, and living fully, 34, 118–119,
    122, 159
Life After Life (Moody), 123

life force, 127
Lifeline (program), 191
light, 124, 167, 168–169
lightning, 123–127, 168, 170–171
Lightning Sonata (Cicoria), 126, 127
linear time, 28–35, 43, 45–48, 77,
    89–90, 121–123
Little Big Horn battle, 43
Locale II (non-earthly environment),
    181, 185
Luther, Martin, 57

M

MacGuffin (plot device), 114
Man: a Machine (Mettrie), 30
Mann, A. T., 55
Martin, Ann, 8
mass murder cults, 12
materialism, 30, 85, 108, 152
matter, mind *vs.*, 88–89
maturity, emotional, 34, 35, 76
Mayans, 6–7, 28
McDurmon, Joel, 14
McKenna, Terence, 7–8
McKnight, Rosalind A., 161–162
measurement, 62–63, 73, 89–90
mechanism, 30, 85, 108, 152
medical materialism, 84–87
memes, 79
Memories, Dreams, Reflections (Jung),
    19
memory, 96–97
Mettrie, Julien Offray de la, 30
micromania, 61
midlife crises, 122–123, 126, 134,
    164

Miller, William, 5

Mind into Matter (Wolf), 73–74

mind *vs.* matter, 88–89

Moen, Bruce, 207

monotheism, 31

Monroe, Nancy (Penn), 183, 186

Monroe, Robert

    on acquiring different overviews, 102–103, 206

    audio technology developed by, 183–184, 185

    background and first out-of-body experiences, 163, 164–166, 169

    biographies on, 163–164

    childhood out-of-body experiences, 170

    Earth-Life System theory, 155

    entities of, 93–94

    on fear, 118, 181

    institutes of, 183

    nonverbal communication theories, 144

    out-of-body experience, description, 135

    parallel world visits, 180–182, 190

    research and experimentation, 176, 178–180, 185–191

    Second Body theories, 184–185

    skepticism, 161–162

Monroe Institute, 183

Moody, Raymond, 123

Moses, 167

Mother Earth, 195

Mount Megunticook, 5

Multiple Self, 147

musicophilia, 125–126

myths, 17–18, 95–96, 195

N

Native Americans

    circle-destructing events, 51–52

    circle of nature views, 28–29, 76

    control concept and time, 65–66

    counterparts, 150–151

    death views, 23

    heyokas, significance of, 205

    in-seeing beliefs, 78

    on knowledge and nature, 82

    nature views, 83, 84

    power gift visions, 128–129

    psychic naturalism, 156

    universe reality visions, 145–146

nature

    Aristotelian view of, 49, 50

    Christian view of, 82–83, 106

    as circular, 28–29

    collective mentality and, 66

    destructive force of, 19

    Native American views of, 82, 83

    power of, 128, 129

    primitive culture view of, 49–50

    religious *vs.* scientific view of, 61

    Taoist view of, 83–84

Neanderthals, 24

near-death experiences (NDEs), 123–127, 160, 184

Neihardt, John, 26, 28, 146

Nerburn, Kent, 26–27

Newton, Sir Isaac, 30, 58

Newtonian theories, 29, 87

Nietzsche, Friedrich, 118, 177, 178
9-11, 15, 70–71
Noble, Sandra, 28
nonverbal communication (NVC),
144
no-self, 111–112

O

OBEs. *See* out-of-body experiences
Oglala Sioux, 26, 28–29, 39, 82
Ohiyesa, 26–27, 150, 156
Ojibwe, 151
Omaha, 26
Oneness, 112
Ortiz, Alfonso, 27
oscillating universe hypothesis,
96–97, 98
out-of-body experiences (OBEs)
channeling nonphysical entities
as, 93–94, 137–142, 161–162
(*See also* Seth)
childhood memories of, 170
consciousness constriction and,
185–186
descriptions and experimentation
of, 174–180
as dreams, 199–204
Native American visions
including, 52, 128–129,
145–146, 170–171
near-death, 123–127, 160
parallel world visits, 181–182, 185
as revelatory insights, 134–136
Second Body theories, 184–185
traditional dismissal of, 103
visiting dead, 180–181

P

pain, as manifestation of call, 166
Paiute, 51–53
parallel worlds, 137, 148, 180–181
Park, The, 181, 190, 191
past-life traumas, 146
Pearce, Joseph Chilton, 99, 172
Pegasus, 44
People's Temple cult, 12
perception
development of, 102–103, 107, 137
as habit, 97
memory recall and, 95–96
of self, 110–114, 145
Persians, 42
pessimism, 37–41
philosophy, 25, 30–31, 37–41, 57, 79,
117
"Physical Universe as Idea
Construction, The" (Roberts),
136–137, 144
physics, 58, 72
Piaget, Jean, 97
Plato, 19, 48
polytheism, 31
power, 128–131
Power of the World, 28–29
precognition, 67–73, 85–86, 137,
150, 169
probabilities (probable selves), 103–
104, 137, 147, 148–149
Protagoras, 90
Protestantism, 57
psychic naturalism, 151–152, 153,
155–157
Psychic Politics (Roberts), 143

psychological time, 90–91, 103

Q

quantum theory, 29, 87–89, 91–92, 172
Quinn, Daniel, 50
qwiffs (quantum wave functions), 92

R

Radha, Swami, 161
radical empiricism, 187
radical iconoclasm, 187–188
Rajneesh group, 112
Realities of the Dreaming Mind (Swami Radha/Sylvia), 161
reason and rational inquiry, 57, 58–59, 151, 155, 172, 178
reincarnation and rebirth, 43, 48, 146–148, 150
related, organized, thought-energy (ROTE), 144, 192
relegere, 82
religare, 82
religion. *See also specific religions*
  definitions and word origins, 81–82
  dualistic divisions of, 171–172
  Eastern views of life cycle, 43, 48
  external Authority of, 110
  human consciousness, 107
  as outdated system, 79
  precognition and, 72
  psychic naturalism views, 155–157
  science competing with, 152–153
  view of nature, 61
renunciate moralities, 112

Ridall, Kathryn, 140
Ring, Kenneth, 123
Roberts, Jane
  channeling, term usage, 141
  on consequences of accepted beliefs, 133
  entities of, 138–140 (*See also* Seth)
  on humanity and consciousness, 65
  on interior *vs.* exterior universe, 133
  James ruminations, 154–155
  karma views, 148
  limitations of knowledge without experience, 109
  on mainstream traditions, 133
  psychic naturalism, 151–152, 153, 155–157
  on questions as limitations, 172
  reincarnation views, 147–148
  research and experimentation, 137–138, 142–143, 146, 178
  revelatory experience of, 134–137, 160
Rorty, Richard, 113–114
Rosicrucians, 12
ROTE (related, organized, thought-energy), 144, 192
Russell, Bertrand, 25, 141
Russell, Ronald, 59–60, 163, 183, 184, 192
Ryan, Leo, 12

S

Sacks, Oliver, 125
science

Cartesian method, 58–59
    dualistic terms of, 172
    evolution view, 31–32
    external Authority of, 110
    human consciousness, 59–60,
        108–109
    materialism, 58–59
    nature views, 61
    precognition and, 72
    psychic experience *vs.* subjectivity,
        85–87
    religion competing with, 152–153
    time, 29
    value-neutrality, 31–32
scientism, 152–153
Seattle, Chief, 26
Second Body theory, 184–185
Second Coming of Jesus, 5, 9
self. *See also* consciousness;
        consciousness, non-ordinary
        states of
    Buddhist views of, 147
    denial of, 117–118
    in different time periods, 149–151
    experience of being alive as, 118
    formula for, 127
    I-There and clusters of, 190
    knowledge and search for, 113–
        117
    Multiple Self myth, 147
    no-, 111–113
    as perception, 110–114
    postmodern plasticity of, as
        personal freedom, 114–115
    power interconnection to, 130
    probabilities/probable selves, 103–

        104, 137, 147, 148–149
    Source (true self), 118, 144, 149,
        150, 190
    self-knowledge, 107, 108–110, 113,
        116, 117–118, 130
    self-transformation, 101–104, 115,
        196, 206–210
September 11, 2001 attacks (9-11),
    15, 70–71
Seth (entity)
    on aspects of self, 148–149
    defining, 143–144
    discovery and development of,
        138–140
    on psychological *vs.* physical time,
        103
    on reality, 145
    time loops and encounters with,
        94–95
*Seth, Dreams and Projections of
    Consciousness* (Roberts), 135
Seth Material, The (Roberts), 95, 134–
    135, 148–149
Shakespeare, William, 37, 39, 40
shamanism. *See also* Native
        Americans
    channeling practices, 140–141
    end of world views, 101
    knowledge and, 89
    lightning bolt initiations, 168–169
    nature and, 82
    soul flight, 43, 135
Shamans, Healers, and Medicine Men
    (Kalweit), 168
Sioux, 26–27, 28–29, 39, 82, 150
Sisyphus, 35

Sitting Bull, Chief, 43
Smoots, 90
Social Transformation of American Medicine, The (Starr), 85
society, 13–16, 76, 127
Socrates, 2, 3, 48, 102, 141
soul
  Buddhist views of, 147
  death and afterlife, 24, 25, 27
  materialist theory of, 59–60
  Mettrie theories on, 30
  symbols of eternal, 48
soul flight, 43, 135. *See also* consciousness, non-ordinary states of
Soul of an Indian, The (Eastman/Ohiyesa), 27
soul-retrieval, 191–192
Source (true self), 118, 144, 149, 150, 190
spectator psychology, 10–11
Specter, Michael, 60
Standing Bear, Luther, 82, 84
Starr, Paul, 85
Star Trek (television show), 18–19
Steiger, Brad, 52
Stockton, Bayard, 164
stories, 95–96, 99
suffering, 37–41, 111
suicidal cults, 12
Swann, Ingo, 68–69
Sylvia, Ursula, 161
synchronicities, 172–173
systems, 79–80, 83

T

Taoism, 83–84, 186
Tart, Charles, 135
telepathy, 137, 150
There (non-earthly environment), 181
Thomas Gospel, 84
thought, 75, 80, 97, 144, 192
time
  character of, 63
  circular *vs.* linear, 28–35, 43, 45–48
  control and mastery of, 64
  future seeing, 67–73
  holomovement theory and, 89–90
  as loop, 73–74, 91–96, 99–100
  measurement of, 62–63, 90
  modern perception of, 62
  Native American, 65–66
  psychological *vs.* physical, 90–91, 103
  relativity of, 29, 72, 87
  simultaneous, 146
  Taoist view of, 83
time loops, 73–74, 91–96, 99–100
twin spirits, 150–151
Tzu, Chuang, 83

U

UFOs, 12, 94–95, 117–118
Ultimate Journey (Monroe), 93, 186, 188, 192
"Unknown Reality," The (recordings), 149

V

vibrations, as manifestation of call,
167, 174
visions
as extraordinary experiences,
168, 169
Native American experiences,
128–129, 145–146, 170–171,
205
precognition, 67–73, 85–86, 137,
150, 169
Visions of Innocence (Hoffman), 67,
119

W

war, 42, 43
Watkins, Sue, 94
Weatherford, Jack, 65–66
Weber, Renée, 88
wheels of fire/terror, 42–43
Whig history, 31
whirling dervishes, 203
White, Rhea, 104

White Goddess, The (Graves), 82
Wholeness and the Implicate Order
(Bohm), 87
Wilber, Ken, 39
Wilson, Colin, 102
Wolf, Fred Alan, 73–74, 91–92,
95–96, 99
Woolger, Roger, 146–147
word play, 80–83
world (term usage), 16–17
World of Tomorrow, The (radio show),
9
Wounded Knee massacre, 51–52
Wovoka, 51–52, 62
wu wei, 83, 186

Y

Yeats, W. B., 38
Yin and Yang, 83

Z

Zoroaster and Zoroastrianism, 45–
46, 48, 55–56

ABOUT THE AUTHOR

Joseph M. Felser, Ph.D. graduated *summa cum laude* and Phi Beta Kappa from Boston University and received his doctorate in philosophy from the University of Chicago. He is currently Associate Professor of Philosophy at Kingsborough Community College of the City University of New York, in Brooklyn.

The author of numerous articles on parapsychology, religion, myth, and the paranormal, his writings have appeared in scholarly and popular journals, including: *The Journal of the American Society for Psychical Research*; *The Journal of the American Academy of Religion*; *The International Journal of Parapsychology*; *Collingwood Studies*; *Exceptional Human Experience*; *Mythosphere*; and *The Anomalist*. Hampton Roads published his previous book, *The Way Back to Paradise: Restoring the Balance between Magic and Reason*, in 2005.

He and his wife, along with their golden retriever, make their home in suburban New Jersey but get away to Maine whenever they can.

You can contact Dr. Felser via his website: *www.everythingtriestoberound.com*.

Hampton Roads Publishing Company
. . . for the evolving human spirit

Hampton Roads Publishing Company
publishes books on a variety of subjects,
including spirituality, health, and other
related topics.

For a copy of our latest trade catalog,
call 978-465-0504 or visit our website at *www.hrpub.com.*